Bill
+ Jamie

Thanks for all
the support -
Looky forward to our
new Business

Keep the Power
moving to the right!

S Sch...

POWER
PRINCIPLES
for
SUCCESS

America's PremierExperts® *share their biggest success secrets*
for a life of health, wealth, happiness and prosperity.

For more information, please write:

CelebrityPress™,
520 N. Orlando Ave, #44,
Winter Park, FL 32789

or call 1.877.261.4930

Visit us online at **www.CelebrityPressPublishing.com**

POWER
PRINCIPLES
for
SUCCESS

America's PremierExperts® *share their biggest success secrets* for a life of health, wealth, happiness and prosperity.

Table of Contents:

Power Principle #01
The 10 Secret Steps To Guaranteed Success
by Mitch Levin.. 13

Power Principle #02
Focus On The Finish Line to Fulfill Your Dreams
by Scot Ferrell.. 25

Power Principle #03
Align Your Dreams, Goals & Values
by J.W.Dicks 33

Power Principle #04
Earning Potential Is Your Most Valuable Asset
by Brian Tracy 47

Power Principle #05
The Power Of Team Training
by Scott Schumann 55

Power Principle #06
Start With Creating More Value
by Dan Liebrecht and Tony Dietsch.. 65

Power Principle #07
It starts With A Smile
by Lisa Peters-Seppala 73

Power Principle #08
Your Net Worth Is Determined By Your Network
by Marco Kozlowski.. 79

Power Principle #09
Process Yields Progress
by Nick Nanton 91

Power Principle #10
The Importance Of Mastering Follow Up
by Clate Mask 101

Power Principle #11
Refine Your Systems
by Richard Seppala 109

Power Principle #12
Power Up Your Online Communication
by Vesna Sutter 117

Power Principle #13
Find Something You Love To Do, And Then Figure Out How To Make Money Doing It
by Jennifer Burg 125

Power Principle #14
Success Is A Verb!
by Donna Galante 131

Power Principle #15
The Power Of Perseverance
by Ken Hardison 139

Power Principle #16
The Principle Of Kaizen -- Growth
by Michael McDevitt 147

Power Principle #17
Become A Business Warrior
by Brad Hess & Tyrell Gray 157

Power Principle #18
Prepare For Insurance Disaster
by James Murphy 167

Power Principle #19
Power A Tax-Free Financial Future
by Chuck Oliver 173

Power Principle #20
Take Action
by Rutherford De Armas 185

Power Principle #21
Set Power Goals
by Darren Mish 195

Power Principle #22
Content Is STILL King
by Lindsay Dicks 203

Power Principle #23
Develop Funnel Vision
by Scott Martineau 211

Power Principle #24
The Power Of Paradoxical Liberation
by Richard Seppala 217

Power Principle #25
Dare To Begin
by Chuck Boyce 223

Power Principle #26
Be A Jerk With Your Time
by Ben Glass 231

Power Principle #27
Principles Of Entrepreneurial (Small Business) Success
by Kimberly Moore 239

Power Principle #28
Maximize The Day With Personal Management Skills
by David Hoines 249

Power Principle #29
The Power Of Forward Thinking
by Michael Biancone 255

Power Principle #30
Join The Virtual Revolution!
by Kimberly Morgan 265

Power Principle #31
Flip It Like A Pancake!
by William Umansky 277

Power Principle #1

THE TEN SECRET STEPS TO GUARANTEED SUCCESS

by Mitch Levin, MD

The secrets to success are ...wait, <u>there are no secrets</u>!

Success, no matter how you define it, is out there for everybody. And the not-so-secret formula also is available for everyone to use. Here it is: One, do the right thing. Two, take decisive action - NOW! Three, exercise discipline. Four, know yourself. Five, follow the pattern. Six, get some money. Seven, you are not average. Eight, keep it simple. Nine, avoid the big and common mistakes. Ten, it's not about the money. And for a *bonus* – well, read to the end. Let me explain more fully.

<u>**First:**</u> <u>Doing the right thing means doing what you are supposed to, and not doing what you shouldn't, even when nobody is watching.</u> It means doing what you would do as if somebody were watching. It means doing only those things you don't mind getting into the national press or that your mother might find out about. It means "doing well by doing good".

It means following the first grade or kindergarten tenets -- don't lie; don't cheat; don't steal; keep your hands to yourself. That's what I mean by doing the right thing. Don't think when you do the right thing that does not include trying to get something for nothing or trying to beat the clock or be something that you're not. When selling something, anything, do it in a consultative fashion. The "buyer" will gain value and that will bring value to you. Your buyer may be your employee or your boss or your customer or your family. <u>Remember you have to give to get.</u>

Second: <u>Action is better than perfection</u>. And decisive action is best. Take fast action and adjust later. Slow to decide means low success rates. Failures fall prey to "paralysis by analysis". Action means that you go out there and you fight the fight, according to Winston Churchill. You play the game. You do what you're supposed to do and you take part in life. Most of us by now have heard the Woody Allen quote that "half of life is just showing up."

By not taking action and by not constantly planning, you set yourself up for frustration and failure – Dwight Eisenhower said, "Planning is everything. Plans are nothing." You have to plan. But you have to take action. If all you do is plan and plan for perfection and pursue perfection, you will never take any action.

Good enough is good enough. And Voltaire said it in *Candide* that "better is the enemy of good". How many times have you had a good golf swing and you decide to help that ball a little bit at the bottom? What happens? You blade it, you chunk it, you hook it, you slice it. Good enough is good enough. *But planning and plans with no action is meaningless.* Take decisive, massive action – now.

Third: <u>This is the "eat your vegetables" part. Discipline is possibly the hardest and least common of all.</u> And it is the one most likely to translate from desire to reality. It means doing the difficult things and doing them first. Discipline means when you are taking a course of action and you are off course that you adjust and get back on course. Discipline means doing what others are incapable of doing but you are capable of doing. It includes controlling your emotions and urges, and recognizing it is not all about you. Forget feeling entitled. Entitlement too often leads to a sense of victimization.

Discipline means making that extra call, reading that extra book, writing that extra report. It means going the extra mile for your patient or your client or your customer. It means reviewing the books or going over that flight check list one extra time. Discipline means knowing your numbers. *It means knowing where you are all the time so that you can make adjustments, therefore, you can get where you want to go.*

Fourth: Knowing yourself means you have to take some time to 'contemplate your navel'. You have to know who you are, what type of person you are and what your goals are. And you probably have heard it before (and it may be apocryphal or it may be true), but *you must write down your goals.*

But your goals have to be SMART. And by smart goals I mean: S – they have to be specific with perfect and precise clarity. To make more money is not specific; to lose 12 pounds is. M – they have to be meaningful and more importantly measurable. To play better tennis is not measurable if you are not competing. A – they have to be achievable. It is not achievable to have as a goal to earn $1 Million per year if you are a teacher. R – they have to be realistic. It is highly unrealistic for me to have a goal of being an NFL star. And T – they have to have a completion time associated with them. For example, to increase the number of books you read by two each month beginning next month is an appropriate time frame.

And when you have these goals and you write them down, write down the keys to success. What are your keys to success of a particular goal? These keys ought to be clear and consistent with the objectives. In addition to that, write down what achieving the goals mean to you; how will they benefit you. Now, your goals can be spiritual. They can be physical. They can be financial. They can be social. They can be in business. You may have goals of three goals for each aspect of your life. It doesn't matter as long as they are SMART.

But if you don't write the goals down, if you don't write the keys to success, and if you don't write down what achieving those goals will actually mean for you personally, then you are unlikely to ever achieve those goals.

Fifth: Following the pattern means you should identify those people who you judge to be successful, and after whom you would like to pattern yourself. And hang around with them and learn from them; and if they're the kind of person that you want to be with, then it is likely they would be more than happy to mentor you.

Know that your mentor does not have to be older than you and your mentor does not have to be more educated than you. One of my mentors is almost half my age. Another one of my mentors has far less than half my formal education. It doesn't matter. They are experts in what they do.

But if you follow the pattern, if you do what they do, if you do what experts in other fields do, and if you associate with people that you like, people that you admire, people that you think are pretty terrific, then you should be able to achieve success. The unfortunate corollary is that if you associate with people who are unsuccessful, or negative, or who do not affirm your goals, they will drag you down. Avoid these people at all costs.

Sixth: Get some money means that you should spend and live within your means. I'll tell you a story, a true story about two surgeons. One made $250,000 a year and bought a $1 million house. The other made $1 million a year and bought a $250,000 house. The first one had to sell his house and is still having to work at age 60. The second one retired in his forties and was able to build a multi – million dollar house.

Get some money. You can and should save money at any income level (see number three). There are tremendous wealth transfers waiting to deprive us of what is rightfully ours. Save your money, keep your money, protect your money. It's easy to be poor, it's easy to feel entitled to something. But remember, eventually if you feel entitled to something you will also feel victimized.

How many people do we know who's parents or grandparents left them a trust fund and became the ne'er-do-wells? The Paris Hiltons of the world whom few of us respect? The drunkard, or the drug addict who went to a top-ranked boarding school? Get some money. You can do it. You should do it. You must do it.

Not that money buys happiness -- but it sure is hard to be happy and successful and feel fulfilled when you are wondering how to make your next mortgage payment.

Seventh: You are not average. By reading this book, by definition you're not average. But let's talk about what average really means in terms of finance. The median annual household income of all tax-payers is around $70,000 a year and only 3% of people are able to retire on that same amount. According to the IRS, the top 10% of household income is on the order of about $90,000 a year. The top 5% is about $150,000 a year and the top 1% is about $300,000 a year.

If you're reading this book chances are you are making a six-figure income if not a high six figure or even seven figure income -- or you have the desire to do so. So when the typical (average) financial media are telling you to take this strategy or take that strategy, remember they are not talking about you, they are talking about average. You are not average. You are above average. And following average advice will only make you average or below average.

Eighth: <u>Keep it simple</u>. But remember, simple is not easy. How many of us are overweight? Too many. And more than likely, those of us overweight are well aware of the bad health consequences. Yet how many of us don't know what to do to lose weight? Exactly. Everybody knows what to do. It's pretty simple. Eat less, move more.

To be a little technical that means just take in fewer net calories. That is pretty simple to do but it is 'pretty darn difficult' or there wouldn't be Weight Watchers and there wouldn't be all these diet things. And Dan Marino wouldn't be talking about this and that. And there wouldn't be Thigh Masters and so on and so forth. Keep it simple; but simple is not easy. (See number three).

The best way to keep it simple is to obtain more education. You can never learn everything. And try not to feel like you are the smartest person in the room. Read voraciously, attend seminars, and listen to your clients, patients, staff, bosses, family, clergy, and anyone who can give you valuable information. Not the technical information either. That -- you can hire. No it is the leadership and growth information you need to update. The resources are voluminous. The more I learn, the more I realize how little I know, and how much I continue to learn from those I teach and coach.

Ninth: <u>Avoid the common mistakes</u>. You are going to make mistakes. Everybody does. You are going to make "doozies". And they are going to hurt and they are going to be costly. That's okay. Just don't make the common ones. Don't make the ones that could be avoided. Don't make mistakes when you don't know what's involved.

For every action you take, especially every big action, understand the risks, understand the benefits, understand the alternatives, and understand the likely outcomes. Because the common things do occur commonly; and the common outcomes are more likely to occur. So if you are swinging for the fences odds are you are going to strike out. Avoid those great big mistakes because they'll be the killer on your way to success.

Tenth: <u>It is definitely not about the money</u>. Oh, true we all need and want money; and money can add to our success; and money can help us feel better about ourselves; and money is a way to keep track about how we're doing; and money is a way to help others; and money is a way to give us a sense of security; and money is a way to get us the toys and joys that we look for.

But it is not about the money. *The money will happen simply by doing the right thing*. You will "do well by doing good". <u>If it's all about the money you will never be successful</u>. Money is the result of the success. The money is not the cause of success. Don't mistake the relationship between cause and effect and between success and money.

And as a bonus…

Bonus Rule # 1: <u>Use a decision making process that works for you.</u> … *And keep to it!* Some find it useful to list pros and cons, or risks and benefits, about the big decisions. Others find it useful to list the alternatives and give ranking or level of importance to each pro and to each con involved in the alternatives.

This is actually how I decided some of the most important decisions of my life. When I was done, there was a clear-cut number that enabled me to make a proper choice. For example, when I was thinking about first moving to Texas in the early 80's, weather had minimal importance but was a positive. It was not outweighed by the negative of moving away from my support system of familiarity, family, and friends. Yet overall, the number and weight of the positives associated with moving to Texas was greater than the alternatives. And it was a great move.

Bonus Rule # 2: I suggest -- no, I implore, that you invest wisely. By investing wisely I mean prudently and using a process. This will lead to prosperity. Know the three signs you may be gambling and speculating:

- stock-picking

- market timing

- track-record-chasing

Avoid these wealth-killers. Diversify so you are prepared for all eventualities (especially the ones over which you have little or no control). Measure, manage, and know your risks, and get paid for them, consistently, reliably, and predictably.

That means you should understand what asset classes are and what makes an asset class. Basically, there are three things that make an asset class:

1. They have to be compositionally stable.

2. They have to be unique.

3. They have to behave in the same way so that one asset class behaves differently from another asset class.

And then make sure your assets are properly allocated using a disciplined approach, avoid the market timing by any other name, avoid the scares. This time is not different. This time is never different.

Find an advisor who will not be merely an order-taker, or will not enable you to make the big mistakes. Don't invest in any one thing in which you can make a killing; therefore, you won't be able to invest in any one thing in which you get killed. If it's too good to be true don't invest in it. Get yourself a good financial coach. Get somebody who can make sure to keep you on track so that you don't lose what you worked so hard for, what you've earned and what you deserve.

Watch out for those predators, creditors and bad actors. Watch out for *the worst predator, the worst creditor, the worst bad actor* (your Uncle) who wants 30, 40 and 50 cents of every dollar you have earned and then some. And then your Uncle will devalue your hard earned wealth through inflation. Yikes.

Watch out for the people who want to sue you. Protect your assets. Make sure that your investments are held in the proper pockets. Should they be held in limited liability companies or family limited partnerships or some other type of account?

And make sure you have appropriate and sufficient insurance in varieties of ways to cover those assets. Because asset protection will not help you avoid a lawsuit but will help you keep what is yours when one comes. In this day and age it only takes a few hundred bucks to go down to the courthouse and file suit against a ham sandwich. And probably some moron judge will allow that suit to take place.

Unfortunately, only a very few of us will attain success. And only because too many do not engage in the 10 crucial steps.

Following these secrets, which really are not secret, is the recipe for true success.

About Mitch

Mitchell Levin, MD, CWPP, CAPP, the Financial Physician™, is a Financial Wealth Coach, and is founder and CEO of Levin Wealth Systems, LLC (www.LevinWealthSystems.com) and is Managing Director of Phipps Lane, LLC, (www.PhippsLane.com) a Registered Investment Advisory firm. Mitch has recently been named CEO and Managing Director of Summit Wealth: Florida's Premier wealth management strategists.

He is dedicated to "empowering investors to achieve Healthy Investment Returns™ and to build, protect, and preserve your prosperity through your own Financial Fortress".

Dr. Mitch is an "A" rated Florida State Representative of the Asset Protection Society, and is a member of the Wealth Preservation Institute, the National Association of Professional College Advisors as well as the National Association of College Financial Advisors, and the Financial Planning Association.

Best-selling author, speaker, trusted advisor: Dr. Mitch is the co-author on many articles and several other books, including: Shift Happens; Cover Your Assets; How to Build, Maintain and Protect your Financial Fortress; The Lies My Broker Taught Me; 101 Truths about Money and Investing; and Secrets of a Worry Free Retirement. He has appeared in several educational CD's **(The Seven Deadly Investor Traps, How the Really Smart Money Invests)**, and in the acclaimed documentary movie "Navigating the Fog of Investing" alongside several Nobel Prize Laureates.

Also, Dr. Mitch has been featured on ABC, NBC, CBS, Fox Affiliates; The Wall Street Journal, Newsweek, USA Today, The Orlando Sentinel; Astral Media's 86 syndicated radio stations; various podcasts; webinars; and teleseminars.

In addition, Mitch is certified in Florida to provide Continuing Professional Education credits to Certified Public Accountants. Some of his speaking engagements include, "The Myths of Investing", "College Funding Solutions", "This Time is (Never) Different", "The Affluent Survival Guide", "Why Mutual Funds Stink", "Why Your Insurance Agent is Costing You Tens or Hundreds of Thousands of Dollars", "How to Prosper in the Reign of Error", and "Your Asset Protection is Inadequate".

His clients are nice, affluent successful people, who actually may be furious when they discover - too late - the poor outcomes, outrageous and hidden fees, and unnecessary taxes they have to pay. And the excessive risks they're taking—that's another conversation completely. They're bombarded with mixed, or negative, or outright fearmongering messages. They sometimes wake up in the middle of the night in a cold sweat. These people feel cheated ...(is that too strong a word?).

Some are worried sick about the markets ups and downs... and their futures don't look so rosy anymore. How to pay for college, retirement, eliminate their mortgage burden.

They're looking for new ideas and don't know who to turn to.

Still others may be having trouble admitting they're failing miserably in their invest-ments, trying to pick stocks, or time the markets, or chase mutual fund track records. They would stop, but no one has the guts to provide a viable alternative, to tell them the truth, to tell them they're wasting time while losing lots of money. They'd have a better chance at the roulette wheel, without the fun.

Is any of this familiar to you, or someone you know?

Mitch's mission is to **"Empower investors to achieve financial fulfillment and peace of mind"** as your "Chief Financial Physician™". Help stop the financial mal-practice and facilitate the cure for financial cancer. Progress from scarcity, losses, fear and frustration, to abundance and peace of mind; Mitch provides a completely independent Financial Second Opinion™.

While in medical school, Mitch was instrumental in setting up the first (and completely student financed) long-term endowment campaign through insurance and derivative products. He was recruited by then Orlando Regional Medical Center to open the first full time eye surgery practice at one of its facilities. The practices grew to several locations with dozens of employees, including several now prominent surgeons. He has lived with his family in Central Florida since 1986, and has been involved profes-sionally in the financial world since 2005.

A small business owner, Mitch has built, grown, bought and sold several other busi-ness entities. In addition, he is a successful commercial real estate investor. Dr. Mitch is a major donor to charitable organizations, and has served as an officer on several Boards of Trustees. The knowledge he gained through these experiences contributed to his personal financial success and the ability to pursue his passion of educating and assisting others in their quest for financial freedom. Contact: info@levinwealth-systems.com

If you take nothing else from this book, we hope you take away enough motivation (if you need it) to become pro-active:-

(a) when developing an appropriate and effective investment policy statement;

(b) when implementing your investment plan; when trying to protect your assets;

(c) when trying to save on income, estate, and capital gains taxes;

(d) when trying to more efficiently and effectively run your business, or your family enterprise; and....

(e) when you plan for transitioning your wealth.

That motivation, along with fortitude (or help from your coach), can allow you to avoid the Big Mistakes that wind up costing loads. It is our intention that you will have discovered for yourself the secrets to building and maintaining your financial fortress. That you find it useful to fulfill your purpose for your money. For control, clarity, comfort, and confidence. In short, for independence and dignity... **through Financial Freedom.**

Power Principle #2

FOCUS ON THE FINISH LINE TO FULFILL YOUR DREAMS!

by Scot Ferrell

"Success is not measured so much by our accomplishments in life, but what we had to overcome in the process." ~ *Booker T. Washington*

Throughout my life, I've always believed that everyone needs a "finish line" to keep them focused on their dreams and the desired outcome, whether the outcome is health, wealth, happiness or prosperity. When I sit down with a new client, I always ask one question – What do you want? This may seem like a very easy question to answer, but for some reason, for most people, it is the equivalent of climbing Mount Everest.

Most people only focus on what they currently have and what they think they can achieve, not what they truly desire. Every human is born with a God-given desire and dream, yet so few ever actually realize it. Why?

In my early 30s, I was diagnosed with bipolar disorder, and, like most people diagnosed with a psychological disorder, I had absolutely no idea which direction to go with my life. Unfortunately, from the moment of my diagnosis on, I allowed outside forces to dictate everything that happened in my life until several years ago, one rainy afternoon, driving home from my psychiatrist's office. Here I was, a teacher specializing in behavior management, and I was the one allowing other people to control my life. Throughout that period, I had stopped asking myself what I truly wanted out of my life.

During the 45 minute drive home, I replayed in my mind everything that my psychiatrist and I had discussed during my visit. With tears running down my face, I heard his voice in my head constantly repeating that I should go on disability and give up my dreams of having a "normal" life – being a high school basketball coach, getting married, having a full time job, and having a healthy mind, body and soul. I allowed him to hand me the "death sentence" of my dreams. Here I was, in my late 30s, letting someone tell me that, for all practical purposes, my life was over.

I know my doctor thought he was doing me a favor that day, but how can it be helpful to you if your support networks are the ones trying to steal and crush your dreams? For some reason, people think that they are helping us by telling us to "live in the real world" and that our "dreams aren't possible." When I got home, I walked around and screamed at the walls for a while (I didn't have a cat to kick), and decided I could either be a whiner or a winner. For years, I had been telling my basketball players, "The only thing that can beat you in life is you." I decided that I had to put up or shut up.

Right then and there, I decided I would beat bipolar disorder and nothing would stop me. For the first time in many years, I was very clear on what I wanted with all of my heart.

Viktor Frankl was able to sum up exactly what I felt and what I needed to do, in this quote: "Everything can be taken away from a man but one thing: the last of the human freedoms – to choose one's attitude in any given set of circumstances, to choose one's own way." This was a Jewish man who had been imprisoned in a Nazi death camp during World War II and had watched as his entire family was put to death, in addition to many others around him whom he befriended. He was starved, frozen, abused and tortured, and when I read what he had endured, it made me think, "Why am I complaining? All I have to do is beat bipolar disorder!"

Now that I knew what the "finish line" was, how would I get there?

"Appreciation can make a day, even change a life. Your willingness to put it into words is all that is necessary." - Margaret Cousins

The first step in seeing the "finish line" is gratitude. I had to be grateful for what I currently had and express appreciation for the things that I knew were coming. I started to get up every day, thanking God for everything in my life, big or small, good or bad. When you have an "attitude of gratitude", it begins to focus your attention away from the negative things in your life and gives energy to the positive thoughts you are expressing. The best time to express gratitude is always! It is impossible to be negative and grateful at the same time.

I also thanked God in advance for helping me develop a process that I would use to beat bipolar disorder. I'd like to point out here that at this stage, I had absolutely no idea how I was going to beat bipolar disorder. I was attempting something that appeared to be an impossible goal. But, I knew where I was starting and I knew my "finish line."

"Change your thoughts and you change your world." - Norman Vincent Peale

The second step for me was figuring out how to change my thoughts by writing down everything that I wanted - not what I thought I could have, but the deepest desires of my heart. I got out a pad and wrote with as much detail as I could about what I wanted my life to look like – a life free of bipolar disorder, a hot, flashy sports car in the garage, a meaningful career I loved that provided me with a chance to help children and adults overcome their own obstacles, the financial abundance that would reward my entrepreneurial efforts, the house of my dreams, someone I could love with all my heart who would love me unconditionally and ways I could use my purpose to serve God.

"What makes us human is our capability to imagine, to cast ourselves as the heroes in the mental adventures of our own design. When one stops dreaming one might as well die, for there is nothing for which living is more worthy than one's imagination." - Odic Henderson

The third step is visualization. During visualization, it is not actually what you think, but what you feel that is critical. You have to give a future event a "present day" emotion. The emotion has to be so strong and vivid that if you're thinking about jogging, you're actually sweating! If it's a new car you dream about, smell the leather, feel the seat warmers, hear the Metallica playing on the radio, see the scenic countryside and taste your favorite hot beverage as you drive. Do you want someone special to share your life? Remember your first kiss and how you spent hours imagining how it would be and how much passion you felt over something that had not happened yet? Then, it happened and you continued to re-live the moment in your mind and you may even still think about it today!

Now apply that same passion to your visualization of that ideal man or woman you have been searching for. Ladies, if you're searching for your mate, here are some ideas: Go to the men's cologne department and pick out a scent that you would like your future man to wear. Smell this as you visualize the touch of his hand embracing yours. Feel the passion as he looks in your eyes and your lips touch for the first time. Be sure to put the amount of passion and feeling that you just put into the thought of that first kiss into every visualization exercise you perform on a daily basis. I do my visualization exercises every morning when I get up and every evening before I go to bed. I want to start and end every day with the "finish line" firmly planted in my thoughts and emotions. If you don't feel it and believe in it, it is pointless to think about the "finish line."

"Only in our easy, simple, spontaneous actions are we strong." - Ralph Waldo Emerson

The critical fourth step is action. Without action, thoughts and feelings will always be fantasy, not reality. I had to develop the steps to get me to the "finish line" of beating bipolar disorder. The process took me years to accomplish, one day at a time, completing the action items I had identified. <u>Success, in any area of your life, is not just about feelings. It's about doing.</u> It takes a winning formula of the big four – gratitude, thoughts, feelings and action.

Just to reiterate this point, research shows that successful people train their minds to think only about what they want to happen in their lives and then they put action behind their thoughts. I don't want to insult you by implying that you haven't taken the time to write out your plan or goals to get you to your "finish line" at some point in your life. However, that "finish line" and your dream may have completely changed, or you may need help getting restarted and/or re-focused on your dream.

Here's how I stay focused on my dream and the ultimate "finish line:" I keep a set of 3 x 5 note cards with me at all times. Each morning, I write down four actions that I need to take that day to bring me closer to the "finish line." I do not end my day without completing the four action steps that I wrote earlier that morning. This prevents me from confusing "busyness" with productive, focused action that will move me a few steps closer to my dream. I feel very strongly about this method and here's why: *it works!*

I'm sure by now, you're wondering if I ever made it to my "finish line." The answer is yes.

I took my thoughts, combined it with the visualization of my feelings and developed action steps that actually began to make my dreams begin to come true. The more I focused on my dream with every fiber of my body, the more all of the unknowns became known! Each step of the way, someone I did not know would appear to help me. Remember, I said I had no idea how I would ever get to my "finish line."

I didn't need to know, because God knew and He provided every single thing I needed to get me to my "finish line." It's okay to not know how you are going to get to your "finish line." That's how everybody starts. You just have to have enough faith in God and yourself that no matter what happens, you know you'll get there.

So, what did my "finish line" look like when I got there?

The "finish line" had my doctor sitting beside me, telling me that all of my neurotransmitters were at normal levels and that I was completely free of bipolar disorder. The "finish line" was far greater than anything I could have ever imagined. I went out of his office that day with much different emotions than the ones I had that rainy afternoon several years prior. I was finally free. I was free to be whoever I wanted to be and dream anything I wanted. I had just beaten an illness that many say couldn't be beaten. I knew at that moment, that whatever I dreamed in life, I could have and achieve. It's true. By the way, I did find the girl of my dreams, we're now married and we write books together. Remember, the only person who can defeat you is you.

"No one can cheat you out of ultimate success, but yourself." - Ralph Waldo Emerson

I now teach my clients that they can have anything they want. They just have to be able to combine gratitude, thoughts, feelings and actions and if they stay focused, they will see the "finish line."

About Scot

Scot is a nationally recognized inspirational author, speaker, mentor, as well as radio show host and television guest, teaching people how to overcome life's obstacles and achieve their dreams. He provides clients with the tools to create spiritual, physical, mental, and emotional health. His process teaches clients how to overcome the behavioral barriers that have hampered their lives and destroyed their dreams. In addition, Ferrell teaches a scientific, "results-oriented" process to overcome disorders, such as Clinical Depression, Bipolar Disorder, Anxiety Disorders, ADD and ADHD.

Utilizing a process he developed for his own personal life, Scot works with pastors, executives, athletes, individuals and families, guiding them to more satisfying life experiences, attitudes, behaviors and performance, utilizing behavioral management concepts. He provides consultation and training to families, to provide adults, guardians, parents and children with the tools they need to successfully develop the problem solving and self-management skills required to overcome their unique challenges.

Scot is also the author of "*The Success Guide to Bipolar Disorder*", which teaches people the process to overcome, not manage, not only Bipolar Disorder, but Clinical Depression as well. In 2010, he will be releasing his three new books, "*What Men Don't Get about Women*", "*What Women Don't Get About Men*" and "*Defeat Your Demons*". He will also be a contributing author to "*Power Principles for Success*" due for release in July of 2010. Ferrell also hosts a weekly radio show on blog talk radio on Monday evenings at 6:30 PM Eastern. Listeners can call in to talk with Scot, listen live or download archived episodes. His show, The Success Guide to Life, can be accessed through http://www.blogtalkradio.com/thebehaviorexpert. Ferrell previously hosted The Success Guide to Life on WNIV, a Christian talk radio station in Atlanta, Georgia.

Scot himself is completely recovered from Bipolar Disorder using the process he developed and now teaches others to utilize in their own lives. He works with businesses, churches, pastors and private clients, educating them about psychological disorders as well as mentoring clients through his scientific, "results-oriented" process to defeat what he terms as "dream-destructive" behaviors.

Scot Ferrell, psychological disorder and behavior management expert, is one of only a handful of participants selected for America's Premier Experts and participating in The Ultimate Celebrity Branding Experience™.

Power Principle #3

ALIGN YOUR DREAMS, GOALS, AND VALUES FOR LASTING SUCCESS

by J.W. Dicks, Esq.

In the many training sessions I have hosted over the years, I have noticed a great number of people have a difficult time with goal setting. They understand intellectually the value of setting goals, but they can't see how it applies to their own lives.

Maybe this sounds self-evident, but I'll say it anyway: Before you can set a goal, you have to understand what a goal is. Simply put, _a goal is a dream fixed to a certain time._ The dream is something you desire. The time element affixes it to your personal world and your reality. The dream is no longer simply floating in space; now it has a real "time meaning" attached to it, and it must be dealt with.

Second, the goal must relate to a personal value. Goals are the answer to the question, *"What is important to you in life?"* Values are the answer to why you want to accomplish those goals. If you don't relate your goal to your values, that goal will remain as lost – floating in space – as it was before you attached it to the reality of time.

This is one reason why you can't simply adopt someone else's goals for your life. The chances that you'll share that person's deepest values are incredibly small. Therefore, a goal that makes sense to another person isn't likely to make much sense to you.

It is also why it is foolish for parents to push their children onto a particular career path, or – worse – into accomplishing something that they had not been able to achieve for themselves. Why? Because the goal that is being set for the child is based on the *parents'* dream rather than the child's. Yes, you can help someone nurture his or her own dreams, but you can't dream for someone else. The most rewarding thing a parent can do for a child is help that child discover their own dreams and learn how to fulfill them.

SHAPE YOUR DREAMS

In order to reach a goal you set for yourself, you must first learn to *define it specifically*. If you are unsure of your objective, it will be easy for you to become distracted. For example, if you start only with the general desire to "make more money," you may achieve that goal – but chances are you won't *keep* the money. You'll soon discover that there is no end to the amount you can spend if you don't relate it to certain standards. The 2,500 square-foot house will become the 5,000 square-foot house. The "first new car" will evolve into the "first luxury car," which will evolve into the "top of the line new car traded in every two years."

Because you have no specific goal, you will be trapped on the 'up escalator'. You will spend more and more, because you think that the very acquisition of things will make you happy. Yes, you will find yourself in new, more luxurious surroundings – but instead of worrying about how you are going to make your $700 per-month house payment, you'll be worrying about how you will make the $4,000 per-month house payment.

You achieved your vague goal – *more money* – but somehow things got worse. The topic of worry (lack of money) has stayed the same, but now the practical burden you bear has become far heavier. You had a certain number of options to find replacement cash flow for the $700 per-month payment on your smaller home. But now that your payments are $4,000 per-month, the options available to you for producing that much money are far fewer.

To stay off the up escalator – to avoid the "more money" treadmill – you need to decide what you do want, and in very precise terms. You need to *shape your dreams* by attaching them to time frames and specifics. At the same time, you need to make sure that the goals you set are aligned with your values.

Why? Because your values are the focal point of your internal happiness. If you set and achieve a goal that is in conflict with your values, not only will you be unhappy about having obtained that goal, but the result will have a negative influence on your desire to set and achieve *other* goals. Psychologically, you will begin to regard goal setting as an unhappy experience, even though that wasn't the problem in the first place. The *real* problem was that you didn't align the goals with your values.

I have some very good friends who worked for years to build a large company out of an idea they came up with together. They longed for the day when they could buy a huge house on the water in a very exclusive area of our town. Because of their diligence and hard work, the company prospered, and they achieved their goal of purchasing their dream home. Unfortunately, the achievement of that goal didn't make them happy. Why not? Because that purchase separated them from their friends and their church, both of which – as it turned out – were things that they valued far more than that new house on the water.

And just to make things worse, they began to feel guilty about their newfound wealth. They worried that people might think they were showing off – even though that had never been their intent – and that people might become less friendly toward them. And in fact, their friends did begin to associate with them less frequently – in part because of their own feelings of jealousy and insecurity, and in part because their old friends now seemed different in their fancy new house. They seemed guarded and defensive rather than open and friendly.

While this couple came to understand the causes of what had happened, it didn't make them feel any better. The mistake they made was not in buying a big house on the water. (There's nothing inherently wrong with that goal.) The mistake they made was that they had defined and achieved a goal that didn't match their values. How do you keep your goals and valued aligned?

I have summarized the process in a series of seven steps:

1. Create a list of goals and values.

2. Prioritize your goals.

3. Establish a plan to achieve your goals.

4. Take action on your goals.

5. Create success habits.

6. Rebalance your key objectives.

7. Enjoy, actualize, and repeat the process.

GOAL-SETTING STRATEGY NO. 1: CREATE A LIST OF GOALS AND VALUES

Values are what you believe about yourself. Goals, on the other hand, are targets that should capture those values and – once achieved – reinforce those values. In the case of my friends who became isolated, their goal was a hollow one, because it took them away from their fundamental values of friends and church. The goal was clearly at odds with their values. Without an alignment between values and goals, there will be no satisfaction. In fact, the only possible outcome is dissatisfaction.

Discovering your own values is one of the most important things you can do. And yet, very few people have ever even considered their values. Here is a short helpful exercise. Sit down in a quiet room and write down five personal values that you consider important. Don't think too hard about it – just start writing what comes into your mind. They will come to you. If you put down more than five, that's fine (you won't be graded!)

If you need help getting started, that's OK, too. Just glance at this list of values shared by many people. Remember that while lists of values may overlap (in other words, you may use the same words as someone else), the order of the words and the weight you place upon them make the lists very different.

A close relationship with your mate

A good relationship with your family

36

A meaning of life

A relationship with God

Being highly regarded

Control of your destiny

Fame

Friendships

Giving to others

Good health

Happiness

Influence

Living to old age

Peace of mind

Possessions

Power

Purpose to work

Respect

Retirement

Security

Sense of accomplishment

Travel

Wealth

YOUR VALUE LIST:

1._____

2._____

3._____

4._____

5._____

Now that you have made your list, rank your values from more important to less important (even though every value on this list is important).

Look at the result. Did you get it right? Are you happy with this summary of your values? If so, congratulations, because coming up with this list may be the most important thing you will ever do. Why? *Because it is truly your road map to happiness.*

Here's why. Let's assume that your number one value is a close relationship with God, and your number two value is a close relationship with your family. And let's also assume that at the present time, you are pursuing a career that pays well and earns you lots of kudos and recognition but requires you to spend a great deal of time away from your family.

Well, if that job doesn't somehow help you to develop a closer relationship with God, you are likely to be one miserable human being – and chances are, you won't even know why. Most likely, you are working hard, banking a lot of money, and feeling mostly empty inside. Your values are your essence. If you hope to achieve a happy life, you have to live a life and aspire to a future that captures and expresses those values.

Assume for a moment that a certain individual (let's call her Jane) has the following values:

1. A close relationship with God

2. A close relationship with family

3. Peace of mind

4. Security

5. Good health

Conspicuously absent from Jane's list is anything about "making lots of money." True, you could make the case that goals 3 through 5 presuppose financial security. But the point is, "making money" didn't make Jane's list.

Can you see the importance of this discovery? If Jane spends all of her time trying to become a millionaire, she is almost certain to be a very unhappy millionaire (if, indeed, she ever gets there). For Jane to be successful in her own eyes, her goals must be aligned with her values. To sharpen the point, let's consider the following question: Which of the following goals, if achieved, would make Jane happier?

1. Making $1 million

2. Setting up a faith-based charitable foundation with an endowment of $1 million

See the difference? Putting $1 million in the bank would probably make Jane feel OK, up to a point. But wouldn't endowing a faith-based charitable foundation do a lot more to make Jane feel satisfied with her life?

Let's take this illustration a step further. What if you changed the second goal to read: "Setting up a faith-based charitable foundation with an endowment of $1 million, in which all of my family members would work together." Wow! Do you see what that would mean to Jane? The better she understands her values, the more likely it is that she can set the right goals, give herself a life's mission, and live her life with passion.

So here's our next exercise, which builds directly on the last one, as well as on Jane's example. Take a few minutes to review the values you've written down and ranked. Now write down five goals that, if achieved, would capture and reinforce those values.

LIST GOALS

1._____

2._____

3._____

4._____

5._____

GOAL-SETTING STRATEGY NO. 2: PRIORITIZE YOUR GOALS

Now that you have established a list of goals, rank them. Renumber them as you did your values list, lining them up in their order of importance to you. And although we don't want to complicate the assignment too much, we encourage you to think about making two such lists: one ranked in order of importance, and the second ranked in order of urgency. Which goal is of the greatest enduring importance to you, and which do you want (or need) to accomplish first?

For example, if one of your goals is to build a $2 million retirement nest egg and another is to put your kids through college five years from now, it doesn't make a great deal of sense to concentrate on your retirement plan when you have a much more urgent need – unless, of course, the retirement plan is of far greater importance to you. If the goals are of equal importance, then urgency takes over, and your priority quickly becomes the tuition bills.

GOAL-SETTING STRATEGY NO. 3: ESTABLISH A PLAN TO ACHIEVE YOUR GOALS

You have your goal. It is your top priority. Now, what are you going to do about it?

When my children were younger we went on trips by car, I would call the American Automobile Association – "Triple A"— and ask them to do a trip plan. In a couple of weeks, AAA would send back a nice, bound series of maps that told us the best way to get to our destinations. (Now, of course, you can do it all online.) If there was construction along the way, AAA would either suggest detours or carefully mark the construction area and advise us that there was a bumpy road ahead.

Wouldn't it be nice if life were like that? You could set your goal, call up AAA, and get a plan laid out for you. Unfortunately, life isn't quite that easy. But with the help of the simple concepts you can learn how to do the plan yourself. The key to reaching any financial goal is to have a plan. Surprisingly, it's not so important that you pick the perfect road or the perfect investment system. Instead, the important thing is to pick a specific plan and stick with it until you reach your destination.

How do you create a plan to achieve your goals? The same way that you create a plan for a trip. You write down the moves that you need to make, step by step, to get to your destination. Just as you follow a map from AAA to get to a geographic destination, you follow a specific plan to get to a goal destination.

GOAL-SETTING STRATEGY NO. 4:
TAKE ACTION ON YOUR GOALS

My father always said, "A turtle never gets anywhere unless he sticks his neck out." He was right. Ultimately, we have to take action. Otherwise, all our values, goals, and plans aren't worth the paper we put them on.

But taking action proves difficult for a lot of people, because they are filled with anxieties and insecurities. Did I put down the right goal? Is my plan a good one? These doubts paralyze the worrier, just like a deer caught in headlights.

Nevertheless, you must take action on the plan you create. Think of it as something like scaling a cliff. If you had to climb a cliff for the first time, how would you do it? You'd start out slow and easy. You'd pace yourself, going up foot by vertical foot. You don't have to break any speed record or take any unnecessary risks. Well, it's the same with acting on a goal plan. You don't have to reach your goal overnight. Success is an endurance event – a marathon rather than a sprint. Take off slowly, build to a comfortable pace, and stride to the finish.

How do you get started? It's easy. Take a look at your goals list. Pick the one goal on your list that seems the easiest to accomplish and also has near-term importance. Let's say that you wrote down, "Make $10,000 more this year." That's a good goal. It's near-term, and it's specific. So let's use it to take action. Below your goal, create a plan to achieve the goal by listing the specific action steps you'll take to get there:

Goal:- Make $10,000 more this year

Plan:- Increase salary by $3,000

Action Step 1: Ask for a raise.

- Create a list of reasons I deserve a raise.

- Make an appointment with my boss.

Action Step 2: Start a small business.

- Research businesses of interest.

- Pick a business in 60 days.

- Start the business in 90 days.

If you are like a lot of people who have never properly learned the techniques of goal setting, this method is likely to come as a pleasant surprise. For the first time, not only do you *see* your goal, but you see specific action steps that you can take to achieve it.

While the goal may seem difficult, the action steps to achieve the goal are often much easier. You will discover that taking each step puts you closer and closer to your goal, which in turn makes the goal appear easier and more attainable the closer you get to it.

GOAL-SETTING STRATEGY NO. 5: CREATE SUCCESS HABITS

Sometimes, with the best of intentions, parents do their children a disservice. One example of such a disservice is continuously linking the words habit and bad. For example:

Quit biting your nails. It's a bad habit.

Stop smoking. It's a bad habit.

Don't drink so much. It's a bad habit.

Have you ever heard anyone praised for developing a good habit? Not often, and yet, good habits are critically important. The tennis star's consistent stroke, which leads to victories on the court, is the result of a good habit. The student who studies consistently and makes top grades has developed good study habits. In fact, any repetitive pattern that brings success deserves to be recognized and applauded, and should be built into one's system of goals: I will continue this action until it becomes a habit.

Vital habits can be developed to help you maintain your success. For example, in investing, diversifying your portfolio, setting limits on losses, resisting the temptation to get greedy – all are proven goal rules that build both protection and consistency into your goal plan. If you take the time and effort to transform these goals into habits, you will profit substantially from the improved performance of your portfolio and the added protection they give you.

GOAL-SETTING STRATEGY NO 6: REBALANCE YOUR KEY OBJECTIVES

I hope that, by now, you have been impressed on the importance of values and goals when it comes to your success. You should also understand that while some values may be consistent throughout your life, others may change. When they do, both your goals and your plans to reach those goals need to re-evaluated and rebalanced, in order to get your new value/goal structure into alignment. If you don't rebalance, it will be like deciding to stay on the road to New York after you've decided to go to San Francisco instead. Yes, you're still moving along a path, but you're sure to arrive at the wrong place.

To help you spot these changes as they occur in your life, I suggest that you set a particular time each year to rebalance your objectives. I have found the two weeks after Christmas to be a perfect time for this activity. Business always slows down during that time of year, and the decrease in activity gives you an opportunity to reflect.

Note the consistency in this approach. By consistently rebalancing your objectives at the same time each year, you have made this activity into a habit. While that time might not be good for you, pick one that is, rebalance your objectives, and (if necessary) refocus your life.

GOAL-SETTING STRATEGY NO. 7: ENJOY, ACTUALIZE, AND REPEAT THE PROCESS

If you incorporate the six strategies, or steps, just outlined into your life, you will find a new sense of gratification and enjoyment. Now that your life is in alignment with who you are, you should begin to feel that you are headed in the right direction – much like the driver with the AAA road maps. Take the time to enjoy this newfound sense of satisfaction.

At the same time, be prepared for that sense of satisfaction to ebb and even disappear. Just as the wheels on your car lose their alignment over time (and far more quickly if you hit a curb!), our lives also get "out of alignment" because of life's curbs. It is just a part of human nature: We get caught up in all sorts of things that we never intended to get caught up in.

What's important, though, is simply to understand that we must (1) enjoy things when they go well, (2) understand that misalignment will happen, and (3) get realigned when we hit that curb (or when life's twists and turns gradually lead to misalignment).

By repeating this process, you will enjoy your life more and continually refocus yourself on the things that are truly important to you. **Once you are properly focused, it is easier to let go of those miscues that don't fit into your grand plan.**

About J.W.

JW Dicks is an attorney, best-selling author of 15 books, entrepreneur and personal branding business strategist. He has spent his entire 38-year career building successful businesses for himself and his clients producing sales of over $500 million worth of products and services.

Today, JW serves as a consultant to business professionals and entrepreneurs to position their business and grow it through the power of personal branding, a concept he has developed and pioneered.

Through the use of proprietary methods , JW works with a client to create a vision and branding position for their business that is centered upon the client as the expert in their field. Once the branding position is set, JW helps the client develop a step by step business development system designed to reach their monetary and lifestyle goals.

JW is co-founder of Dicks & Nanton Agency, a new media, marketing, and branding company which implements online and offline business growth strategies for clients to help them get more new clients while increasing the value of the ones they have. The company uses its patent-pending formulas to get their clients guaranteed mass media credentials such as being quoted in major publications like USA Today, Newsweek and the Wall Street Journal, appearances on television shows created for ABC, FOX, NBC, and CBS along with becoming Best Selling authors in their field.

Although technically proficient in several disciplines, JW's clients consider his greatest attributes to be his business vision, creativity and ability to design and implement multi-layered profit centers for their businesses.

JW's business address is Orlando and his play address is his beach house where he spends as much time as he can with his wife, Linda, of 38 years, two daughters, son-in-law, and two Yorkies. His major hobby is fishing-- although the fish are rumored to be safe.

Power Principle #4

EARNING POTENTIAL IS YOUR MOST VALUABLE ASSET!

by Brian Tracy

What you are about to learn changed my life and it will change yours as well, in a positive way.

When I first heard the question, *"What is your most valuable asset?",* I immediately thought of my car, my furniture, my house, my investments and money in the bank.

But these are not your most valuable financial assets. Your most valuable asset is your "earning ability." It is your ability to earn money each day, week, month and year. It is your ability to enter into a competitive market place and use your acquired and accumulated talent, skills, intelligence and ability to achieve results for which people will pay you 'good money'.

You could lose your house, your car, your job, and all your money, ending up penniless on the street. But, as long as you have maintained your earning ability and were able to re-enter the marketplace, you could pump tens of thousands of dollars back into your life. You could make it all back, and more besides.

Because of our rapidly changing economy, and the continuing obso-lescence of knowledge and skills, your earning ability can be either an "appreciating asset" or a "depreciating asset". If your earning ability is an "appreciating asset," you are becoming increasingly valuable every week, month and year. You are continually upgrading your existing skills and adding new knowledge and skills. These will enable you to get even better results for which people will pay you even more money.

For most people who are not aware of the importance of their earning ability, they have a "depreciating asset." It is continually losing value year by year, because the individual is not getting better and better at what he does. Even worse, most people are getting worse in the essential skills required by their jobs. They are progressively worth less and less.

Pat Riley, the basketball coach, said, *"If you're not getting better, you're getting worse."* No one stays in the same place in a time of rapid change.

Peter Drucker said, *"The only skill that will be of lasting value in the 21st century will be the skill of learning new skills. All other skills will become obsolete with the passing of time."*

YOUR MOST PRECIOUS RESOURCE

Here is another question: *What is your most precious resource?*

It is not something tangible or material. Your most precious resource is actually your "time." Your time represents your life itself. Your life is made up of the minutes and hours of each day. Once time has passed, it can never be retrieved. Once a minute or an hour has gone by, that amount of your life has passed as well.

One more question: *What is your very best investment?*

Answer: The very best investment you can make is to invest your time into increasing your earning ability. There is nothing that will improve the quality of your life, boost your income, and enable you to enjoy a better lifestyle than by "getting better" at what you do today to earn your income.

You have heard about the 80/20 Rule. This rule, the "Pareto Principle," says that 20% of your activities will account for 80% of your results, and 20% of the things that you do in your work will account for 80% of your income.

This rule also says that the top 20% of people in any society earn and control 80% of the wealth. The bottom 80% of money earners have to struggle and get by on whatever is left over by those in the top 20%.

Why does this happen? Why do some people earn several times the income of others? As it happens, everyone starts off roughly at the same point. We have roughly the same education, intelligence and opportunity. Like a marathon, we all line up on the starting line and then the gun goes off. In the months and years ahead, some people move to the front, the bulk stay in the middle, and many people fall to the back, not even completing the race until everyone has gone home.

INCOME GAP VERSUS SKILLS GAP

There is a good deal of talk today about the "income gap" in our society. But Gary Becker, the 1993 Nobel Price winning economist, has pointed out that we do not have an "income gap" as much as we have a "skills gap."

The people in the top 20% are simply those who have learned the essential skills that they need to achieve a high level of earning ability. The people in the bottom 80% are those who, having had the same opportunity, failed to develop those skills.

Many people have gone from rags to riches by realizing this critical fact, and then dedicating themselves to become very good at what they do. You must do the same.

Every person who is serious about their future, especially their financial future, should commit to being in the top 10% of their field. What we have found is that anything less than a commitment to excellence condemns a person to being mediocre.

It seems as if there is a "default setting" on human performance. If you don't decide to become the best, you simply become average. Nobody sets off in life to be "average" or below. But by failing to dedicate yourself totally, especially in the formative years of your career, and by failing not to becoming absolutely excellent at what you do, you default into the bottom 80%, where you worry about money all your life.

In the 21st Century, you are a "knowledge worker." You do not work with your physical body, making and moving things. You work with your mind, applying your intelligence and personality to your world to make a valuable contribution that others will pay you for. <u>The key to becoming an effective knowledge worker is for you to continually upgrade your knowledge and skills in the work that you have chosen to do</u>.

KEY RESULT AREAS

In each job, there seems to be about five to seven *Key Result Areas* that account for performance, effectiveness and results in that job. You may perform dozens of small tasks in the course of a day or a week, but there are seldom more than five to seven key tasks that determine your success or failure.

For example, in <u>Management</u>, the seven *Key Result Areas* are:-

1) Planning; 2) Organizing; 3) Staffing; 4) Delegating; 5) Supervising; 6) Measuring; and 7) Reporting. Your success as a manager can largely be determined by how well you do your job and perform these functions in each area.

In <u>Selling</u>, for example, the seven *Key Result Areas* are:-

1) Prospecting and getting appointments; 2) Establishing rapport and trust; 3) Identifying customer needs accurately; 4) Presenting your products persuasively; 5) Answering customer objections and concerns; 6) Closing the sale and getting the customer to take action; and 7) Getting resales and referrals from satisfied customers.

In summary, this is what we have discovered: <u>Your weakest key skill in your field determines the 'height' of your income and your success</u>. Your weakest essential skill is what holds you back from performing at your very best in all of the other areas. By identifying your weakest skill, and then becoming excellent in that area, you can often surge ahead rapidly in your career and move up into the top 10%.

YOUR MOST IMPORTANT SKILL

How do you determine the skill that can help you the most? You ask this question: "What one skill, if I was absolutely excellent at, would help me the most to double my income?"

If you are not sure about your answer to this question, you must find out as quickly as possible. Ask your boss. Ask your coworkers. Ask your friends. Ask your customers. *You must know the answer to this question or you cannot move ahead in your career.* It is impossible for you to get into the top 10% in your field unless you know with great clarity which skill, or lack of skill, is holding you back.

Once you have determined the one skill that can help you the most, write it down as a goal using these words: <u>"I am absolutely excellent at this particular skill by (such and such a date)."</u>

Then, make a list of everything you could do to develop this skill. Organize the list by sequence and priority. What do you need to do before you do something else? What is more important and what is less important? A list of activities, organized by sequence and priorities, becomes a plan. With a goal and a plan, you will start to make more progress in your life than you can imagine today.

The next step is for you to take action immediately on your new goal - that of becoming excellent in an area where you are still weak. <u>Then, to complete your success, you must do something every single day that makes you a little bit better.</u> Read a little bit in your field. Listen to audio programs in your car. Attend seminars and courses. And most of all, practice, practice, practice until you finally reach the top.

JOIN THE TOP 10%

When I first learned that I would have to be in the top 10% in my field in order to enjoy the highest possible income, I immediately felt discouraged and disappointed. I had never been good at anything before. I had been kicked out of high school in the 12th grade and had worked at laboring jobs for several years. When I got into sales, I knocked on hundreds of doors, cold-calling, and made almost no sales at all.

Now, a top sales professional was telling me that I would have to be in the top 10% to really enjoy all the riches and rewards of the selling profession. Then I learned something that changed my life. I learned that everyone who is in the top 10% started in the bottom 10%. Everyone who is doing well was once doing poorly. Everyone who is at the top of your field today was at one time not even in your field, and did not even know that your field existed.

Here is a great discovery:

All business skills are learnable. All sales skills are learnable. All management skills are learnable. All business building and entrepreneurial skills are learnable. All success-skills and money-making skills are learnable.

Everyone who is good at them today was at one time poor in every area. But they made a decision, set a goal, made a plan, and worked on it, over and over again, until they mastered the skill. *And what hundreds of thousands and millions of other people have done, you can do as well.*

NO ONE IS SMARTER THAN YOU

Remember, no one is smarter than you and no one is better than you. If someone is doing better than you today, it simply means that they have learned the essential skills they needed before you have. And anything anyone else has done, you can do as well.

When you follow this formula, concentrating on your most important and desirable skills, disciplining yourself to persist until you have mastered those skills, you will open up your whole life. You will put your career onto the fast track. You will increase your earning ability rapidly.

As you get better and better at a key skill, your self-esteem will increase. Your self-image will improve. You will like and respect yourself more, and you will be liked and respected more by the people around you. You will feel a tremendous sense of personal power and pride as you get better and better at what you do.

Sooner or later, in a month, six months, or a year, you will have mastered that key skill. Then what do you do? You repeat the process with the next one!

Once again, you ask, *"Now, what one skill will help me the most to double my income?"*

You write it down, make a plan, and work on it every day. <u>You turn</u>

<u>yourself into a do-it-to-yourself project.</u>

FAST TRACK TO SUCCESS

Thousands of chief executive officers of large and small companies have been asked, "What qualities would most mark a person for rapid promotion in your company?"

Fully 85% of them give the same answer. They say: "The most valuable people in my company are those who set priorities, work on their most important tasks, and get the job done quickly and well."

As you develop new skills, increasing (a) your earning ability, and (b) your levels of knowledge and skills, you must then apply what you know to getting important jobs done quickly.

<u>There is nothing that will cause you to stand out in your field more than by developing a reputation as a hard worker who does things quickly and well</u>.

In a short period of time, you will become the 'go-to' person in your company. When your boss, or other key people, want or need something done quickly, they will come to you. Along with these additional responsibilities will come additional authority, opportunity and increased income. *Your goal should be to become one of the most effective, most competent, most respected, and highest paid people in your business.*

The good news is that <u>there are no limits to what you can accomplish, and how far you can go</u>, when you dedicate your working life to continually increasing your earning ability. You will soon become one of the highest paid people in your field.

About Brian and Brian Tracy International:

Brian Tracy is Chairman and CEO of Brian Tracy International, a company specializing in the training and development of individuals and organizations.

Brian's goal is to help you achieve your personal and business goals faster and easier than you ever imagined.

Brian Tracy has consulted for more than 1,000 companies and addressed more than 4,000,000 people in 4,000 talks and seminars throughout the US, Canada and 40 other countries worldwide. As a Keynote speaker and seminar leader, he addresses more than 250,000 people each year.

He has studied, researched, written and spoken for 30 years in the fields of economics, history, business, philosophy and psychology. He is the top selling author of over 45 books that have been translated into dozens of languages.

He has written and produced more than 300 audio and video learning programs, including the worldwide, best-selling Psychology of Achievement, which has been translated into more than 20 languages.

He speaks to corporate and public audiences on the subjects of Personal and Professional Development, including the executives and staff of many of America's largest corporations. His exciting talks and seminars on Leadership, Selling, Self-Esteem, Goals, Strategy, Creativity and Success Psychology bring about immediate changes and long-term results.

Prior to founding his company, Brian Tracy International, Brian was the Chief Operating Officer of a $265 million dollar development company. He has had successful careers in sales and marketing, investments, real estate development and syndication, importation, distribution and management consulting. He has conducted high level consulting assignments with several billion-dollar corporations in strategic planning and organizational development.

He has traveled and worked in over 80 countries on six continents, and speaks four languages. Brian is happily married and has four children. He is active in community and national affairs, and is the President of three companies headquartered in Solana Beach, California.

Brian is also the President of Brian Tracy University, a private on-line University for sales and entrepreneurship.

Power Principle #5

"THE POWER OF TEAM TRAINING"

by Scott Schumann, D.D.S.

"Individual commitment to a group effort. That is what makes a team work, a company work, a society work, a civilization work." ~ *Vince Lombardi*

The 2010 Super Bowl. The Indiana Colts were heavy favorites to win, thanks to the football fan frenzy over legendary quarterback Peyton Manning. And for while, it looked like the Colts would do the job – despite some score see-sawing during the first three quarters, the Colts kept coming back to take the lead.

Then, in the fourth quarter, Tracy Porter of the Saints intercepted a Manning pass, ran for 74 yards and scored a touchdown – this was the play that took the Colts down for good.

And there's only one reason it happened – because Porter was prepared. In the days leading up to the big game, he had watched film of the Colts playing over and over – and over.

"It was great film study. We knew that on third-and-short they stack, and they like the outside release for the slant," said Porter. "It was great film study by me, a great jump, and a great play."

In other words, Porter prepared for that moment mentally, even though that moment might never have come. When it did, however, he was ready for it – and provided the big turning point.

When a team is that highly trained, it's hard for anything to go wrong. People working together at peak performance make magical things happen.

Imagine your staff working at the level. Imagine what that would do for your business.

Well, actually, I'd rather not just imagine. *I'd rather make it happen.*

Which is why I do everything in my power to make sure the staff at my dental office works at a Super Bowl level. And I must be doing something right, because my team beat out 1200 other dental practices to win team of the year in a nationwide contest last year.

Frankly, my business is a lot more important to me than any Super Bowl – as I'm sure yours is too. So shouldn't we all train our people as well as the Saints train theirs?

CREATING THE RIGHT CULTURE

Tony Hsieh, CEO of Zappos.com is someone the business world really admires when it comes to creating a positive and effective employee culture. He prides himself on making amazing customer service a vital aspect of his brand – and gives his people a list of 10 core values he expects them to take on board. He encourages every one who works for him to Twitter, to help keep Zappos front and center in the social media arena.

He was asked, does he monitor his employees' "tweets" to make sure they don't say anything negative or inappropriate about Zappos? His reply was 'no – because he makes sure to hire the right people'. When a person is hired, if it doesn't seem like they will fit in with the Zappos ethos after their training period, they're actually offered $2000 to leave – because Hsieh thinks it's worth the pay-out to protect his overall culture.

Now, you might think this would create an overbearing, oppressive atmosphere to work in. I mean, the guy's lecturing his employees on values? He imposes a "culture" on them? Isn't that basically some kind of fascist thought-control?

Well, apparently, the employees don't mind – because the company was named by "Fortune Magazine" as one of the "100 Best Companies to Work For."

And I believe the reason they do love working at Zappos is because they're, by nature, positive, productive people. They *like* doing their job well – or they'd be sitting at home watching the Game Show Network while they count their 2 grand instant-severance pay. It has nothing to do with trying to control people who don't want to work hard – it has everything to do with inspiring and motivating *people who want to get the job done.*

Hiring a new person on your staff involves a huge investment on your part in terms of time, money and effort. Not only that, a negative personality can throw off the performance of the rest of the staff – especially if they get away with 'bagging on the business' and doing less. I actually think the Zappos' two thousand dollar pay-off is a bargain – because the wrong person can create a million different problems in a million different ways.

There are a series of important questions to ask when you're considering any staff hiring – is this the right person for the job? Is their work ethic what I need it to be? Will they fit in with the rest of the office? Even in this era of high unemployment, it's still hard to find good people – because it's *always* hard to find good people.

I've been lucky enough – and maybe relentless enough – to find a lot of them over the years, enabling me to build an outstanding team that takes care of the 'small stuff' so I can concentrate on the 'big stuff'. What worked for me? Let me share a few thoughts on why I was able to create an award-winning group of great employees.

BUILDING YOUR TEAM

Here are what I believe to be crucial factors to building an all-star staff:

- **SUPERSTAR, NO – ALL-STAR TEAM, YES!**

Remember "The Mary Tyler Moore Show?" Or "The Bob Newhart

Show?" Now imagine them without Mary Tyler Moore or Bob Newhart. Tough sell, right?

Now think about the TV version of "M*A*S*H" (it shouldn't be hard if you're as old as me – it was on CBS with Mary and Bob on Saturday nights in the 70's) - a show about two military surgeons, Trapper John and Hawkeye Pierce. Only about three years in, the guy playing Trapper John decides he'd rather be a businessman than an actor and quits. The show not only goes on, but becomes more popular than ever.

That's because "M*A*S*H" was an ensemble show that could – and did – survive major cast changes. Same as other great long-running ensemble shows such as "Cheers." Main players could leave and the show would chug along, barely missing a beat.

Keep that in mind, because you don't want your office to be "The Debbie the Receptionist Show." Or "The Max the Accountant Show." When one superstar employee dominates the office, suddenly no one – including your other staff, your clients and customers and even you – can imagine the business going on without that person. They can even end up with as much perceived power as you – which can obviously be a bad situation.

That's why it's important to groom a *team* of all-stars who can consistently deliver, so it doesn't matter if one is missing or ends up leaving your business. Consistent quality across the board makes for an efficient, productive team. A dominant "superstar" ends up weakening the other employees and makes the office dependant on their presence.

You should be the main superstar of your business, no one else. It's your business, just like those were Mary and Bob's shows. Remember when Fonzie took away "Happy Days" from Richie Cunningham? You don't need that in your life.

• OUTSIDE EYES SHOW WHAT YOU CAN'T SEE

I'm a big believer in using things like "Mystery Patient" services. If you're not familiar with "Mystery Patient" (or "Mystery Shopper," depending on what business you're in), it involves an outside company hiring someone to either call or actually come in to your office posing as a new customer. No one, including the head of the business, knows who this person is going to be or when it's going to happen. Every interaction is recorded when they do approach your business, so you can check just how well your people do in terms of giving them good customer service, and working to convert their visit into a sale.

Oh, and you can also check how well *you* do if you interact with clients/patients as I do. I don't let myself off the hook in this process, and neither should you.

This is incredibly important because, when you do the day-to-day day-in and day-out, you and your staff often lose sight of the basics of customer service. It happens to all of us – we get lazy and don't stay on top of things.

That's why a set of outside eyes, showing you what you might be missing about the way you deal with your clients, makes a big difference – both in helping you recommit to core principles you've already taken on board, and in developing new techniques to help you keep and convert customers.

And, by the way, this is another aspect of my practice that I'm proud of – when our Mystery Patient came in to check us out last year, he was so impressed with our operation, that he booked a real appointment, and drove an hour to come back and have his dental work done by us, instead of his local dentist!

• DELEGATE AND AUTOMATE

You don't want to spend your entire day micro-managing your business. It drains your energy, distracts you and keeps your eye off the big picture. That's why it's important to create the kind of systems that allow your office to run without your direct intervention. It's a fantasy to think you'll never have to get involved – but, if you do it right, you'll avoid the lurking nervous breakdown that's just around the corner from your office.

I know that from personal experience. When I began really marketing my dental practice in earnest, it grew in leaps and bounds. I didn't get it right away and I still tried to do everything myself. It soon became clear to me, though, that if I didn't delegate and create some efficient systems, my business would never be able to get to the next level – I wouldn't be able to handle any more growth.

If your staff is big enough, designate team leaders to take charge of certain functions in your office – for instance, at my practice, we have a front office team leader, a clinical team leader, a hygiene team leader and we will shortly have a practice administrator. When that happens, we will have the front office, the back office and hygiene running their own areas and reporting back to the top administrator, who will watch over the entire operation for me, keeping me in the loop and allowing me more time to work on my business. Make someone like that accountable to me for running the practice means I only have to talk to one person instead of chasing down 10 or 12.

In line with that, also look into hi-tech automatic solutions to common office tasks that will both free up you and your staff, and also ensure that certain things get done. For instance, on the marketing side, I use "The Bridge" system provided by "The ROI Guy," Richard Seppala. Richard provides me with different toll-free numbers for my different marketing placements. When generated leads call these numbers, their contact information is automatically captured by "The Bridge" and also automatically transcribed and uploaded into our Infusionsoft Customer Relationship Management software. This enables us to do fast and easy follow-up customized marketing to the database we create and grow.

This ends the uncertainty of relying on your staff to actually ask during incoming sales calls for the prospect's contact information, and to enter that information into your computer program. It all gets done without human error being involved, or being forced to find that "special quiet time" to catch up on the fun task of data entry - which makes both you and your staff's lives a lot easier.

The right systems lower the stress levels for both yourself and your staff – when things are defined, there's no confusion. I always say the goal is to decrease the stress associated with the chaos and enjoy the freedom that the systems give you. Everyone knows what's expected of them and does what they need to do. And, again, you free yourself up to actually run your business instead of feeling like an employee yourself. And isn't that why you went to work for yourself in the first place?

- **CREATE GREAT EMPLOYEE TRAINING SYSTEMS**

This is my current passion – to make it possible for a person who's never been in your office before to come in and immediately be able to go to work in an effective, efficient manner. How do we do that? By giving them the tools so they can train before they come in the door. Through videos and written instructions, posted online, we can effectively "break in" a new hire, or a temporary worker, without wasting a lot of actual work time.

The trick is to make these, excuse the expression, as "idiot-proof" as possible. We all have days where we end up with a clueless, unmotivated temp – and if we can at least get them familiar with how our businesses work, they can function at an acceptable level.

I'm now in the midst of creating the systems for these kinds of online training tools for businesses to implement, because we've been so successful with what we've done at my practice. By accurately documenting what each worker does and how they do it – down to such basic info as to where things are located in the office – anyone can completely familiarize themselves with a workplace.

For example, for someone working in the front of the office at the reception desk, we would document the entire procedure for what needed to be done with a new patient, so there's no doubt or hesitation – the information is immediately accessible to the new or temporary employee. The same for dental assistants working in the back of the office in the patient treatment rooms – we can provide them with what they need to know about our procedures *before* they need to know it.

This saves an incredible amount of time when it comes to giving a new person on-the-job training. Naturally, there will still be a little bit of a learning curve, but by making available the information they need to know beforehand, and expecting them to know it *before* they come in, it prevents a lot of needless time from being wasted during working hours. This also helps people who have been trained in doing things a different way to adjust to the systems we've created at my practice – although there are always those who just want to do things their own way and *not* try to adapt. Our joke around the office is that we have a "rogue" staffer secretly teaching new people or temps their own systems to short-circuit our own!

I'm excited to be able to share the secrets of how we 'roll' at my practice, Grove City Dental. I believe we have taken our operation to an incredible level and I know other businesses can learn from my experience in getting to that level.

Let's go back to my original point about the Super Bowl. The Saints' organization ran the Colts game film so many times for Tracy Porter that, by the time in the fourth quarter, when the interception opportunity presented itself, he didn't have to think about the opportunity. He just reacted because he knew what to do.

A great football team works like that – they run the plays forward and backward until they're lodged in their brains and it's second nature. I believe that's how a great staff should work together as well. With the right training, you can have an office full of Tracy Porters – all ready to take the ball and run with it when the moment presents itself.

About Scott

Dr. Scott Schumann, a native of Columbus, Ohio, grew up loving the Buckeyes, playing sports, and collecting rocks. Dr. Schumann and his wife Robin live in downtown Columbus with their dog, Bourbon, the boxer. Dr. Schumann loves supporting the local arts, sponsoring little league teams, golfing, fishing and attending concerts as well as NASCAR events.

Dr. Schumann graduated from Ohio State University Dental School in 1989 and then completed his residency training at University of Texas Health Science Center at San Antonio in 1991, with training and certification in advanced dental techniques, dental implants and sedation dentistry. He also received a fellowship in Hospital Dentistry, helping him to excel in assisting his medically compromised patients. After returning to Columbus Ohio, Dr. Schumann started his career and began teaching in the Advanced Dentistry Clinic at the Ohio State University, teaching dental residents advanced cosmetic, implant, hospital, and sedation dentistry for ten years.

An active member in the Columbus Dental Society, Ohio Dental Association, American Dental Association, Academy of General Dentists, American Academy of Cosmetic Dentists and the American Dental Society of Anesthesiology, Dr. Schumann and his team have kept up to date on the latest developments in dentistry.

Dr. Scott Schumann's office in Grove City, a suburb 8 minutes south of downtown Columbus, Ohio, is often referred to by clients as "fun" and "cool"—2 words not often associated with dentistry. Dr. Schumann and his staff are well known for their love of helping their patients achieve the smile they always dreamed of. Now through his innovative systems, Dr. Schuman is helping dentists around the country achieve the lifestyle and success they always dreamed of while helping patients change their lives. His professional team and his facility, with amazing new technological advancements, makes each patient visit as 'fun' as possible without guilt or embarrassment while allowing him to leverage his time and experience to grow his dental practice.

Dr. Scott Schumann has been published in multiple research journals, as well as featured in *21 Principles of Smile Design* and *Shift Happens*. He has presented at various conferences and events and has been quoted in the Wall Street Journal, USA Today, and Newsweek and well as appeared on America's PremierExperts® TV show on NBC, CBS, ABC and FOX.

To learn more about Dr. Schumann and how he helps to grow dental practices visit www.dentalofficesystemsmadeeasy.com

Or call toll-free 888-496-1250

Power Principle #6

'START WITH CREATING MORE VALUE!'

by Dan Liebrecht and Tony Dietsch
Clean Guru LLC

"How to Beat Price-Cutting Competitors… Without Cutting __Your__ Price!"

Things have changed!!!!

Y ou know it. We know it. And every service business out there today can see and feel it.

What is it? It's simply this…

The <u>old</u> ways of growing a successful service business simply DON'T work any more.

For example, 20 years ago, when we started our janitorial-cleaning business, nearly anyone could do pretty well for themselves and have a sizable customer list, just by knocking on doors, word of mouth and, of course, delivering a reliable service.

Frankly, it was really about that simple!

Growth and profitability were within relatively easy reach; hard work and a good reputation would get you more jobs and at prices… that made you money!

NOT ANY MORE!

Today, there are three changes virtually killing many of the once-strong, independent service businesses; the small and mid-size companies that used to be the business backbone of this country.

1. The first is the economy.

No question about it; with companies desperate to reduce expenses, few service contractors can escape the "chopping block". But, <u>you</u> don't have to lie down and quietly resign yourself to that fate… at least not without a fight.

That's right, there are specific 'things' you can do now to greatly im-prove your chances of coming through the current economic meltdown in good shape; still adding new business and at prices that keep you profitable. We'll explain how in a moment.

2. The second's the widespread use of illegal workers by unscrupulous contractors.

HERE, EVERYONE SUFFERS.

From the sometimes unsuspecting home and building owners, exposed to potential legal problems, to the frustrated, legitimate contractors, justifiably angry about having to compete with the ridiculously low prices offered by these unscrupulous contractors - when it comes to the use of an illegal workforce, nobody really wins.

and

3. The third change destroying independent service businesses is the rise of empty-promising <u>national management companies</u> and <u>franchises</u>.

To us, their business strategy seems no more complicated than this:-

Low-ball the price to get the job…then quickly dump it on some des-perate, local guy who needs the work! (And, oh yeah, good luck to <u>that</u> guy on trying to make a profit!)

Sadly, it's about that simple; those national "sell it and sub it" management companies " know in <u>this</u> economy, they'll get plenty of struggling building owners and managers to "bite" fast and hard on their price-slashing pitch!

And, the slick talking franchises with their glossy brochures know it too!

But here's the catch:

Frantic, knee-jerk decisions to drastically cut costs without getting the facts first (verifying references, as well as confirming quality, training and management methods) quickly <u>backfire</u> when frustrated customers discover they've been sold a bag of empty promises!

"Sure", you might say, "but what can I do about it? - I'm just a small business, how can I possibly compete with these "big guys"?

WELL, THE GOOD NEWS IS... PLENTY!

You see, in just a minute, we're going to reveal a powerful strategy we used in our own cleaning company to beat those price-cutting "big guys" without having to cut your own price. You can use same strategy to <u>avoid falling into the "lowest price" trap</u>.

What's that? What's the "lowest price" trap?

Well, it's when, out of fear or lack of knowing any other way to compete, service businesses frantically drop their price as a way of fighting off equally desperate competitors... to levels so ridiculously low that even if they do get the job, they're unlikely to ever make money on it.

You see, we know how it feels to be broke and desperate.

We started out with next to nothing - like a lot of folks out there today. In fact, less than nothing - frequently having to use credit cards to cover payrolls and monthly bills!

BUT, THEN... WE GOT "LUCKY".

We discovered a set of insider strategies that when used together quickly moved us 'out of the red of debt'... and 'into the black of profitability'!

Here's one of the "game-changing" strategies, we used to grow our own profitable $2,000,000/yr. cleaning service business; beating our price-cutting competitors without having to cut our own price:

CREATE MEASURABLE GUARANTEES OF PERFORMANCE

As buyers, we're all the same.

We're looking for someone who can show they have *real answers* to our *real problems*... and be willing to guarantee it!

We call these real answers - **Measurable Guarantees of Performance** or **MGP's** for short.

Over the years, we've read a number of other marketers explain similar concepts called USP's, which stands for Unique Selling Propositions or UCA's, which stands for Unique Competitive Advantages.

But, we prefer our term, MGP, for a couple important reasons:

1. MGPs emphasize the importance of <u>MEASUREMENT</u>. Anyone can make broad claims. Measurable ones are more difficult to create, let alone guarantee. But that's why they're so much more powerful and effective.

2. MGPs emphasize the importance of <u>GUARANTEE</u>. This speaks for itself. You might <u>say</u> you'll do something, but will you stand behind it?... with your checkbook if necessary!

3. MGPs emphasize the importance of <u>PERFORMANCE</u>. And in the service business that's where, as they say, the "rubber hits the road" – namely, performance.

Here's an example of an MGP from the cleaning industry dealing with the important topic of quality:

<u>Our Quality Guarantee:</u>

"You'll Be 100% Delighted With The Quality Of <u>Each</u> Cleaning Visit...

or it's FREE"*

*That's right! To guarantee you get the quality of cleaning you deserve, your building will be inspected after each visit using our fast, yet effective, "QC Check" form, which will be graded, faxed to our office and placed on your desk. If you disagree with a daily "grade", or feel you were not cleaned properly on any visit... it's FREE!

Now, here's an example of what an MGP in the landscaping business might look like:

Our Service Satisfaction Guarantee:

"To Guarantee Your 100% Satisfaction, Your Lawn Will Be Completely Trimmed, Edged And 'Blown Clean' After Each Mowing... or it's FREE!"*

* That's right, a properly mowed lawn can only look its best when it's also been trimmed, edged and blown clean, so that's why we include it automatically and at no additional charge for every lawn we maintain. Ever catch one of our lawn technicians forgetting to do it; and we not only want to know about it... we'll give you that complete mowing service visit - FREE!

Bold?...Yes!

Hard to create the systems required to support making this kind of strong statement and guarantee?

Absolutely!

But think about this for a minute...

How different would your company be if you could offer a set of 3, 5, or more of these MGPs hitting on every single one of the most important "answers" to problems your prospects are desperately looking for?

YEAH, VERY DIFFERENT.

In fact, we believe developing a set of powerful Measurable Guarantees of Performance may be the *single most important thing* you can do to quickly move your service business ahead of the competition... and out of the "lowest price trap"

What's that? What is the "lowest price trap"?

Well, simply put, it's the misguided and reckless strategy of chasing after your competitors by lowering your prices below what's reasonable or profitable to win the job or land the account!

It's easy to fall into if you feel your only way to get and then keep work is by doing the same work for less.

BUT, IT'S NOT.

Your MGP's or Measurable Guarantees of Performance are the reasons why you're different than the rest of the 'low-balling' pack!

You <u>don't</u> offer the "same" service – you offer a better service... and you're willing to guarantee it!

MGP's create value for your customers. Prospects are willing to <u>pay more</u> for businesses who <u>offer more</u> ... value!

Taking the time to create your own unique MGP's will allow you to quickly move the conversation from PRICE to VALUE. And that's where you want to be.

By the way, if your experience ends up being anything even close to ours, you have little to fear in offering these bold MGPs;

Your worst nightmares of customers lined up to "pounce" on you to take advantage of your generous guarantees by demanding refunds... are seldom realized.

And an occasional refund having to be paid to a customer, where you did, if fact, drop the ball, may be a <u>good</u> thing now and again - a 'wake-up' call to keep you on your toes, force you to re-evaluate your systems and avoid ever becoming complacent.

Plus, the cost of an occasional refund should be <u>far outweighed by the incredible customer satisfaction, loyalty and referral business</u> resulting from the strong guarantees you promote, and the systems you use to make them possible.

Frankly, over our many years in business, we probably didn't have more than a handful of clients who either legitimately deserved a refund due to our mistake (which we gladly credited them for), or on their own actually called us to take us up on any of our powerful guarantees.

In reality, human nature generally shows that the great majority of customers are not waiting anxiously to "hold your feet to the fire" to demand a refund; on the contrary, most want things to work out between the two of you.

Creating Measurable Guarantees of Performance is one of the first and most important strategies in beating the price-cutting "big guys"; but only if it's used the right way.

That's why the 6 <u>other</u> Strategies in our book, ***Discover the Guru in YOU!*** *The 7 Insider Secrets to Finding, Landing and Keeping Profitable Cleaning Jobs*, are so important.

Used together, the 7 insider strategies can rescue you from the "Lowest Price Trap" and deliver you safely to improved profitability.

About Tony

Tony Dietsch is Co-Founder of Clean Guru LLC and the CleanBid Online Program. He is co-author of the book, **Discover the Guru in You**, *The 7 Insider Secrets to Finding, Landing and Keeping Profitable Cleaning Jobs.* After graduating from the University of Toledo, Tony became an automotive engineer with a Fortune 500 Company where he was awarded a U.S. patent for his work. Subsequently, he, along with his business partner Dan Liebrecht, built a successful janitorial cleaning business in Ohio. Tony now uses his technical background to create powerful online tools for independent cleaning businesses. Tony, and his wife Christy live in Temperance, Michigan. They have four children.

About Dan

Dan Liebrecht is Co-Founder of Clean Guru LLC and the CleanBid Online Program. He is co-author of the book, **Discover the Guru in You**, *The 7 Insider Secrets to Finding, Landing and Keeping Profitable Cleaning Jobs.* After graduating from the University of Toledo, Dan worked in HR and Operations Management in Colorado. Returning to Ohio, he, along with his business partner Tony Dietsch, built a successful janitorial cleaning company. He has authored numerous articles about the cleaning business, including an in-depth look at janitorial bidding software published in a leading industry periodical. Dan, and his wife Jennifer, live in Sylvania, Ohio. They have three children.

Power Principle #7

"IT STARTS WITH A SMILE"

by Lisa Peters-Seppala, D.D.S.

"Because of your smile, you make life more beautiful."
- Thich Nhat Hanh, Vietnamese monk

Julia Roberts. Brad Pitt. George Clooney. What do all these people have in common?

Besides being rich and famous, they all have amazing, dazzling smiles.

I call them "Celebrity Smiles."

Watch the Oscars or the Golden Globes or the Grammys, and you can't help noticing all the straight, white, perfect teeth. At least I can't – I'm a dentist! But I'll bet you've seen it too. Famous people might come in all shapes, sizes and colors these days, but a great smile is almost a requirement. And this doesn't just apply to movie stars and models. Successful people from all walks of life – from business leaders and politicians to waitresses and salesmen – all rely on their smiles as one of the secrets of their success.

Which can be bad news for people whose smiles are less than perfect.

In a world where everyone is trying to make an impression, to connect with people, to get ahead, a smile has become an essential tool.

When you smile, you send a message to whoever you're smiling at – whether it's an audience of millions or a single person -- saying that you're happy and confident. …that you're friendly and approachable. …that you feel good about whatever is about to take place, …and you're engaged in the process.

And if you don't smile? You miss out on making that connection. Maybe people perceive you as unfeeling, or uninterested, or just unhappy.

Even if you're not.

To me, there's nothing sadder in the world than people who are afraid to smile because they are ashamed of their teeth. They go through life in the background – simply because they are uncomfortable opening their mouths.

That's why I do what I do. My job is to give ordinary people Celebrity Smiles – and all the power and confidence and success that come with such a powerful transformation.

And it is powerful. Being a dentist may not be especially glamorous, but for me, it's the best job in the world. Because a great smile really does open doors – I've seen it happen over and over again. And there are all kinds of ways to get one, from the standard dental care that keeps healthy smiles looking great to restorative procedures like veneers and implants that transform unsightly teeth into beautiful smiles.

In some cases, those types of procedures actually change people's lives. Which makes my job especially rewarding.

O's STORY

I don't think of myself as being an especially scary person. But a lot of people are afraid of the dentist – to the point where it starts to affect their teeth. Instead of getting problems taken care of, they're so afraid to let a dentist look inside their mouth that they let them get worse and worse until their teeth become unattractive, and even painful. That was the case with the patient I'll call 'O'.

Since having a bad experience in the dentist's chair as a child, 'O' was basically terrified of having any work done on his teeth. This was especially strange because he worked for a plastic surgeon, and had no problem going under the knife to make changes to his face and body. I guess he didn't find surgeons scary. But the dentist...that was a whole other story.

If you're like 'O', I want you to know that today; you don't need to be afraid to go to the dentist. Because from a simple cleaning to major reconstruction, we can do everything we do without pain. In fact, I can give you a whole new smile while you're sound asleep. That's what we were able to do for 'O'. We completed all of his dental work while he was under sedation, and when he woke up, he saw his straight, white teeth and started to cry. Which almost made me cry too. The moment was that powerful.

The funny thing was, these weren't even his "real" final teeth – just some temporary veneers that we installed to stand in until the beautiful porcelain ones being created specifically for his mouth were ready. And now, since he got those real veneers, every time he comes into the office, he shows me a new picture of his new big white perfect grin that he takes on his iPhone in the waiting room. It's kind of a ritual. And it makes me smile.

J's STORY

Of course, fear of the dentist is only one factor that keeps people from having Celebrity Smiles. One of the most common reasons people lose their smile is something we all consider inevitable -- the aging process. Getting older is a good thing – it definitely beats the alternative! But as we age, our teeth change. And a lot of seniors accept losing their teeth as a part of life – their grandparents probably wore dentures, and they expected that as they got older, they would wear them too.

But what they might not have expected is that dentures sometimes make a really, really bad substitute for natural teeth. They can look obvious and ugly, they're uncomfortable, and it can be hard to eat and talk while wearing them – let alone smile.

That was the position 'J' was in when she came to see me. But 'J' was ready for a change. She had decided she didn't want to settle for her uncomfortable, ugly partial dentures anymore, and was ready to get rid of them forever.

And she could, thanks to dental implants – artificial teeth that are implanted in the jawbone, so they work much more like natural teeth than dentures do.

Dental implants are the current state-of-the-art technology when it comes to tooth replacement. They can be used to replace a single tooth, an entire mouth full of teeth, or anything in between. And since they're implanted in your bone instead of sitting on top of your gums like dentures, they feel and act almost exactly like natural teeth. For people who have lost teeth, it really is like a miracle.

We placed dental implants in all the areas where 'J''s natural teeth were missing – and it was all done under sedation, so she didn't feel a thing. When it was all over, she was totally and completely ecstatic – she could finally throw her partial dentures in the trash! Now, she can eat whatever she wants, because her dental implants feel and work like natural teeth. And the best part is, she also looks ten years younger.

Which gives her plenty of reason to smile.

With older people living longer and being more active than ever before, dental implants are emerging as a great alternative to dentures. They keep seniors' mouths as young as the rest of their bodies, so they can continue to work, see friends, travel, volunteer and do whatever they want with confidence. It feels really good to be able to give seniors Celebrity Smiles – in fact, some wind up with better-looking teeth in their '60s and '70s than they had in their '20s and '30s!

C's STORY

You can take great care of your teeth and not have any major problems, but that doesn't guarantee your smile is going to be beautiful. The size or spacing can be off. Plus heredity, aging and other factors can yellow teeth over time and keep them from looking their best.

But that doesn't mean you can't have a Celebrity Smile.

A lot of people don't realize that less than beautiful teeth can easily be fixed. Maybe you're one of them. Maybe you've learned to live with the physical imperfections, even if those imperfections make you feel uncomfortable. Even if they make you reluctant to smile.

But the fact is, nobody has to settle for less than beautiful teeth anymore. Anyone really can have a Celebrity Smile.

This happened with a patient of mine I'll call 'C'. She had come in for her regular cleaning and checkup and nothing more – while her teeth weren't perfect, she was diligent about taking good care of them. But her diligence could only take her so far. Her teeth were a dingy, dark yellow color. Some of her fillings were visible. So she wasn't exactly confident about her smile.

Well, while she was in the chair, I asked 'C' if she might be interested in seeing what she would look like with a Celebrity Smile. I offered 'C' a chance to look at a complimentary before and after picture that we put together with computer imaging. She agreed, and soon she had a preview of how she would look with a beautiful, white smile.

The change was really dramatic, and 'C' was so excited by what she saw that she started porcelain veneer treatment right away. Today, she has a beautiful, perfectly white Celebrity Smile – and looks and feels younger than she has in a long time.

These are just three of the many success stories that have made me feel incredibly fulfilled in my profession. Dentistry has come a long way in the last generation, which is why I'm so excited to be a part of it.

When I was a kid, all the dentist did was keep teeth healthy and solve problems like gum disease and decay. Today, we still do all that, but I also have the power to give patients new, improved Celebrity Smiles – and the extra confidence that comes with them.

Which definitely keeps *me* smiling.

About Lisa

Dr. Peters graduated from Southern Methodist University Undergraduate College in Dallas, TX in 1992, where she obtained a business degree and her pre-dental education.

After moving to Key West, and then to Orlando, she worked as a Dental Assistant for two years before attending the University of Florida Dental College in 1994. She graduated in 1998 with a Doctorate of Dental Medicine and is a member of the American Dental Association, the American Academy of Implant Dentistry, the Florida Dental Association, the Academy of General Dentistry, and the Central Florida Dental Association. In addition, she is licensed in conscious dental sedation.

Dr. Peters opened her dental office in July of 2001 and along with continuing education, enjoys attending seminars to remain current on new technology and procedures to improve the comfort and quality of her patients' dental visits.

Power Principle #8

YOUR NET WORTH IS DETERMINED BY YOUR NETWORK

by Marco Kozlowski

"You can afford anything that moves your dream forward"
~ Marco Kozlowski

THE SIZE OF YOUR NET WORTH IS DETERMINED BY THE SIZE AND QUALITY OF YOUR NETWORK

What the heck is THAT supposed to mean? Look, we all want to be the heir to 'bazillions'. I often fantasize if Donald Trump, The Queen of England, Bill Gates and the Sultan of Brunei had a baby and it was me, what would my life be like?

Do you dream of getting rich? I mean, 'wiping your *heinie* with $100 bills rich'? How does one become THAT wealthy? Is it by accident? By design? Luck??

And who the heck is Marco Kozlowski anyway? ...and why should you listen to him?

79

(I like to talk about myself in the 3rd person sometimes…makes me feel way more important than I really am.)

Well over the last decade, I've gone from needing $1632 in my bank account to BE BROKE to multi-millionaire…my "success" vehicle? Luxury Real estate.

I control and sell Luxury homes all over the world using NO money, no credit and have a TEAM of people that WANT to make me RICH (when I make money, they do as well). Yes, I, with my team, turn Mansions into Mountains of Money.

I take properties that are not selling for whatever reason and leverage Auction companies to sell them for me lighting fast. Auctions work well provided the *perfect* marketing campaign is launched (that's a lot of words meaning *uber* expensive and risky unless you know exactly what you're doing). After 10 years of trial and error, I finally figured out how to NEVER risk a penny again in ANY luxury home transaction. Neither do you want to. (Read on if you want to find out more).

Love to imagine hundreds of really rich people fighting over ONE house they ALL NEED NOW. Looks like piranha on a carcass (amazing and disturbing simultaneously).

No matter what the economy is doing, there are always rich people that NEED things NOW. In fact more millionaires and billionaires were created during the great depression than any other time in history.

I get my jollies by being sticking as many rich folks in the same room fighting over a property I simply control and don't even own…its fun getting rich this way, you might want to try it someday…

WHAT SUCCESS SKILL I'D LOVE TO EMPOWER YOU WITH TODAY

Enough about me, let's talk about myself…just kidding.

This chapter is more about you then me. I know you don't really care about me, I haven't earned your trust or respect yet, however you can learn from my mistakes if you wish to avoid the near fatal ones I made. Its **infinitely** cheaper for you to learn from mine than your own (that goes for any lesson…wise people learn from others' failures so they can succeed)…you learn the same lessons 'any way you slice it'.

I'd LOVE to illustrate how you can leverage a simple idea into helping a whole lot of people around you (sellers, buyers, agents, my team and their families), generate millions in revenue out of thin air, *at will*, and do it as many times as you want.

I'm going to break down the simple yet powerful concepts that I re-tooled, to help me and my family generate millions harnessing the power of Luxury real estate. I went from dead broke meager musician to mansion magnet very quickly when I applied the principles I'm about to share with you…Funny thing 'this success thing'…once you reach the top, you want as many people with you as possible. Will you be one of them? I REALLY hope so…

ARE YOU LAZY ENOUGH TO BE RICH?

WHAT? LAZY? Yes. Lazy. But the RIGHT kind of lazy…do you delegate what NEEDS to be done to the right people so EVERYONE around you has a chance to shine and get rich WITH YOU?

In my real estate business, I'm VERY lazy. Look, I used to be a musician   they don't get any lazier than us….if I could wake up at the crack of noon, and just scratch all day long…I would…

You should never be lazy setting up your team, but LAZY getting in the way of people doing what they love to do best! I have others find my deals (like agents), have others negotiate them (they get paid when I get paid) and use the top auctioneers in the world to sell many of the properties I tie up.

Everyone on the team LOVES what they do, does it extremely well and I am NEVER involved in the process…as such, my laziness pays off!

I simply have a contract on the properties that I have others find (I never quite own 'em, just tie them up)…I do get a piece of the profit for putting the deal and the team together…in effect **I delegate 100% of the work, but receive 50% of the profit** (that's a "writer downer").

I'm like the conductor of the orchestra…that's the guy who gets paid the MOST in case you were wondering….

ARE YOU READY TO CONDUCT YOURSELF TO SUCCESS?

We all get paid at the same time, we work TOGETHER to get rich TO-GETHER…except others do all the work, I simply put them together ONE time, and get paid over and over and over again…

Are you OK with setting up something ONCE that pays you for a lifetime?

Are you Ok with replicating someone else's proven processes, leverage the BEST people in the world at what they do to ALL make money together??

It's a trick question…

Before I continue, a quick disclosure: I have HD-ADHD…for those of you left in the dark never hearing of such a preposterous affliction, it stands for *High Definition* Attention Deficit Hyperactive….(Look! there goes a chicken!.)..Disorder…

I go off on creative tangents…I've harnessed it into a success trait, not a weakness…

THERE IS ONLY ONE THING THAT THAT MAKES A DREAM IMPOSSIBLE TO ACHIEVE: THE FEAR OF FAILURE….

I didn't learn how to make 6 figures at will by accident. I didn't win the lottery to get seed money (If you can't make money without money, you can't make money WITH MONEY) and its not as hard to make large sums of money as you might think…

Anyone, I MEAN ANYONE, regardless of economic situation can achieve financial success. You just need the right knowledge, applied action and team (ah, the TEAM, the NETWORK of people around you is one of the 11 herbs and spices that will get you success and abundance FASTER than Amy Winehouse into rehab). Thankfully, all of the above (not the rehab) are readily available to those who have a need and desire to achieve complete financial success.

I've been teaching people success techniques for the past two decades (I was a piano teacher for the 1st one) and the most difficult lesson for people to absorb, yet the easiest one to understand is belief. Success Faith. Simply getting YOU to believe YOU WILL achieve better results in a shorter period of time than I or any successful person has, if you are empowered with the recipe... YOU JUST NEED TO FOLLOW IT.

WORK A DAY AND GET PAID FOR A DAY...OR WORK ONE AND GET PAID FOREVER??

Success leaves clues. You just need to follow the handful of lessons. Had I not followed them, I would have left me as broke as Mc Hammer and Vanilla Ice's managers.

My Success, as with anyone else's (I'm really not that special...although my mommy says I am), was thanks to a healthy cocktail of:

- perseverance

- planned luck (I wrote a book on that)

- mistakes

- fear

- getting back up after even more mistakes

- learning and growing from the industrial quantity of mistakes made by me

- learning from others' mistakes

- adapting my "dead-broke rotten" attitude that the world was pickin' on me

This left me to realize that I was chasing the WRONG thing. I realized the MORE I was chasing it, the less I had it...I bought into a lie. What lie you may ask? That to get rich, I needed to **chase** the buck.

The more I chased cash, the less I had it. It felt like getting rich was like going fishing with bear hands. You can do it day in, day out and STILL catch nothing. Starvation.

Yes you worked hard, yes you tried, but you still starved...until you learned from your mistakes and invented a net…then you feast…

My friends, many of my teachers and family all said the same…work hard, and you'll get rich…

That's kinda true, but also not the full story. Like seeing a beautiful woman 'and realizing a li'l too late about the Adams apple that really shouldn't be there' (…did I just really write that??).

I'm all for hard work. I did it for years and that kept me broke. I was working very hard - but the wrong way and on the wrong thing. I wanted, as I'm sure you do, to be able to provide for my family, have more fun and have all the money I needed to be as generous with money and my time as I wanted…

Having a JOB was absolutely NOT the way to do that… obviously.

I realized its NOT how HARD you work, but how SMART you work that is key. The foundation of financial abundance is simply working ONE time setting up GREAT systems and teams - and get paid for a lifetime.

WORK ON THE BUSINESS, NEVER IN THE BUSINESS.

If your income is a result of daily activities that you MUST do for the business to grow, you are an employee. You are not really free.

To be free – you need to set up the business ONCE so it pays you FOREVER.

If you buy stock in Google, do you have to know how to program computers? Know anything about search engine optimization? Nope. You own a piece of the company and you enjoy the profits.

Isn't it time to own your own company that PAYS you for owning it???

YOU NEED A TEAM, A NETWORK OF PEOPLE THAT NEED TO MAKE YOU RICH.

Before you haul me away in a strait jacket and throw me in the 'loony bin', let me explain this bold statement.

There is no I in team. (Yeah, I know its overused, but are you DOING THAT?) Are you able to take a day off, week off, month off or even a full year off and **make the SAME OR MORE** in your absence?

No? Then you are part of the team. You need to fire yourself immediately. You suck as an employee…you need to OWN the business, not WORK in the business.

Why? Who makes more – the owner of the Yankees or the players? Owners ALWAYS make the most. Stop being a player, start being the owner.

Build your team NOW!

Show me a self-made millionaire, I'll show you a liar. Every success story has someone that has helped them along the way. You must surround yourself with *the best*. People that will push you, people who are more knowledgeable who can give you good constructive criticism and guidance. If you ask broke people on how to get rich, what kind of response do you get? Rich people *think* rich…

How can you fly like an eagle when you are surrounded by turkeys?

Teamwork is the ability to work together toward a common vision. It is the ability to direct individual accomplishment towards organizational objectives. It is the fuel that allows common people to attain uncommon results.

INTERESTED IN MAKING NOW MONEY NOW IN THE MOST PROFITABLE UNTAPPED MARKET? (MARCO KOZLOWSKI STYLE?)

I don't usually peel back the curtain and show people the inner workings of how I've revolutionized how wealth is made in Real Estate that is accessible to the common person.

I'm about to share with you a hugely automated yet profitable system I use daily, allowing me to generate mountains of money in my mansions business.

'Lock the doors, grab a coke and put the kids to bed….we're runnin' out of daylight over here…'

First the key players, The Real Estate agents.

I use Realtors A LOT to locate deals for me. How many Luxury Houses do you think are on the market right now that are NOT selling?

Ya, no kidding…TONS…. 'Kazillions'. (…you get the idea.)

If a house has been on the market for weeks, months or even years, are the sellers makin' money or losin' money? Yes, losing money. Who likes 'bleeding' cash? Ummmm… no one…

Do rich people in this 'pickle' NEED help? Obviously. Do rich people pay for good service? YES! You know what that means when affluent people need help immediately and can afford to compensate you for the service you can provide them by having your network in place??? Yep, you got it! Opportunity!

(I can teach ANYONE how to make an obscene amount of money helping people. Just go to www.MarcoKozlowski.com for more information if you are interested in helping luxury sellers out of a pinch and making a 6 figure check in the process...lets get back to this agent in your team example - 'cuz my HD-ADHD just kicked in).

Ok. Ok. Ok. Back to luxury houses that are NOT selling scenario…

MOST AGENTS ARE NOT TRAINED TO BE EFFECTIVE.

Now I love and respect agents, I feel bad for most of them. If you ask any agent how many hours of marketing classes (on "how to sell houses ") agents get in Real Estate school , guess what that number is?

ZERO! Zip, Nada, Bubkis, big fat doughnut!

I remind you that houses don't sell due to lack of buyers, but lack of MARKETING, and most agents never get the marketing training they need to become highly effective agents – now that's really not fair at all to the agents now, is it?

Its like wanting to become a dentist, going to dental school and never seeing a tooth!

Where do Most agents learn to sell houses? Yep, other agents. Who in turn have learned from other agents, '…going all the way back to Moses'!

Selling Luxury is a COMPLETELY different game than the small houses, it takes 'beaucoup' dollars and a detailed marketing campaign to do it right. Most agents don't know how, and wont spend the cash to get the result….that's why I LOVE auctions…but not every auctioneer is created equal…that's why it took me 11 years to recruit the BEST ones…ones you can use 'if you chose to play in this sandbox', as I give my students get full access to them…

Lets step back now and look at 99% of the agent listings out there….

Why agents NEED AND WANT to work with YOU.

How do Real estate agents get compensated? Correct, Commissions. Paid by the seller. (…might there be more motivation after many months of being on the market unsuccessfully?)

So buying a house that's been on the market forever (my way), and using an agent costs you nothing. The agent doesn't get paid UNLESS the house CLOSES. And the agent WANTS to get paid. We want to get paid. And if we all work together to help the seller, we ALL get paid… VERY, VERY well!

How many agents WANT/NEED commissions to survive and thrive? All of them…but, like anything else, some agents are better than others… finding the best ones cost you 'the EXACT same' as the laziest ones up front…but the BEST ones obviously get you deals FAST, so they MAKE you money instead of the opposite…losing you time and money.

There is another success lesson here…

USING THE BEST PEOPLE, GETS THE BEST RESULTS.

That principle transitioned me from 'pauper' to powerful "prince" pretty promptly. (OK, that was a bit nerdy…)

Lets take it one step further…What if the word on the Real Estate Agent street was that some "insane" investor (you) is paying out $50,000 bonuses (everyone gets paid when you close the deal, so relax) to agents who find deals that are not selling, are under market value, and meet 3 other criteria. (Oh! the average city has THOUSANDS of theses opportunities in case you were wondering…you can hop on your computer and go to www.Realtor.com and pull up houses on the market over 6 months and see for yourself the "house candy" available to us…)

How many agents want to make not only their commission on the houses they CAN'T sell, but a HUGE bonus just for handing you the opportunity on a silver platter BECAUSE you have the network in place to help the seller AND them???

Obviously …_all_ the agents I've ever known scramble at this opportunity!

Let's re-cap what I've covered so far:-

(A)   Be lazy, delegate 100% of the work, but generate 50% of the profit so your team gets rich WITH you.

(B)   Your winning team:

> 1. Mr. T…no, that's the A-Team…sorry

> 1. **Real Estate Agents** bring you deal after deal after deal, so they can help their sellers - and they get rich at the same time you do.

> 2. **The Sellers** win by getting a result which they could not before.

> 3. **Your Negotiators** win by helping put the deal together and sharing in the profits of the company.

> 4. **The Auctioneers** win by profiting from the sale of the house.

> 5. **Your team** wins.

> 6. **You** win.

> 7. **Your family** wins.

Looks like you are now a winner by helping A LOT of people win…

That is how you can go from broke to rich almost as fast as you want to. Simply orchestrate the "musicians" into a thundering performance. Everybody wins.

Build as many people into your network that all want to increase their own net worth….you don't have a choice but to be dragged along with them in the wild whirlwind ride of helping people, which in turn will give you abundant success.

"Everyone is living in either results or excuses" – anonymous

About Marco

Marco Kozlowski was a struggling musician, under constant pressure to make ends meet and virtually bankrupt before a late night infomercial led him to real estate. The promise of wealth intrigued him, but it came with a steep learning curve. After buying 119 houses in his first year he found himself upside down — paying more out than he got back in rent. But in his 'zest' to move a luxury property no one could sell, he witnessed firsthand the power of auctions. It was then that he began to unravel the secrets that would make him millions. That was more than 10 years ago. Now he focuses exclusively on finding, controlling and selling luxury property without risk. Best of all, he's created and perfected a system that allows others to do the same.

Power Principle #9

PROCESS YIELDS PROGRESS

by Nick Nanton, Esq.

"The journey of a thousand miles begins with a single step." ~ Lao Tzu

I am willing to bet that almost every single one of you reading this chapter has read the above quote – or had it quoted to you – in the course of your life. You're starting college and it's rough – somebody tells you about that first step. You're having trouble getting a new business off the ground – somebody tells you about the first step. Whenever you're at the initial stage of anything – you hear about 'that thousand miles' and 'that first step'.

And to be fair, you can't argue with it – it's true. That 'thousand mile journey' starts with that first step.

What people don't discuss, however, is the 4634th step. Or the 5489th step. When you're so far from the beginning that you're in danger of forgetting where you're going – and when you're still so far from the end, you think you'll never make it there.

When you're in the middle of the grind – when it feels like the pay-off will never come – and when you may be so tired you don't think there ever will be a pay-off – that's when it can be incredibly difficult (maybe the *most* difficult) to take the next step.

I firmly believe that when you get to that tough slog where it just feels 'like you're grinding it out for no reason', that's actually when you're in the middle of the real hard work that's going to ultimately validate your efforts. This is when it's most important to follow through on the process and systems you've set up – and not forget what got you as far as you already are. That's when you <u>need</u> to power through with your process and get what you originally wanted with it.

But let's not start with the 5489th step. Let's take Lao Tzu's advice and start with the first.

THE FIRST STEP AND WHY IT'S CRUCIAL

Someone who I recently learned of, and am enamored with, has become an inspiration to me and a whole lot of other people, …former UCLA basketball coach John Wooden. He always had an interesting first step for his players at his 'first talk' of the season. It probably wasn't so interesting for the seniors to hear the exact same 'first talk' they heard when they were freshman - but Wooden was a man who believed in the proper process, which is one big reason he was voted "Coach of the Century" by ESPN.

That first talk of the season was not about the goals for the team, who the captains would be, or any of the usual rally cries of a typical coach, nope, it was all about Wooden demonstrating, in meticulous detail, how the players should properly put on their socks and their shoes. Yes, he would actually show them how to do it. And yes, you usually don't get that kind of instruction after you're two or three years old – especially from one of the best college coaches of all time. Frankly, most coaches at any level above elementary school would think it was too trivial to deal with – and college boys should know how to dress themselves!

Wooden, however, knew that most good players ended up on the bench because they ended up with blisters from gameplay. And he knew most of those blisters could be prevented *if players would simply take the time and put on their socks and shoes correctly.*

Hence the lecture every year – even to the players who had already heard it!! It was a vital first step to Wooden's process – and do you re-

ally argue with a guy who ended up with an over-80% win record? ...
who won ten national championships? ...who is regarded as America's
'winningest' coach? I certainly wouldn't!

By building from that base, Wooden created teams that knew basketball inside and out. He gave them a process that enabled them to do
their very best – and turned him into a legendary coach.

It's what all of us need to do in our individual businesses. Your first
steps, in any venture, should be about finding out what works, from the
bottom up. 'Fine-tuning' will obviously come as you continue along
the way, but if you nail down the process that works for you personally,
it's a template that can take you to where you want to go -- *if you learn
the basics, remember them and continue to implement them.*

Some aspects of that process are generic – they're essential to anyone
trying to do what you're doing. Others are personal – making use of
your specific talents and what works best for you. Out of all of it, however, you build your own unique process by seeing what's effective and
what isn't. Once you have it all put together, you drill that process into
your brain at every given opportunity. And you never forget why you
use the process you use – because it works ...for you! No, not for the
guy down the street, or somebody two office doors down from yours...
but for YOU!!!!

And it has to be the process that's going to serve you all the way down
the line. I have to hand it to my four year-old son Brock's T-ball coach,
Coach Will, because he showed me this power principle in action and
how it's relevant at any age.

The kid that was playing pitcher (no, really, in T-ball they have one, they
just don't actually pitch!) in the game ran from the pitcher's mound to
run down another kid running to home plate – and pulled it off. He got
the out. But the coach told the pitcher that's not what he wanted to see.
That's not how the game is played. It'll work out in T-ball, but that play
won't work when the kids get a little older, and a little faster. He said,
"You might get an out this year with that play, but we're not here to get
outs, we're here to learn how to play baseball." Wow! Now that's what
I'm talking about! Coach Will wanted them to learn how to play the
right way for the long run – not just what worked for now – so as they

moved on, they could power through with the proper process.

With any first steps, you should be doing the same thing – finding out how whatever "game" you're learning works, and how best to play it - whether it's the game of life, the game of business, or a true game. *The principle is the same.*

THE FIRST STEP AND WHY IT'S OVERRATED

No, I'm not getting into an argument with myself, it's true…first steps are absolutely crucial and also amazingly easy!

First of all, people are always incredibly encouraging when you start something new (unless they know you well enough to sense you're heading for disaster). It's exciting to them and they live vicariously through you trying something for the first time. Why? Because you have to do all the hard work and all they have to do is watch!

Seriously, how many quotes and advice do you see on beginning something, whether it's a business or a relationship or just a work-out regimen? Whereas, when you're in the middle of something and whining about it – well, everybody's in the middle of something and whining about it. And they'd rather listen to themselves whine than listen to you do it!

The first step also often means *you're not putting that much at stake.* There's not a lot invested in it emotionally, physically or financially yet. It's basically setting a goal and beginning to figure out how you can achieve that goal.

Taking that first step usually means:

- You're beginning something you want to get done.

- You haven't faced serious opposition to your goal.

- You've psyched yourself up to get going – so you're 'pumped' to see it through.

- Nobody expects a lot from you – because you're just beginning to find out how it's done.

In other words, sure, you're nervous – but you're okay to start that long 'thousand mile' journey, whatever it is. It's not so bad. You're choosing to do it. And nobody will be too hard on you about it.

The first step is also generally *not that complicated*. Remember what the first day of school or a class was like? It was the teacher telling you what you were going to be doing the rest of the semester or year and that's about it. You didn't have to worry, at that point, about having homework done or passing any tests. You were just there – trying to stay awake until the bell rang. Hey, even with Coach Wooden, all they had to do was figure out how to put on their socks and shoes the first time he talked to them! Most of us can handle that kind of pressure.

And one last thing about the first step not really being all that bad – **you can totally 'bail' before the second step**. Seriously, most things won't have horrible consequences if you bail early (guys, this is not an excuse the day after that bachelor party, don't even think about it!). Maybe you say to yourself, "Hey, I want to learn Mandarin Chinese (I use this example in honor of Lao Tzu)." You take that first step – maybe you get an introduction to a beginner's Mandarin Chinese book – and then the bolt of lightning hits your brain....."Hey! This is hard! I'd rather spend the effort on _____ (fill in the blank with your next goal)."

What did you lose? ...that $9.99 you spent on the book? ...and those ten minutes it took you to realize it was hard enough for you to learn English? ...let alone this.

Taking one step on the thousand mile journey and changing your mind? No big deal. Getting five hundred miles down the road and changing your mind? Enormous deal. That's why you can't...

DON'T JUST MUDDLE THROUGH THE MIDDLE

So let's talk about being five hundred miles down that thousand mile road. That's what I like to call the unsung hero of heroic struggles – the middle.

They say the closer you get to the summit, the harder it is to reach it. I've chosen to consciously disagree, and you can too with the right mindset – and I talked about this a little at the beginning of this chapter. When you're so far along, you forgot why you started - but you're not far enough to see where you're going - it's easy to feel like you're stumbling around in the dark, going through the motions, and completely not getting anywhere.

And that's where you have to power through with your process. That's where you have to put your socks and shoes on correctly and keep doing what you're doing, if you've proven to yourself that it works. You may need some adjustments – that's normal, because the world is always changing – but in general, you have to 'keep on keeping on'.

I'm speaking from personal experience on that point. For example, a big part of our business involves me speaking at different events all across the country. They are great because they usually generate a lot of interest in our business and we get to build a list of prospects who were interested enough to come out and hear me, and give us their contact information to stay in touch – so it's almost always a good decision to accept invitations to speak at events. It's something I've learned works for us and it's definitely a big part of my process.

Well, I was invited to speak at what was billed as a major seminar event in California – and I was told there might be a lot of influential people there that would be interested in doing business, and many of them had very large fan bases (sounds good, but believe me, I've heard it before and the delivery of those elements is usually far less than what has been promised). So I thought about it. It was a big commitment (a week in California, away from my family in Orlando), and a big financial commitment (not that it was overly expensive for the trip, but because of my marketing budget at the time, I had to choose between this trip and a new marketing campaign I really wanted to launch).

The California trip, more and more, just felt like a big hassle to me, and an inconvenient one at that. I was ready to skip it, when I remembered that this kind of thing – speaking at places where I could widen my circle of influence and boost my network – was really a vital way that we grow our business. So, I agreed to it.

When I got there, I was amazed at the number of top-tier speakers and writers that were in attendance – it was a room of about 100 people who were all seven figure speakers and authors. I won't drop names, but I would be willing to bet you'd know at least half of the people in the room. We're talking about men and women who literally fill STA-DIUMS with rabid fans wanting to hear them speak, and others who had collectively sold over 100 MILLION books! It was insane! Don't get me wrong, the seminar was hard work – sessions night and day – but out of that came lots of things, including an invitation to speak at another event which proved to be a huge windfall, and there are many other opportunities still being fleshed out, all because I didn't forget my **basic principles**, even when I was reluctant, and **I powered through with my process.**

PROP-UP YOUR PROCESS WITH PRINCIPLES

When I was thinking about whether or not to accept that speaking engagement, I didn't think about making important new contacts or generating more business. I concentrated on the expense, the work and the inconvenience. Obviously, big mistake on my part. Fortunately, I got back on my thousand-mile road because I remembered that the process didn't exist for its own sake – the process brought results!!!

*And that's what we all have to remember. We must continually perfect the process – and sticking to that process is more important than anything else...**because the process gets us to the goal line***

When Coach Wooden gave his annual "socks and shoes speech," some older players would start to feel insulted that he was still teaching the ins and outs of footwear. They didn't want to listen to it all over again.

But consider this – **do you think Coach Wooden really wanted to tell players how to put on their socks and shoes every single year?**

Don't you think maybe one season, he said to himself, "Maybe I don't have to do this anymore. Maybe these college kids can figure this out for themselves." I'm willing to wager he did – and that he also went back to doing it because he once again realized that this was his process, it worked and he should stick to it. **...and because it was also important to his players' process.**

After the newness of whatever you're in the middle of wears off, it's tempting to forget all the building blocks that got you there. It's easy to be distracted by turn-offs on the thousand mile road and take another route ...that will take you somewhere you really don't want to go.

Both behaviors are dangerous to your business. Sticking to your the principles that you used to develop your process helps you avoid them. Maybe you have a choice between a lunch with somebody you like but isn't going to do much for your operation – and somebody else you don't know that well but could do an awful lot for you. You're better off seizing the second opportunity, even though you'll have to invest some time and energy in getting to know this person and selling them on you and your business.

Making productive choices that will further your process means you'll keep getting the results you want. And, hey, you can always have lunch with the other friend on a day when there isn't a conflict.

When the pay-off isn't necessarily in sight, you simply have to trust that what you're doing will work – and that your process will, in fact, see you through to the other side.

I will leave you with some very wise words from Coach Wooden: "Don't be too concerned with regard to things over which you have no control, because that will eventually have an adverse effect on things over which you have control."

You have control over what you do and how you do it. You can't control the outside factors. Even if you've made your process the most powerful it can be, it still won't work every single time. But if you fixate on the things that could go against you, you'll have a hard time achieving what you want to achieve.

Life is all about making the odds work in your favor – *and having a process that will allow you to power through to the end of whatever road you're on - which means that chances are you'll get what you're after.*

<u>So pull on those socks and lace up those shoes the right way – so you can win the game!</u>

About Nick

Nick Nanton, Esq. is known as "The Celebrity Lawyer" for his role in developing and marketing business and professional experts into Celebrity Experts in their field through personal branding -- to help them gain credibility and recognition for their accomplishments. Nick is recognized as the nation's leading expert on personal branding. He lectures regularly on the topic at the University of Central Florida, and his book Celebrity Branding You® is used as the textbook on personal branding at the University.

Nick serves as the Producer of America's PremierExperts® television show and The Next Big Thing® radio show, both designed to recognize the top Experts in their field and bring their solutions to consumers.

Nick is an award winning songwriter and the co-author of the best-selling books, Celebrity Branding You!®, Big Ideas for Your Business, and Shift Happens. Nick also serves as editor and publisher of Celebrity Press™, a publishing company that produces and releases books by top Business Experts. Nick has been featured in USA Today, The Wall St. Journal, Newsweek, The New York Times, Entrepreneur® Magazine, and has appeared on ABC, NBC, CBS, and Fox television affiliates speaking on subjects ranging from branding, and marketing and law, to American Idol.

Nick is a member of the Florida Bar, holds a JD from the University of Florida Levin College of Law, as well as a BSBA in Finance from the University of Florida's prestigious Warrington College of Business. Nick is also a voting member of The National Academy of Recording Arts & Sciences (NARAS - Home to The GRAMMYs), and spends his spare time rooting for the Florida Gators with his wife Kristina, and their two sons, Brock and Bowen.

Nick can be reached at 800-980-1626 or Nick@CelebrityBrandingAgency.com.

Power Principle #10

THE IMPORTANCE OF MASTERING FOLLOW-UP

by Clate Mask

The greatest "principle of success" I ever learned was revealed to me (and my business partners) in the early stages of growing our business. It's all about **follow-up. Follow-up** is the secret. **Follow up** is at the heart of growth and success. *Lack of* **follow-up** *kills most businesses. The following article is on what to do about it.*

But what exactly do I mean by **follow-up**? Let me start from the beginning…

Many years ago, my software company was providing customized software to small businesses wanting to use the power of automation to grow. We built all sorts of custom software applications. Most of them had a customer management component to them.

Then one day, a guy (Reed Hoisington) came to us and asked us to help him manage his contacts more effectively. He was trying to follow up with his prospects and customers, but he was making lots of mistakes. He was having 'one heck of a time' keeping leads, responders and customers straight. He couldn't track things properly and **follow-up** was 'hit-or-miss.'

After collaborating with Reed, we built a software program that could automatically **follow up** with prospects and customers, segment contacts based on interests, behaviors, and actions, and track all communication.

Reed was thrilled with the results and he left happy. But…he soon returned.

You see, Reed had a handful of clients who realized what his software was doing, and they were eager to have the same system built for them. So, we "productized" the software and sold it to a few dozen entrepreneurs. They, in turn, raved about the software. And for the first time, things were really moving forward.

But that was a drop in the bucket compared to what happened next…

You see, not long after creating our signature product, our sales skyrocketed. Why? Because we actually started using the software. With our own **follow-up** features, we were able to send emails, letters, faxes and voice broadcasts to our entire database. We reconnected with our prospects, started them on educational follow-up sequences, and soon, prospects were calling us, ready to buy.

That's when I knew we were on to something.

And our business has never been the same since. Today, thousands of people use our software to **follow up**, educate their prospects and customers, cultivate lasting relationships and maximize the value of their prospect and customer lists.

And **follow-up** marketing is at the heart of it all.

Since that time, we have tried all kinds of techniques to drive our business success. Still, nothing has ever compared to the success we've experienced by following this one simple principle: **follow up continually with all your prospects and customers.**

You don't need an army of telemarketers to do this. But if you want to achieve the incredible growth we did (1,100% in just three years) then you do need to know the proven secrets to mastering **follow-up**.

Follow-up is the one "principle of success" that has never failed me. And I promise you that when you fully comprehend **the concepts of follow-up**, it will change the way you do business. It will super-charge your marketing and sales in ways you never believed possible.

Now, before I get into the **follow-up** concepts, I want to ask you a question:

Have you been diligently **following up** with your prospects and customers?

Nine times out of 10, the response to that question is a guilt-ridden "no!" I say guilt-ridden, because most entrepreneurs and business owners <u>know</u> that they have severely neglected their prospects and customers. They know that keeping in touch with your contacts is important to building a business, securing a positive reputation and creating beneficial relationships.

Plus, they know that in failing to **follow up** with customers and prospects, they're 'leaving money on the table.'

I've spoken with thousands of entrepreneurs who have confessed to me that if they could just figure out how to **follow up** more consistently, they would have much more profitable and dependable businesses.

Unless you're the rarest of exceptions, you're in the same boat. When you fail to keep in contact with your prospects and customers, you're letting go of perhaps the biggest opportunity in your business.

I want to help you change that. So, here are the 5 concepts behind *Follow-up Mastery*:

1)   The Real Definition of Successful Marketing

There are three and only three factors that really have an iron grip on the profits of any successful marketing efforts. The smartest marketing minds on the planet have boiled down these factors to this simple, but incredibly powerful formula:

(i) The Right Message…(ii) To The Right Market…(iii) At The Right Time

Most businesses miss one, two or all three of these factors, and as a result have very ineffective marketing and advertising results. Heck, just miss one of them and you're looking at the wrong end of a marketing disaster. It's like a three-legged stool: take any one of the legs away and you're flat on the ground, right?

The objective of your marketing efforts is to generate leads--people that you can follow up with. When you convey the right message to the right market at the right time, you generate leads. And that's when the whole follow-up process should begin…the moment you acquire a new lead.

After all, you provided this person with a message they wanted to hear. You connected with them. <u>Now</u> is the time to build that relationship.

Unfortunately, that's not what usually happens.

2)   "Cherry Picking" and the Three Types of Leads

Every time you get a new batch of leads, whether it's from your website, a conference, a mailer, etc., you can divide your leads into three categories. They are:

a. Hot Leads- the leads that seem anxious and ready to buy.

b. Warm Leads- leads that show interest, but may not be ready to make a purchase just yet.

c. Cold Leads- leads that have no immediate interest in your services or products.

Now, if you're like most business owners, you immediately reach for the hot leads. And that's to be expected. After all, you have sales to close. You can't be wasting your time on people who won't be making a purchase. You've got a business to run and that business demands sales…now!

But here's the problem, as you race 'from hot lead to hot lead', your warm leads have seriously begun to cool. By the time you've interacted with all your hot leads, every other contact has lost interest and disappeared. At this point, there's nothing more for you to do but seek out new leads.

The challenge with this model is two-fold. One, you're always going to need more leads. Which means you'll be spending time and money just trying to track down new ways of filling your funnel. Two, when your warm leads decide they *are* ready to buy (and they will), guess who they won't be taking their business to? That's right, the company that neglected them.

But you can do so much better. With *effective* **follow-up** in place, you will always have hot leads, because you'll constantly be working with and building relationships with warm and even cold prospects.

3)   Timing is Everything

You'll notice that Secret #3 is closely associated with Secret #1 (the right message to the right market at the right time).

Most people tinker with their message and their market and end up with something that works okay. But they forget how critical timing is in the whole mix.

See, they simply forget this one simple truth:

"People buy when they are ready to buy, not when you are ready to sell."

But how do you know when a prospect is ready to buy? You don't. So you just have to be standing there the moment someone wants to make a purchase. If you're not, one of your competitors will be.

You don't want to leave new business up to chance, not unless you like being poor or losing to your competitor. No one does! But the one thing in this situation – staying in front of the prospect – is probably the single greatest challenge in your business.

The fact is, **'follow-up'** is a gut-wrenching, time-consuming, tedious and labor-intensive task that is almost impossible for the human mind to keep straight. The good news is that you can easily annihilate this problem…and when you do, you'll see a massive jump in your business success.

4)   Transform Your Sales Strategy From Outbound "Hunting" to Inbound "Harvesting"

This secret is critical to your business success because it puts you in a position to land customers quickly. It shortens the sales cycle, increases your capacity to handle more deals or sales and improves your closing ratio because you spend more time talking to highly qualified prospects.

See, when you're in "hunting" mode, you're dialing for dollars. You feel resistance at every turn. Rejection is common. You get "price-shopped" against competitors, and you waste tons of time working with leads who simply aren't ready.

On the other hand, when you're in "harvesting" mode, you're working smart and scooping up sales right and left. You're like the expert fisherman with the irresistible bait, drawing your prospects to you.

So, the BIG question is…how can you spend more time working with hot leads and less time – *even NO time* – with cold leads?

To understand how to do this, you need to know about a fundamental business problem at the heart of nearly every company in the world. This problem is: *How does a company balance its marketing and sales efforts?*

You see, in most companies, the marketing department's job is to get the leads and the sales department's job is to call on the leads and close the sale. But in between getting the lead and closing the sales, there's a huge gap.

If you close the gap, you'll make the shift from hunting mode to harvesting mode… And your business will see unbelievable success!

5) <u>You Must Have a Living, Breathing Customer Database</u>

Okay, so by now you understand why you must **follow up** with all your prospects and customers if you want to see your business achieve even greater success. But before you can **follow up** with your customers, you have to have people to market to.

If you're like most business owners, you want to build a business that doesn't rely heavily on outside marketing efforts. You want to maximize referrals and repeat business so that you don't have to spend your time chasing down leads and convincing folks that they should do business with you.

When I ask entrepreneurs what they're doing to make this dream a reality, too often they answer with something like:

"Well, Clate, the longer I'm in the industry, the more customers I will work with and the more I'll get repeat business and referrals."

I cringe when I hear that! Because, bottom line, your customers and prospects just aren't thinking about you. That's the cold, hard truth. No matter how great your services or products are, your customers are busy living their lives.

If you want a strong customer base that is the backbone of your business, you must actively, systematically and methodically build your customer base. And you need to be adding to that customer database every day, every week, every month. These are the people you'll want to keep in touch with.   .

And if you put into practice this important technique, your customer database will become your #1 asset, bringing you added business for weeks, months and years into the future.

When it comes right down to it, the only reason people care about you is because you ask them to. The only reason you and/or your business achieve success is because you consistently and effectively reach out to your customer base.

Today, consumers are searching for one thing, a relationship with you. If you are unwilling to build that relationship, you're missing out on your opportunity to let your prospects and customers propel you forward!

About Clate

Clate Mask, JD/MBA from BYU, is the co-founder and CEO of software company Infusionsoft, the leader in email marketing 2.0. He raised nearly $17 million in venture capital funding from Silicon-Valley-based Mohr Davidow Ventures and vSpring Capital after bootstrapping Infusionsoft from 2001 to 2007.

Clate's mission is to revolutionize the way small businesses grow.

More than 16,000 small business subscribers use Infusionsoft's SaaS marketing automation solution, which comes with a 'Double Your Sales' guarantee.

POWER PRINCIPLE #11

REFINE YOUR SYSTEMS - "THE ONE-TWO PUNCH"

by Richard Seppala, "The ROI Guy"

Y ou have probably heard the expression, "Build a better mousetrap and the world will beat a path to your door," attributed to Ralph Waldo Emerson.

Well, in my opinion, you can have the best mousetrap possible – and it does you absolutely no good if you don't have a way to lure the mouse into it.

This is the ROI Guy here with another chapter and another Power Principle – that it's important in business to make sure you take care of both the front and the back of all your systems. It's what I like to call "the one-two punch."

Focusing and fine-tuning one half of a system can make this half completely perfect – but it doesn't matter if you don't pay any attention to the other half. In a football game, for example, you might have an awesome quarterback – but he could be ready to tear his hair out, because the receiver couldn't hold on to the ball if you attached it to his hands with a nail gun.

Or think about the classic "I Love Lucy" episode, where Lucy and Ethel are working on the assembly line of the chocolate factory - and

109

they have to wrap the candy up as it comes out from the manufacturing process. Nothing wrong with how the factory is making the chocolate – but a lot wrong with how Lucy and Ethel handle the situation (even though it's a pretty yummy solution).

Front to back. Both sides have to be effective. And both sides have to deliver. That's what makes a successful system, especially when it comes to providing your business with the right kind of marketing muscle.

THE POWER OF INFUSIONSOFT

Hopefully, you've already read the chapter by Infusionsoft CEO Clate Mask. Infusionsoft creates a lot of great CRM (Customer Relationship Management) software that's perfect for small businesses and entrepreneurs. It enables you to take your database of contacts and do some awesome automated follow-up marketing whenever you want.

If we're talking about building a better mousetrap, this is about the best one you can think of in the marketing arena. Not that you should think of your prospects and clients as rodents – it's just a metaphor, folks! But a system like Infusionsoft does allow you to have the marketing power of much bigger companies at a much more affordable price.

With Infusionsoft, you've got a powerful back half of a system. Combine that with an equally powerful front half and you've got a dynamite marketing system that sells your product or services.

That front half should entail focusing on efficiently and effectively generating and capturing the leads to feed the funnel into your Infusionsoft - with marketing that's tracked and targeted. If you can't feed your funnel with fresh, quality leads, eventually you'll be at a marketing dead end.

That's where the ROI Guy comes in.

"THE BRIDGE" TO A COMPLETE MARKETING SOLUTION

I've created an integrated front-end solution that works with the Infusionsoft packages to automatically capture quality leads that can be immediately turned around and marketed to, in your next campaign.

It's called "The ROI Bridge." Why is it important? Well, can you afford to *lose* a sale – or a potential new long-term customer – in these tight times? That was pretty easy to answer, I'm willing to bet – with a great big fat, "NO!" But how much money is slipping through the fingers of businesses all across the country, just because contacts are not captured or put into the sales funnel in a correct or timely way? Marketing info *that's coming directly into them*?

Most businesses simply have someone at their office handling incoming sales calls. That person, who most likely has not had much sales training, will probably not do the best job of selling your product or service – or even of collecting the caller's contact information for follow-up marketing.

I know this through experience - part of my services to clients includes providing "Mystery Shoppers" who call a business pretending to be a new customer. We record the calls and the results can be pretty shocking. Most sales calls are handled so badly it's hard to believe anyone gets new customers!

Even if the person handling the sales calls actually does write down the contact info, they'll usually put it on a Post-It note that could easily get lost in the shuffle – meaning you've lost a potential sale just by simple negligence. And I don't mean to be hard on anyone's staff here. This is a common problem. A small business is usually extremely busy, with people stretched to take care of everything that needs to be handled, and sometimes they just don't have the time or the preparation to handle a sales call.

Unfortunately, that impacts your bottom line in a big way. Without the right automated system to handle incoming sales calls and capture contact info, you risk losing quality leads that are *directly demonstrating an interest in what you have to offer* by taking the time to call you.

I'm sure your business can't afford to have that happen on a regular basis. And "The ROI Bridge" makes sure that doesn't happen.

THE PATH TO "THE BRIDGE"

The ROI Bridge process begins with my Lead Generation Hotlines, which I offer in a package with the Bridge. Basically, I provide a business with a certain number of unique toll-free numbers to allocate as they wish.

Those numbers are used for two very important reasons – to feed into The Bridge and to help track your marketing placements. One of my clients will put a different toll-free number on different campaigns and/or placements (print, online, radio, etc.). That allows the client to immediately see which marketing efforts are generating the most leads – and which just aren't worth spending money on. And it helps the client save money by getting rid of ineffective marketing and to better target potential customers by putting more into the marketing that works.

Let me walk you through two very distinct ways that a business can use the hotlines. In both cases, I'll use a dentistry practice as an example.

Let's say this dentist has one marketing campaign where he offers a free 'teeth whitening' treatment to a new patient making an appointment for a cleaning and check-up. The toll-free Hotline number, in this case, rings directly at the dentist's office, where the receptionist schedules an appointment. Meanwhile, our Bridge software has recorded the call, and also the caller's contact information, for loading into Infusionsoft.

The dentist is able to track, thanks to that particular number, how many people called about that campaign and how many of those calls were actually converted to appointments. If the conversion rate is low, the dentist also has the option of listening to the recorded calls and evaluating if the staff needs some sales call training (as I said earlier, that training is usually a good idea!).

The other way that same dentist can use my Hotlines is to put one of my toll-free numbers on an ad for, say, dental implant treatments. The ad has a strong "Call to Action" on it – "To receive my FREE report on 'The 9 Critical Ways Implants Can Improve Your Life,' call this toll-free number and we'll send it out to you."

This time, when someone calls about the ad, the call goes to a pre-recorded message that asks for their contact info, so they can get the free report. That call is then tracked, recorded, transcribed and pushed into the correct follow-up campaign within Infusionsoft, so the free report is sent out and the contact info is retained for future marketing AUTOMATICALLY.

That means the dental staff no longer has to answer the calls and input the information manually into the campaign – which, to be honest, sometimes they do and sometimes they don't. It's usually not a priority of the workday and, if they do input the contact info, it rarely happens right away.

With "The Bridge," it happens instantly. When the lead gets their requested info, they can familiarize themselves with what implants are all about and what they can do for them – making them more likely to buy. This system is the best way to educate potential customers and the most foolproof, as it bypasses the chance of the client or their staff mishandling a call.

Whether you use the Hotlines for a direct call into your place of business – or to a pre-recorded message that captures the lead info – you still capture sales call data in a format easily used for later campaigns, bringing a whole new level of automation to your marketing efforts. That saves you <u>two</u> very valuable things – *time* and *money.*

The ROI Bridge, combined with Infusionsoft, enables you to do the kind of automated marketing that large corporations do – but at a small business price. You're also able to follow up on leads in a timely and efficient way – and you get to measure the effectiveness of your advertising placements at the same time.

AUTOMATION MAKES THE DIFFERENCE

Again, it's very easy to lose valuable sales leads through simple neglect. It's also easy to rely on the same tried-and-true marketing you've been doing for years, without any idea of how well it's really working.

With our Hotline numbers and The ROI Bridge, much of your marketing will become automatic. You'll know instantly from your "ROI Guy" web page which ads are generating the most leads. You'll have all your generated leads automatically captured, tagged and ready for follow-up marketing. And you'll have all the recorded incoming sales call messages at your disposal for return phone calls and staff evaluations.

Believe it or not, you'll generate more and better leads from utilizing a toll-free phone number rather than an online opt-in box. More and more consumers are afraid opt-in boxes just mean that they're opting to get a ton of spam in their email 'inbox'. It's also easier for people to just call from their cell phone when they see an ad, rather than try to remember the website address when they spot your ad and don't have easy access to the internet at that moment.

By making a phone call, the prospect also demonstrates they're more serious about using your product or service – and studies show that conversions over the phone are much higher than through online communication.

It's hard enough to keep your core business organized the way you want it, let alone your marketing. That's why taking The ROI Bridge to an Infusionsoft package is a great all-in-one solution to keep your marketing operation humming – while you're busy working.

Having an automatic marketing one-two punch can leave your competitors 'out cold on the canvas' – while you reap the benefits of more sales. So go for heavyweight status – <u>and make sure you have the right marketing system to help your business 'go the distance'</u>!

About Richard

For over a decade, TCS President Richard Seppala has worked in the Long Term Care arena as V.P. of Sales and Marketing for top providers. During this time, he has developed unique and creative marketing programs consistently exceeding census goals and financial satisfaction.

As a result of his marketing and sales success, Richard has most recently formed Total Census Solutions. A company helping others benefit from his innovative marketing techniques and the newest technologies that have just hit the long term care market.

Grounded by years of direct sales and marketing experience, Richard brings significant value to organizations with creative insight, proven strategies and practical sales and marketing tools that generate results. These tools have generated thousands of inbound calls and qualified leads for multiple providers in multiple disciplines.

Richard has trained thousands of sales and marketing professionals from all over the country, to help them sell more effectively, generate more referrals and successfully convert callers to customers.

All this, combined with an appreciation for quality resident care, customer satisfaction and compassion, Richard Seppala sales and marketing innovations are like no other.

Power Principle #12

POWER UP YOUR ONLINE COMMUNICATION

by Vesna Sutter, D.D.S.

"Communication works for those who work at it."
~ John Powell

It's easy for me to remember how long I've been a dentist – I was pregnant with my son, Nicholas, when I graduated from dental school and he's now 23 years old. And yes, he's certainly grown and changed over the years, as has my dental practice, and I'm proud to say he's now a graduate from Indiana University. I am, of course, equally proud of my daughter Jacqueline who is graduating also from Indiana University this year. No, neither of my children chose dentistry as their career. They both are pursuing careers in business and marketing.

And lately, I'm *very* proud of how they have applied their new knowledge in my business and what they've done for my dental practice, Sunrise Dental Care.

They taught me a very important lesson – that it's just as important to keep up with the technology that enables you to communicate better with your customers (in my case, patients), as it is to keep up with the technology that enables you to provide more and better dental services.

That's where Social Media comes in.

I'd like to share how my kids helped me use social media to continue to grow and deepen my relationship with my patients – and how it could be a Power Principle for your business as well.

WHY OUR PATIENTS LOVE US!

See, when it comes to dentistry, we are always doing our best to be current with the latest advances in dentistry – I feel like I owe it to my patients and myself to constantly keep increasing the knowledge I have, so as to be able to provide superior dental care .

This past January, for example, I bought a new, smaller laser that we use for treating canker sores, periodontal therapy, and trimming tissue. It's more powerful, but smaller and less invasive than past laser treatments. We also use another laser that tests the stains on your teeth to see how far the tooth is broken down by the bacteria – enabling us to catch cavities when they're tiny and in the earliest stages of formation.

A few months ago, we also introduced CariFree, a new screening test that can help us determine how cavity-prone a patient really is by testing the pH in their saliva, and again, allows us to tackle dental problems in the very early stages.

Back when I graduated from dental school – which, you may recall, was 23 years ago! – none of the above technology was even an idea in anyone's mind. It was more like science fiction. Today, however, they are real and important tools for any dental practice – which is why I make it a point to be aware of these new breakthroughs.

The key question though, as a Doctor and a business owner is, "How do I make sure all my patients, their friends, family, and potential patients know about the great things we are doing in our practice?"

My Children provided the Missing Link.

Thanks to my young business graduates, the missing link was revealed to me. What I haven't been doing, until recently, is keeping up with the equally-important breakthroughs in social media – and how people today are communicating differently than ever before in human history.

FACING UP TO FACEBOOK

Let's go back one more time to my dental school days; back then, cell phones were just coming into usage, and they were the size (and the weight) of a brick. Not the ultimate in convenience, and texting definitely was not an option – the closest you could come to that were telegrams. Anybody remember those?

Now, my patients tell me their ten year-olds are asking for cell phones, and everyone, of course, texts and emails. I was up to date with all that – about four years ago, our office went paperless and we began communicating with our patients that way. *They prefer those kind of less intrusive electronic methods to send reminders for check-ups and scheduled appointments.*

Where I 'missed the boat' was Facebook and Twitter.

These two websites grew into internet juggernauts in recent years without any help from me. I emailed a newsletter once a month to my patients and I thought I was doing all I needed to do to keep in touch with everyone about what was happening at my practice.

My children thought differently – since they were learning about, and how to use, social media in business school. I was surprised that was part of their curriculum and it really made me take another look at it more seriously. I thought to myself, if a top-notch university is teaching this to business students, then it's important to my practice. This generation will be running things in a few years and it'll be commonplace. Also, they're going to be my patients and they're going to expect me to be up-to-date with this kind of stuff. The last thing any businessperson needs is to be perceived as being behind the times. The thought might cross my patients minds that if I was behind the times with the computer and technology, maybe I was also old fashioned in their dental care.

Luckily, my son and daughter offered to set up a Facebook page and a Twitter page for myself and my practice. Hey, a freebee is a freebee, so I gave them the green light – they're smart and they know what they're doing a lot more than I would in this area. Plus, they could get it done ten or twenty times faster.

Well, they went ahead and made it happen – even though I was blissfully unaware of exactly *what* they had made happen. I didn't actually have a chance to check out their work for about a month after they had created my pages - then I finally logged into my new Facebook account and took a look at my **Sunrise Dental** page.

And I was shocked!

Let me quickly say that I was shocked in a *good* way. It wasn't as if my kids had 'photoshopped' a moustache on my picture or anything.

What I was shocked by was all the incredibly nice things my patients had posted on my virtual wall (I thought walls had to have drywall and paint to exist – who knew?). They had left warm and incredibly kind comments about how well we had treated them and how they enjoyed their experience at my practice. And they sent me a lot of virtual hugs (again, I thought hugs had to have arms involved somehow…but hey, I'll take them any way they're delivered).

That's when I really felt the power of this new communication channel. I know that some of these patients would have been very embarrassed or at least uncomfortable to say these things to me face-to-face – others just wouldn't think of it at the moment when they were at my offices. Somehow, however, going on the Facebook page made them feel free to give me the kind of compliments that might not have come easily in person.

Suddenly, this wasn't just about how I could communicate with my patients – it was also about how *they* could communicate with *me.* That was a big realization. It is a way of building a personal connection with my patients. The relationship develops from Dr to patient to friend to friend - which is how I wish to treat all my patients (as family and friends). This is not something that's going to happen with a newsletter that you just receive in your inbox. When you're participating in an online community, it's much more of an interactive experience and a great one for both sides.

WHY YOU SHOULD CONSIDER SOCIAL MEDIA

Some people cautioned me against getting involved with social media. You hear a lot of scary stories, such as the one about criminals 'trolling' Facebook to see who was going on vacation in their area, and then breaking into their houses when they were gone. Obviously, you have to be smart about what information you put out there and how you use it – but I really think social media is becoming too dominant to ignore. There is a great video on U-Tube (another huge social media network) called Social Media revolution, you should check it out. It points out some amazing growth numbers with social media. For example, to reach 50 million people it took the radio 38 years, TV 13 years, the Internet 4 yrs, ipod 3 years, and FACEBOOK added 100 million users in less than 9 months. That is huge!

Think about this – if Facebook were a country, it would be the fourth most populated one in the world. Social networks and blogs are the fourth biggest activity that people engage in online – beating personal email! The top three people on Twitter (Ashton Kutcher, Britney Spears and Ellen Degeneres) have more followers combined than the entire population of Austria. And 65% of all marketers spend 5 hours a week or more using social media to deliver their message.

But it's not just about marketing – that's not what really excites me about it. I also believe it's the next stage in the evolution of the relationship between people like me who deliver a service, and their clients.

I wrote a chapter in another book, "Shift Happens," about the importance of the personal touch between myself and my patients. Social media helps continue to bring down the walls (virtual and/or real) between us. It's how good word-of-mouth will spread and business will grow – potential patients can see all the unsolicited (nice) remarks on my pages and trust me to do good by them. _Note: 78% of consumers trust peer recommendations, only 14 % trust advertisements_.

While I still email out my monthly newsletter, I find I can reach people faster and better with Facebook and Twitter. When I get in new equipment like the laser, or a new service like the CariFree screening, I can just mention them on both services without having to "hard sell" my patients on them in an aggressive way. I just inform them of the new things I have learned, and now have available to better treat them. I show them my excitement and then let them be. They can then check them out on their own, and decide if they want to use them. I like feeling like I'm not straight-out selling to them but rather sharing with them – and they can discover these things on their own. It makes for a more true and trusting relationship.

SO, 'POWER UP YOUR SOCIAL MEDIA NOW!'

Social media is continuing to grow, but a lot of people in my age group still aren't participating. From my own personal experience, I wouldn't let the bad things you hear about it deter you from joining in. Just like anything else, as long as you know the limits and you're smart about it, social media can be a huge benefit to you and help you reach and help thousands of people.

And when you do finally decide to participate, drop by the Sunrise Dental Care page and I'll be happy to "friend" you. And of course, don't forget to follow me on Twitter @vesnasutter!

About Vesna:

Dr. Vesna Sutter is not your average run-of-the-mill dentist. Yes, she places implants and crowns, and even does root canals on patients, but her passion is not just "teeth." For the past twenty years, Dr. Sutter has prided herself on changing people's lives. A smile is the strongest and most genuine thing people can share with one another, so she has dedicated her life to helping as many people as she can achieve the smile of their dreams.

Dr. Sutter is a 1986 graduate of Loyola Dental School and completed her undergraduate studies at the University of Illinois, Champaign-Urbana. The field of dentistry is constantly changing, and in order to provide her patients with the best opportunities to change their lives, Dr. Sutter has taken over 500 hours of continuing education in Implants, Sedation, Orthodontics, TMJ Disorders, Cosmetic Dentistry, and Sleep Disorder Dentistry.

Dr. Sutter is an active member of the following organizations:
Dental Organization for Conscious Sedation (DOCS)
American Academy of Cosmetic Dentistry
American Dental Association
Chicago Dental Society
Illinois State Dental Society
American Association of Functional Orthodontics
International Association for Orthodontics
Academy of Dental Sleep Medicine
American Academy of Sleep Medicine
North American Neuromuscular Study Club

On top of her extensive knowledge and education, Dr. Sutter has developed a 'state of the art' dental office. She uses the newest and best technologies the dental field has to offer. She puts it very simply, "In order to provide the best care possible, and make my patients feel as comfortable as possible, having the proper technology is essential."

Dr. Vesna Sutter lives in South Barrington, IL with her husband, two children, and two (Tiny) dogs. Although Dr. Sutter is an Illini at heart , in her kids eyes she has officially been adopted as an Indiana University Hoosier. Both Dr. Sutter's son and daughter are recent graduates of Indiana University's Kelley School of Business.

In her spare time (of which she has very little), Dr. Sutter enjoys cooking, exercising, and decorating. Through Dr. Sutter's devotion, dedication, and overall goal of improving people's lives, Dr. Sutter has established herself as one of the America's *premier* Dentists.

To learn more about Dr. Sutter and her practice in Geneva, IL,
visit: www.SunriseDentalCare.com

Power Principal #13

"FIND SOMETHING YOU LOVE TO DO, AND THEN FIGURE OUT HOW TO MAKE MONEY DOING IT."

by Jennifer Burg

THESUBURBANMOM'S POWER PRINCIPLE

I was never one of those kids who just *knew* what she wanted to be when she grew up. When adults asked me what I wanted to do when I grew up, I could only shrug my shoulders. Dad's response to my uncertainty was that it was fine not to know what I wanted to do when I grew up; after all he was still working on what he would do when he grew up.

You see, dad was (and still is today) an entrepreneur, and even as a kid, I knew this meant dad did lots of different things. I was never much of a speller, but in kindergarten I knew how to spell "entrepreneur" -- I had to have something to write down when I was asked what my father did for a living.

Because dad was an entrepreneur I learned early on that it was o.k. for the ideal job to change, and that sometimes finding the right path meant discovering the wrong ones first. Dad was this and then he was that, but he just kept "going with the flow" picking up new ideas along the way.

Of all the paths to choose, when I was a kid, no one in their right mind would have dreamed that I would find a love for writing and find a career in it, but I discovered a knack for it and here I am. A happy and successful testament to my power principle, **"Find something you love to do, and then figure out how to make money doing it."**

At the age of six, I was diagnosed as a "slow learner" with "severe dyslexia." My parents were told that it would be a struggle for me to even graduate high school. (Now that I am a mom, I can't imagine how devastating that must have been for my parents. What a cruel diagnosis.) But those who counted me out didn't count on my type-A personality, internal drive and a report on *60 Minutes*.

It was a story on *60 Minutes* caught my family's attention and changed my life. It was about a form of dyslexia and how it could be helped with simple colored lenses. (Yes, colored lenses.) The report went on to describe the symptoms exhibited by those with ***Scotopic Sensitivity Syndrome*** (now known as the *Irlen Syndrome*). It was as if someone was describing reading the way I saw it for the first time. I had every symptom listed.

The Irlen Syndrome is not an optical problem. It is a problem with the brain's ability to process visual information. In order to assist the brain in processing visual information, patients are matched with colored lenses that aid the brain's comprehension. Research indicates that as many as 46% of people diagnosed with dyslexia could be helped by the Irlen Method and millions of people are discovering how simple colored overlays change their life every day. It changed my life. Visit www. Irlen.com for more information.

A few days later dad and I were on a plane bound for California to be "tested." And on the plane ride home I read an entire book (*Ramona Quimby, Age 8* – all 208 pages) for the first time in my life with the assistance of colored overlays.

By the time I graduated high school – third in my class of 453 students with an above 4.0 grade point average – I had discovered that I loved to read and I *loved* to write.

My attempt at theater in high school lead me to become part of "the crew." As a publicity coordinator, I put together all of the programs and promotional items for the school's shows. It was my introduction into the world of design and production.

At the University of Florida, as an at-first-undeclared freshman, I discovered the College of Journalism and Communications. Once there, I found that what I loved about writing and production transitioned nicely into a degree in public relations. Upon graduation from UF, also with an A average, I still didn't know what I wanted to be when I grew up. But I had fallen in love with the written word and learned the power of hard work and my own persistence.

My first hand at doing what I loved to do came when I decided to start my own magazine. Having returned to my hometown from Washington D.C., after discovering that I did *not* love working in politics, I needed to find something I could get excited about. I was looking for something I would love to do. As an avid magazine reader, I quickly recognized a void in our area of publications dedicated to women in business. There were several local publications for lifestyle and family, but the local business angle was limited to the newspaper. Recognizing the strength of women in the business community, I created *mzbiz* – a magazine for women in business.

mzbiz's content, production and publication were its successes, but its downfall was advertising revenue. While I loved producing the monthly, full-color, glossy publication packed with useful content and had no problem distributing it to local business community; I quickly learned that I did *not* love advertising sales. Advertising sales is just not my forté. Since a magazine can't survive without advertising revenue to back it, *mzbiz* came to an end after just 10 issues.

But *mzbiz* afforded me the experience that lead to my next opportunity. Still loving the magazine world, I was hired to help a company start its own publication, and for the next five years I used that experience and my passion to produce an 84-page, full-color, national financial magazine. (Yes, financial. A world that I had no inherent knowledge of, but I had become a quick learner.)

In 2008, my path changed directions when my daughter was born. I wanted to stay home with my daughter, to be the kind of mom my mother was to me – driving carpool, volunteering at school, creating big birthday bashes, etc. So a full-time, in-office job suddenly no longer excited me. But after a few months home on maternity leave, I also realized that not doing something didn't work for me either. I thrive on projects and productivity – I needed something to occupy my mind.

In order to become the mom I wanted to be, I realized that I had to fill my idleness with something I could be passionate about. Once again, I was looking for something I would love to do. It came naturally for me to fall back on my first love – writing. So, I started by picking up free freelance projects here and there. It was a wonderful escape into the world of adults and productivity, but the world around me seemed to have changed with the birth of my daughter. My focus had shifted to play dates, laundry, parenting – I was a mom.

Quite by accident, a visit from an old friend drove this point home for me. While my friend regaled my husband and me about tales of travel and adventure, fine dining and his carefree-bachelor life, I wiped breakfast off my daughter's face and told him stories about life with a baby. Pondering how our paths had become so different, I realized he was the same friend we had always known, but I had become something else. I had become a mom. I had become TheSuburbanMom.

In that moment, I knew what I wanted to do. I wanted to write about my new life's passions and share them with other moms. I realized that while my friend couldn't relate to my life in suburbia, moms all over could and would relate. That weekend TheSuburbanMom.com was born – actually she was born the day my daughter was born, but that was the weekend it all came together.

I followed my power principle. I found something I loved to do (be a writer and mom), and I created a way to make money doing it (write about being a mom). My journey with TheSuburbanMom continues to open doors for freelance projects and opportunities to work with national companies to promote products and services geared toward families. Best of all, it affords me the ability to do all of these things and more from home with my daughter.

And I was right; moms all over can and do relate to life in suburbia.

They relate because we are all looking for the same things -- products and services to make life easier, more comfortable or healthier for our families; an escape from our own lives, even for a moment; ways to make our household budget stretch a little further and someone we can relate to and who can relate to us.

People still ask the question, "What's next?" And I can only shrug. I still don't know what I want to be when I grow up, but I love being a mom and I love to write, so that's where I will start. Oh, I have ideas, and I know I won't be idle. I am open to opportunities and excited about who I am – TheSuburbanMom.

So, what will I teach my daughter to call what I do? A writer? A blogger? A freelancer? I like all of those options, and they are all easier to spell than entrepreneur. Most of all, I hope to teach her that finding her own path is a journey and the key to her own happiness and success will be: ***"Find something she loves to do, and then find a way to make money doing it."***

About Jennifer

Jennifer Burg is TheSuburbanMom. After the birth of her daughter in 2008, Jennifer found herself in a place that was familiar to moms around the country, but new to her – she had become a stay-at-home mom. While she loved her time with her daughter and found friendship in other local moms, Jennifer's type-A personality needed an outlet. Since her new world revolved around her daughter, she sought an outlet that would include her daughter and her "new" life as a mom. In one short weekend, TheSuburbanMom was born.

*"So, who is TheSuburbanMom? I'm a SAHM, I'm a WAHM, I'm a WOHM. I'm frugal, I'm green, I'm a toy-picking-up machine. I'm a woman, I'm a wife, I'm a Modern Momma. If you are all of those things and more, YOU are a SuburbanMom"**

With the technical help of her husband, Jennifer created a blog about the life of one mom in suburbia. Knowing that moms everywhere were looking for the same things she was: product reviews, ways to save money, practical ways to be green, free stuff, first-hand DYI accounts and more deals - TheSuburbanMom chronicles all of the things this suburban mom does for her family and more.

In her previous life – pre-kids (PK) – Jennifer was a magazine editor, a human resources director, a consultant and a writer. Today, she uses the skills she learned in those positions to serve her clients as a freelance writer and editor and as TheSuburbanMom. A graduate of the University of Florida's College of Journalism, GO GATORS, Jennifer considers it a privilege and a challenge to balance working from home with caring for a busy toddler. Jennifer lives in the suburbs of Orlando, Florida with her husband, Bobby; their daughter, Kendal; and their yorkies, Bear and Bella.

* SAHM = Stay-at-home mom, WAHM = Work-at-home mom, WOHM = Work-out-of-home mom

Power Principle #14

SUCCESS IS A VERB !

by Donna Galante, D.M.D.

Serving our patients, family, friends and community, with passion and purpose is truly a power principle for success.

When it comes to defining success, the number one power principle for me is the verb - *to serve.* (Yes, we know that technically success is <u>not</u> a verb, but bear with me.)

As practicing Orthodontists, both my husband and myself believe that it is our primary duty to serve our patients, their families, our staff and our community.

Let me give you three examples of serving others that can set you, your business and your life on fire:-.

(A). MAKE EXTRAORDINARY CUSTOMER SERVICE YOUR NUMBER ONE GOAL

... *'Service with a smile!'* and ... *'The customer is always right!'*

Sounds trite, a bit corny and cliché. However, how often do you find service with a smile in your day-to-day interactions with people and businesses?

Customer service is a hot topic today in the business world. We all have our horror stories about poor service that range from absolutely abysmal to just plain unmemorable. Think about the last 4 or 5 customer service interactions you have had recently. What was your experience?

I bet the vast majority of your experiences were basically unremarkable or maybe even downright horrible. Can you think of a recent customer experience that was remarkable? Have you had an experience that you could not stop talking about at dinner with your friends and family?

When you think about this experience how does it make you feel? Do you feel that you were treated in a special way? Do you feel valued? Did the experience make you feel good about your purchase? Did the experience remove some doubt or stress? Did the experience make an impact on your future purchasing decisions?

I know that all of us have had that kind of experience in a business setting. It could be a restaurant, a retail store or even a dental office that gives you extraordinary service.

For example, in our Orthodontic offices, besides providing our patients with a beautiful smile to last a lifetime, we are committed to giving our patients and parents service with a smile.

For us, this means that our staff is expected to treat every patient and parent as if they were the only patient in the office that day. This means seeing patients on time, inviting the parents back into the treatment area to sit and watch what we are doing, spending time with the patient and parent to make sure all their questions are answered, and following up with a personal phone call from the staff (or even one of the doctors), to make sure their appointment went well and that all their questions have been answered.

We make it a point to connect with our family of patients and parents on a weekly basis via email, and make sure we sign off on all printed communication with the words ... 'In Your Service'.

None of this requires a huge investment in a marketing budget. So that is the good news for you and your business. However, there is an investment in you and your staff's time - in providing an atmosphere of true caring, gratitude and service to your clients, customers and/or patients. In other words, you need to fall in love with your customers, clients and patients, and treat them like members of your family.

For your business or practice, can you think of ways to add the personal touch with a phone call, a personal note or email? How is your follow up? Do your customers, clients or patients feel welcome, special and important when they are in your business or practice? Are you providing a service or product that would meet or exceed your expectations to your own immediate family?

This leads me to the next part of the service model. You must make sure you are hiring people with a passion for serving.

(B). HIRE FOR PASSION, PURPOSE AND SERVICE

In our practice, it is imperative that our employees enjoy and have a true passion for people, especially families and children.

In our practice, about 70% of the patients are children and teenagers. The younger children are often apprehensive and scared about getting braces or retainers. Our staff has not only the training and experience to help these patients relax and actually have fun, they are absolutely passionate about it.

For example, if you have ever had to get an impression or mold of your teeth for a retainer or night guard, you may remember some putty placed in your mouth that tasted horrible and possibly made you gag. (I apologize for bringing back those memories, but bear with me here.)

Our younger patients who have never had this experience, but have been told how awful it is by a friend, sibling or parent, are quite apprehensive about the entire process. Sometimes they get themselves worked up so much that they are literally shaking in the dental chair.

To provide a more pleasant experience and one that will not be permanently imprinted in their brain as 'an awful experience', we offer a choice of flavors for the putty that will be placed in their mouth. Furthermore, we use a fast setting material that generally takes 30-60 seconds to set once in their mouth.

Usually just having the flavored putty and a quick setting material is enough to keep them from gagging. Some patients, however, have very strong gag reflexes and a good flavor just does not prevent it!

In those cases we have them hum 'Happy Birthday' to us while the assistant is taking the mold. Sometimes we make them work even harder by having to lift a leg and an arm in the air at the same time and hold it up until the putty is set.

Of course we are all enjoying the rendition of Happy Birthday with a mouthful of putty, and the arm-and-leg technique is a further distraction for the patient. The result is a near perfect mold of the teeth, and an empowered child who realizes that the thing they feared so much wasn't so bad after all.

We take these extra steps as part of our dedication to serve our patients. We want them to go back home or to school and brag how they had a mold and did not gag at all! Meanwhile, the parent is satisfied at our efforts to help their child relax and have a great experience in our office.

Again, there is no advertising cost associated with this process. In fact our staff is proud of the fact that they can get a successful mold of patient's teeth especially when a parent has warned us in advance of their child's terrible gag reflex. The parent is happy and grateful that we took the time and extra effort to make sure their child had a fantastic experience and did not gag!

In your business or practice, does your staff have a passion for service? Do your employees truly care about the customers, clients or patients that they come into contact with each day? Employees with a true heart for service are a key ingredient to success for your business.

Take the time necessary to hire the right people for your business or practice from the start. Remember the title of this chapter, *Success is a Verb*? You can no longer just hire an employee because they have a pulse and present themselves well. You need to have clearly defined personality attributes that you are looking for, in regards to the position you need to fill.

I have found that when I can match a person's passion with the job they are applying for, they will always have the right attitude, be on task, and have passion for the job. The specifics of the job 'at hand' can be taught through training. A sense of purpose, passion and service for a job, is difficult to teach someone in the hopes that they will eventually 'get it'.

(C). SERVE YOUR COMMUNITY, FAMILY AND FRIENDS

The third and final example of service as a power principle for success has to do with service to your community, family and friends. Your business and your practice may be centered on service to your customers, clients and patients, but what about service in your personal life?

Are you serving the ones closest to you? Your relationships with your spouse, children, parents, grandparents, siblings and friends are all part of your overall success. Can you think of ways to serve them better?

As a wife, mother, daughter, sibling, aunt, friend and business owner, there are days when I want to be served and not serve a single soul. Can you relate? However, it is in those moments that we get our renewed source of energy and passion by serving another. Have you ever had that feeling of joy after doing something for someone else - even though you were worn out and spent yourself?

The greatest levels of contentment and self-satisfaction can be experienced when you find a way to serve others. Ralph Waldo Emerson is quoted as saying: *It is one of the beautiful compensations of this life that no man can sincerely try to help another without helping himself.*

Are there causes or organizations that you are passionate about? Many charities have boards that are in need of business people with skills such as marketing, accounting, fund-raising or management. You could also look at opportunities in your church, temple, synagogue or other place of worship to serve.

Even your business can serve a charity or an organization you are passionate about. For example, a company called Toms Shoes donates a pair of shoes to a child in need of shoes for every pair that is purchased. You actually go online and decide what color shoes and what country the shoes are shipped to.

Your family and friends are another area of service. By staying true to your word, giving of your time and energy, and being fully present with your loved ones, you demonstrate your love, gratitude and service to them.

Albert Einstein said: *Only a life lived for others is a life worthwhile.*

People need to feel appreciated, respected and valued. Your customers, clients and patients should feel this way when they interact with you and your business or practice.

How about your family or friends? Are you making them feel appreciated, respected and most importantly loved? Are you showing how much you care and love them?

I can honestly say that this has been an area of service that I had forgotten. Like many business and practice owners, you are pulled in so many directions on a daily basis. Your employees, your clients, customers or patients can often take up the majority of your energy and time. You come home at the end of the day exhausted …and with little left over for your family.

In this third example of service, you will need to learn how to work 'on your business' and not 'in your business'. Michael Gerber, author of The E-Myth writes about how most entrepreneurs and business owners work in their business.

Working 'in your business' means that you are just managing to the accomplish the bare minimum tasks that get your rent paid, your payroll covered, and keep your business in operation another day.

Working 'on your business' means you are being astute enough that your activities will not only maintain, but also actually grow your business. Generating a strategic plan for your business requires concentrated thinking, and deserves more of your time, attention and even respect, than any other activity.

As a business owner and professional, it can be a difficult to give up that power to an employee. However, if you have a plan in place that you systematize and consistently analyze, you can safely delegate to employees and get the desired results.

Once you have the power to delegate, and a great team in place, you will be able to free up your valuable time to serve – serve your community, spend more time with your family, and fulfill your deepest passions and purpose in life.

You probably weren't expecting to hear about serving others in a book about power principles for success. However, if you genuinely seek to make the lives of your customers, clients, patients, employees and family better through serving them with great customer service, life changing products and acknowledgment, respect and appreciation, *success will overflow into all areas of your life.*

Success is a verb??? ? The verb is really… *to serve.* By serving our customers, clients, patients, employees, family, friends and community, we will truly live an abundant life full of love, wealth, health and success.

Service is what life is all about *~ Marian Wright Edelman*

About Donna

Dr. Donna Galante is a Board Certified Orthodontist in practice for over 24 years and currently has 3 locations in the Sacramento area. She practices with her husband, Dr. Paul Cater. They know that they change lives by changing peoples smiles. Their practice is one of the top Orthodontic practices nationwide, and they are dedicated to continuing education and providing amazing service to their patients. They are unabashedly excited about the newest technologies for creating gorgeous smiles that are available today. One of those new technologies is Invisalign, which are clear removable aligners that move teeth effortlessly. Drs. Galante and Cater are Premier Providers of Invisalign, which puts them into the top 5% of all practices nationwide for expertise and experience with Invisalign. You can learn more at www.luvmysmile.com

Dr. Donna Galante is also the CEO of her own coaching, consulting and seminar business, which primarily focuses on women dentists. As a dentist, business owner, employer, wife, mother of two 2 children, sister, daughter, and friend, she understands that women have multiple hats they wear. Having been in practice for over 24 years, she has gained a wealth of experience and knowledge on how to balance all the various aspects and roles women have. She has a passion for sharing this knowledge with women dentists, and teaches and encourages them that they can have it all - without having to sacrifice their practice, their family or their health.

To learn more go to: www.drdonnagalante.com

Power Principle #15

THE POWER OF PERSEVERANCE

by Ken Hardison, Esq.

S uccess in life doesn't come easily. There are many obstacles and failures along the way to reaching your goals. There are all sorts of factors which contribute to success, but there is one that is often more important than all the others….Perseverance. The dictionary meaning of Perseverance is: persisting in or remaining constant to a purpose, idea or task in spite of obstacles.

The world is full of stories of those that have "succeeded" only after years of trial and effort. Thomas Alva Edison, one of the great inventors of the 20th century is famous for his invention of the electric light bulb, among other things.

Edison had close to 10,000 failures before he succeed in finding the secret to make the electric light bulb a reality. Edison was quick to point out that the thing that made him famous occurred after years of not being successful. Note…he never used the word "failure". I have always viewed unsuccessful attempts at projects as learning experiences, not as failures. Of course, some of my lessons were expensive, but they helped me reach my final goal and become successful.

Very few "successful" entrepreneurs, sales people, business owners, and professionals can say they achieved success without trial and error....many errors. In fact, many will admit (if they are truthful) that their success came to them after a long period of time, where they did some pretty foolish things which costs them a lot of time and money.

I have always preached to my associate lawyers that the only way to become a better trial lawyer is to go and try cases. You learn from your mistakes (learning experiences). Below is what I believe are the six Traits and Characteristics of Perseverance.

1. PASSION

Passion is the most important characteristic of perseverance. What I mean by passion is that you have to have that burning desire and really love what you're doing. It has to be fun. It has to be intriguing. When you get up in the morning, you must be excited about getting to work. I've often told my children that if they find something they have a passion and love for, I could easily find a way for them to make money from their passion.

I've also preached to my associate lawyers and staff over the years that if they get up in the morning and dread coming to work, they need to come see me. They're not doing themselves nor our firm a favor. What I do is help them find a job they do have passion for, so they look forward to coming to work.

I have been accused of being a workaholic over the years. But, I have always really enjoyed what I was doing. It never occurred to me that I was working. I was having fun and obtaining a goal that I had a burning desire for.

2. POSITIVE ATTITUDE

Some people see the glass as half empty, and some people see the glass as half full. To have perseverance, you must really be able to see the glass half full. When faced with obstacles, you have to look at the positive. What positive things can you take from this experience? You cannot be doubtful. If you doubt it, then how can you get others not to doubt it?

Don't let other people discourage you or tell you that it can't work. I see successful entrepreneurs and people that are go-getters, ignore the ones that say you can't do it because of this or that. The negative individuals make all these lame excuses of why it can't work instead of seeing how it can work. One key to keeping a positive attitude is to surround yourself with positive people. I have always dreaded, and tried to avoid, negative people and negativity in general. It's a downer. It brings me down. Negative people bring down everyone around them.

As my mother once told me, *"you are who you hang around with."* One of the keys to having perseverance and being successful is to hang around like-minded people. And when I say like-minded, I mean they don't see the glass as half empty. They see the glass as half full. They don't see what can go wrong but what can go right with a project or a goal.

Mark Twain said it most eloquently when he said *"Keep away from people who try to belittle your ambitions. Small people always do that, but the really great make you feel that you, too, can become great."*

3. DISCIPLINE

Another important element of perseverance is discipline. You must discipline yourself to follow through and finish things. You must set goals and understand the necessary steps to meeting those goals. Setting benchmarks is on my favorite things to do.

If I have a goal that is going to take three months to reach, I break it down by weeks and set mini goals. If it's a project or goal that's going to take a year, I break it down by months. I break the months down by weeks, and weeks down by days. This system disciplines you to get things done. It allows you to tackle a big project, one step at a time.

As my father once told me, *"the best way to eat an elephant is one bite at a time"*. Also, no excuses. I've never seen a successful person make an excuse of why they couldn't get something done.

Successful people understand why something didn't get done, and they fix it for the future. Another key element to discipline is organization. I constantly use lists. At the end of everyday, I sit down and write out a list of everything I want to get done the next day. I rank them by A's, B's and C's. "A's" are things that <u>must </u>be done the next day, "B's" are thing that <u>need</u> to be done and "C's" are things that I would <u>like</u> to get done but can wait.

If you do this each day, your "C's" become "B's" and your "B's" become "A's". If I have something that is really urgent, and it's the first thing I want to get done, it is marked "AA's". <u>Always do the hardest thing first</u>. Tackle your biggest and hardest tasks while you're fresh and can get them out of the way. Discipline is a key not only for following through, but by the way you arrange your work each day.

4. KNOW YOUR STRENGTHS AND WEAKNESSES

We all have unique abilities. That means we all have strengths, and we all have weaknesses. One of the keys to success and having perseverance is not wasting your time trying to deal with things you don't have strengths in. Spend more time building your strengths, not your weaknesses.

For example, I'm a great "idea guy", but I'm not that good at actually implementing my ideas. I'm not a nuts and bolts guy. I see the big picture. I can see what the obstacles are going to be, but as far as getting down and doing the step-by-step process that is needed….that's not my strength.

So how do you deal with this? Once you realize what your strengths are, hire people and surround yourself with people whose strengths are your weaknesses. Some people have problems with this because they don't want anybody around them that is smarter than they are in certain areas. This is a 'surefire' way <u>not</u> to be successful. You must be secure in your own talents and abilities. Check your ego at the door.

You say, how can I know what my strengths are? There is a book called Strength Finders, which costs about $50, that has an online test that will tell you what your Top 5 strengths are. It also gives you a guide on how to increase and build on those strengths and how to use them to leverage your abilities to your utmost success.

Surround yourself with people that compliment your weaknesses. Don't micromanage; you have to have people you can trust and know that they can get the job done. You do not want to stifle these people because it will definitely slow the process down and make reaching your goals take twice as long to accomplish, if you ever do accomplish them.

5. TAKE ACTION

"The critical ingredient is getting off your butt and doing something. A

lot of people have ideas, but there are few who decide to do something about them now. Not next week. But today. The true entrepreneur is a doer, not a dreamer. " - Robert Browning

Fear is the main obstacle to people taking action. They are scared of failure. They're scared of the unknown and some people (believe it or not) are actually scared of success. They subconsciously feel they are not worthy of success and happiness. No action gets you no change. A little action gets you a little change. But a massive amount of action brings change and usually success. A good friend of mine, John Morgan, told me that 'the best time to plant a tree is twenty years ago, the second best time to plant a tree is today'! That advice has always stuck with me because it is so true in anything you are trying to do or accomplish in life.

I wrote this chapter in less than 4 hours after only being given one day's notice. I don't like to write, and I'm not really good at it, I could have made excuses and put it off, but I sat down the next day and just did it!

6. NEVER GIVE UP

Do you know who Michael Jordan is? Jordan is the greatest basketball player to have ever played the game. Did you know that Jordan's high school coach cut him from the basketball team? Aren't we glad Jordan didn't give up? We would have missed some of the most exciting moments and games in basketball history.

When you have an ultimate goal, you owe it to yourself to completely follow through and never give up. I remember when I just started my own law firm in 1996. There were several times where I went months without pay. All my friends and family thought I was crazy and was going to go bankrupt…but I never gave up. Eventually, the money came in. All by just not giving up and charging forward in the face of adversity.

George Allen, a great former NFL coach of the Washington Redskins and Los Angeles Rams, said it best, *"People of mediocre ability sometimes achieve outstanding success because they don't know when to quit. Most men succeed because they are determined to."*

<u>Conclusion</u>

There are many factors which have contributed to my success. I consider my perseverance as a major factor in my success. I hope this chapter has given you something to pull from. <u>When things seem impossible and adversity is staring down your throat, always persevere!</u>

About Ken

Ken Hardison is known as The Go-To Law Firm Marketing and Management Expert. Ken practiced injury law for over 27 years. He built a leading law firm in NC from ground up - Hardison & Associates. Through Ken's vision, the firm grew from a small 2 lawyer, 3 staff person firm to a 13 lawyer 42 staff person powerhouse. In a period of 6 years, the firm grew 30-50% EACH YEAR through Ken's ability to market and manage his law firm.

Over the years, Ken has shared his expertise on building and running a successful law firm with countless other lawyers. He has authored books (How to Market Your Personal Injury Law Practice in the 21st Century and Build Your Law Practice with a Book), lectured and presented on law firm marketing matters, coached and consulted other law firms nationwide, and written countless articles.

Ken is an in-demand speaker, teacher, and consultant on marketing and business development techniques for lawyers. His knowledge spans over anything that has to do with growing your law firm - how to generate larger caseloads, how to increase the response and return on your marketing, how to hire the best employees for the job, and how to network to build referrals.

Ken is the founder and president of PILMMA (Personal Injury Lawyers Marketing and Management Association). PILMMA is the only legal marketing and management association exclusively for injury and disability lawyers. For more information, visit www.PILMMA.org.

Power Principle #16

THE PRINCIPLE OF KAIZEN – GROWTH

by Michael McDevitt

"Success is not where you start, but where you finish"

What is success?

I think we can agree that the actual definition varies widely from person to person.

J. Shoop, a business consultant, sums up success as *"the progressive realization of a worthy ideal."* David Carter, the owner of Scramjet Strategies, a business consulting and professional coaching company, thinks that the most important rule for business and life success is *"... always be moving forward. Never stop investing. Never stop improving. Never stop doing something new. The moment you stop improving your organization, it starts to die. Make it your goal to be better each and every day, in some small way."*

Fred Gratzon, an author/entrepreneur, takes a bit of a different view – he says that avoiding work is the secret to his success. Of course, could we expect less from the author of "The Lazy Way to Success?" More seriously, he adds that success is a combination of health, happiness, material prosperity, love of family and friends, wisdom, influence and fulfillment.

Then there's the opinion of Bob Dylan, the legendary singer-songwriter: *"A man is a success if he gets up in the morning and goes to bed at night and in between does what he wants to do."*

It's fairly obvious that success means a lot of different things to a lot of people, so let's check with the final authority on definitions – the dictionary.

According to the Webster's Dictionary from 1828, success was defined as *the favorable or prosperous termination of anything attempted; a termination which answers the purpose intended.* And according to the 2010 Dictionary.com, it also has another meaning – *obsolete* (…in that, once you've achieved success, you're done).

A overwhelming majority of people would probably agree that, in some way, that's true – success means to them that you've made it, the struggle is over and that you've attained some sort of important overall achievement in your life – either personally, financially or socially, depending on what's important to you.

I would argue, however, that true success is an ongoing process. It's the old Satchel Paige dictum, "Don't look back – something might be gaining on you." If you stop working on yourself, your work and your life, you invariably slide backwards.

In this chapter, I'd like to discuss two overall approaches to success that see it as a journey and not a goal. They've been incredibly useful "Power Principles of Success" to me and I hope they will be to you as well.

THE KAIZEN CONCEPT

"Kaizen" is a principle that the Japanese applied to business management that allowed them to create their post-World War II "economic miracle" – and powered companies like Sony and Toyota to incredible global success.

Masaaki Imai introduced the term in his book, "Kaizen: The Key to Japan's Competitive Success" in the mid-1980s. The word 'kai' means an idea of change or the action to correct, while the word 'zen' means good. In other words, Kaizen is an idea of 'continuous improvement' that occurs from a series of small changes, then on to larger ones, and finally into a transformation. Kaizen requires self-motivation, individual dedication and an ongoing commitment to improvement.

And the ironic thing is that this Japanese discipline that Americans like myself study and emulate actually *originated from American thought*. Statistical control method experts from the USA went into Japan after World War II to help them get back on their feet economically. The Japanese simply took the ball and ran with it – taking it a lot further than America ever did.

Entrepreneurs who effectively implement Kaizen will create, over time, positive changes in the quality, the cost and the delivery of the product, as well as growth in the business and greater customer satisfaction.

For example, in order to analyze and understand areas that need improvement in an organization, an individual or a small team can be trained to apply the Kaizen way of solving problems by taking responsibility for getting rid of the negative aspects and improving the workplace. These steps could include helping employees identify their own skill sets, encouraging them to excel in their respective fields and processes, and creating a healthy environment.

The individual or the team can then work together on the improvement areas, coming up with suggestions and implementing them simultaneously. Once the implementation is done, it is essential to convey the changes clearly and concisely.

Although Kaizen is a business philosophy, it is not only limited to business. It can also be applied to your personal life, to help you become more organized or more positive, or at your workplace, to help create a satisfactory and friendly environment for employees to lead a better and healthier lifestyle.

The application of Kaizen is generally viewed in the form of a cycle:

- Standardization of an operation

- Evaluation of the standardized operation

- Assessment of measurements against requirements

- Innovation to meet requirements and increase productivity

- Standardization of the new, improved operations

- Continuation of the cycle ad infinitum

The cycle is otherwise known as the Shewhart cycle, Deming cycle, or PDCA – Plan, Do, Check, Act / Problem finding, Display, Clear, Acknowledge. And again, this was the process originally taught to the Japanese in the late 1940's – by us!

I look at the Kaizen concept as a compounding effect. Just try and better yourself 1% per day and watch how much you improve over the course of 5 years.

THE "BE, DO, HAVE" PRINCIPLE

A good "partner" to Kaizen in working to improve your everyday life is the "Be, Do, Have" principle.

Most of us are in a "Have, Do, Be" frame of mind. We think we need to "Have" certain superficial things that will enable us to be happy, so we "Do" things in order to gain them and then we think we'll "Be" what we want to be. In other words, we think what we get will make us the person we want to be.

In reality, it's the exact opposite. We need to find ways to "Be" happy and productive and come from a place of contentment, rather than dissatisfaction. What we "Do" from this higher state will enable us to "Have" what we want.

But it all sprouts from who you choose to "Be." Making ourselves who we should "Be" inspires us to "Do" what's required to "Have" what we want.

Take a look at your own life and analyze whether you have the following:

- Focus

- Decision-making Abilities

- Financial Security

- Satisfaction

- Happiness

- Leadership

- Clarity

The above-mentioned are some of the important factors that influence a successful life – and not just in business. A mutual balance of these factors can help one lead a happy and healthy lifestyle. Zig Ziglar, a popular motivational speaker, believes that being successful means having a balance of success stories across the many areas of one's life.

"You cannot truly be considered successful in your business life if your home life is in shambles", he says. "There is no amount of business success, or any other type of success, that can compensate for the failure of what is truly important - our relationships with family."

Ziglar, who believes in the 'Be, Do, Have' theory, has an exercise putting it into action:

- Draw two vertical lines on a sheet of paper to make three columns and write the words BE, DO and HAVE on the left-hand, middle and right-hand columns respectively.

- List all the things you really want, or dream to have in life, in the right-hand column. It could be higher education, maintaining your important relationships with your family and friends, traveling around the world, owning a business, buying that latest Ferrari, losing weight, etc.

- Identify the things you have to do in order to achieve the list of things mentioned in the right-hand column and jot them down in the middle column. For example, let's say you want a successful marriage. To do so, you must be willing to show intimacy by sharing your innermost thoughts and concerns with your partner. A lot more goes into the relationship of marriage than your share of the workload - like supporting your partner in achieving his/her own goals, or being there for your partner in good and bad times.

- Go to the left-hand column and identify what you have to BE, in order to DO, so that you can HAVE. To have a successful marriage, some of the things that you must be are faithful, attentive, loving, caring, helpful, empathetic, encouraging, persistent, committed, kind, thoughtful, considerate, and responsible. All these characteristics may not exist in every individual, but can be developed over a period of time with experience (the Kaizen concept can help you here as well).

The point of "Be, Do, Have" is basically to look inward before you look outward. Manifest what's necessary in your own self to make possible what you want out of life – and it will come to you.

SUCCESSFUL ENTREPRENEURIAL PRINCIPLES

Let's apply the "Be, Do, Have" theory to becoming a successful entrepreneur – what must you cultivate in yourself to achieve that particular goal? Here are some traits that I feel play an important role in one's own success:

1. Judgment

Studies show that good judgment is critical to running a business. A combination of knowledge and expertise is important to make the right calls when problems and challenges present themselves.

2. Specialization

Specialization in a particular field helps you leverage that knowledge to running a successful business in that niche. You gain that necessary understanding ideally by a combination of education and prior experience in the respective field.

3. Self-confidence

The difficulties of running your own business can often lead to frustration, despair and dejection, which can dominate your outlook if you don't possess the necessary self-confidence. A successful entrepreneur is one who can roll with the punches and isn't afraid to explore new prospects or to take risks.

4. Perseverance

Entrepreneurs, in many cases, have to focus more on their professional lives rather than their personal lives. A lot of dedication, commitment and hard work are involved in creating a successful business. This requires an ability to persevere, to keep the big goals in sight while tackling current obstacles, and utilize a blend of self-discipline and self-control in order to see things through to completion.

5. Creativity

Industries and niches change all the time, due to new technologies, economic realities and population shifts. Entrepreneurs need to be creative and open to new ideas in order to adapt to these changes, and find innovative ways to grow their business. A new product, a new marketing method or a new venture – these are all essential aspects of the kind of entrepreneurial creativity that's required to take a business to the next level.

6. Leadership

It almost goes without saying that leadership is necessary for an entrepreneur to succeed. By inspiring and motivating your team and your business associates, you earn the kind of backing that enables you to reach the top.

7. Self-reliance

Successful entrepreneurs depend on themselves more than anyone else and hold themselves responsible for their own actions. They are proactive, set goals, and go that extra mile to achieve their goals with the combined effort of their resources and abilities.

Cultivating these aspects of your personality enables you to create the optimum conditions for business success. Using the Kaizen system to improve yourself in these ways on a day-by-day basis enables you to make the change possible. And both systems can be equally applied to achieve whatever you want out of life.

Your life improvement begins with you. Grow the necessary attributes in yourself and you will grow the life you want to have. **The surprising result you may find is that, as you change, your goals will too – as they will reflect your own transformation, allowing you to achieve a more lasting and substantial success.**

About Michael:

Michael McDevitt began his career in the Real Estate Finance Industry at the age of seventeen. He worked late nights at Countrywide where he found his passion for helping people and real estate finance. He continued as a top employee at Countrywide throughout college until the age of twenty-one. During his career at Countrywide, Mr. McDevitt was promoted many times in just four years and became one of the youngest executives Countrywide has seen. He felt compelled to expand his quest for knowledge in this industry and decided to leave; however, he took his time at Countrywide as an invaluable experience as it set a solid foundation in his career. This foundation was made up of skills that he cultivated in every facet of the industry from Portfolio Retention to Correspondent Lending.

Mr. McDevitt then went on to become an Account Executive for a Direct Mortgage Lender and quickly became a top producer in the highly competitive field within 6 months. Again, feeling trapped in the wholesale industry, he moved to Beverly Hills, CA and decided to pursue a more challenging and lucrative position within the trade. Having experience in Correspondent Lending and now Wholesale Mortgage Banking, Mr. McDevitt then began his career in the Retail Aspect of Mortgage Banking as a Sr. Loan Officer and was personally trained by the #2 Originator in the entire Country. He found this experience invaluable and reaped the benefits of hard work in the rewarding real estate finance business. Mr. McDevitt funded over $100 million dollars in loans and generated over $20 million dollars in real estate per year.

In 2005, at the age of twenty-three, Mr. McDevitt co-founded A&M Capital Funding Inc. and for two years managed a boutique multi-million dollar brokerage comprised solely of top producers within the real estate field – while the youngest professional in the firm. Since then, he owned other successful businesses and has thrived as a young entrepreneur. Mr. McDevitt's main focus is now Fidelity Financial Group, a division of McDevitt & Associates, a full service Real Estate Firm that specializes in residential, commercial, and hard money loans.

Michael McDevitt has also accomplished raising millions for many diverse real estate developments, and has quietly cemented his reputation as one of the major players in the industry. Michael is currently retained by several law groups to be their premier commercial loan modification expert. Residential or commercial, no matter how complicated the terms, Mr. McDevitt has the experience to find the best possible deal. Unlike many in the field, he hasn't always been one to 'toot' his own horn, relying instead on strong word-of-mouth from satisfied clients.

For more information about Michael McDevitt please visit: www.Michael-McDevitt.com or www.USFidelityGroup.com or www.twitter.com/MichaelMcDevitt or www.ScovisLawGroup.com

Michael is a best-selling author who is regularly sought out by the media to give expert opinions. He has been featured on NBC, CBS, ABC, and FOX affiliates as well as seen in USA Today, Newsweek, and the Wall Street Journal.

Michael holds a private pilots license flying Cessna aircraft. He is a scuba enthusiast holding advanced levels of certification in deep diving, night diving and search & rescue diver. Michael enjoys racing fast cars, bikes, planes and boats and is an avid student and fan of mixed-martial arts.

Michael graduated from Marine Military Academy in 2000. He attended American Intercontinental University for his Bachelors in Business Administration with an emphasis in Operations Management and is currently pursuing his MBA with an emphasis in Finance.

Power Principle #17

BECOME A BUSINESS WARRIOR

by Brad Hess & Tyrell Gray

E very year thousands of books are sold teaching principles/techniques of success. Unfortunately, most of them overlook the simplest facts; regardless of how effective the techniques are, they will not change lives unless they can be implemented. The majority of people have a hard time visualizing what their true goals are - let alone putting them in writing. In an effort to help, let me start by saying that this next chapter is designed to teach you power principles that will teach you how to make more money. Not just a little bit of money, we are talking retirement kind of money, the type that allows you to do what you want when you want!

Over the years I have watched several businesses mature into billion dollar companies, and they have all used power principles to become "Business Warriors". They become "Business Warriors" by virtue of fighting, engaging, planning, defeating, and overwhelming the competition, industry, markets and clients. I have continued to adjust my business and implement these principles to generate the greatest success possible out of any given situation.

A perfect example of a business that has grown from a mere idea into a billion dollar industry is the Ultimate Fighting Championship

(UFC). The UFC has become part of the main-stream culture, not only in America but across the world. The UFC started as the idea of Art Davie, a producer from California who happened to employ Rorrion Gracie to help get him in shape.

The Gracie family had a long history of MMA (Mixed Martial Arts). MMA has existed for eons in other countries but has only become main-stream in the United States over the last decade and a half. MMA is the mixture of marital arts, striking and grappling. There are many different forms of MMA, but all of them revolve around the same fundamental principles of dominating an opponent with a combination of strikes, grappling and submissions.

When Art Davie was introduced to Rorrion Gracie he became intrigued by the idea of seeing who would be the winner out of all the fighting disciplines. Could a boxer win against a karate expert? Could a Ju-jitsu specialist subdue a wrestler? It really boiled down to the age old question of who is the toughest kid on the block?

Art Davie established a business plan, and with the funds from 28 different investors established WOW, a production company designed to promote the first ever MMA tournament. The first tournament was designed as a single elimination event, with no weight classes (the theory being that a skilled fighter could win regardless of size). The WOW business plans were designed to eventually turn the sport into a television show. Unfortunately, there was no main-stream media outlet that would pick up on the concept. Eventually WOW joined with SEG (a forerunner in the pay-per-view industry) to air the first MMA event. The night of that original production, SEG had 86,592 people purchase the event!

Remember that at this point Pay-Per-View was a relatively new idea, and MMA was completely new to main-stream media; so the massive response to the first event was very exciting. Although, there was an obvious interest in the idea, there were many hurdles that the sport would have to overcome.

One of the largest hurdles was the disapproval of many prominent politicians, including then Senator John McCain. The sport quickly became known as a blood sport or as Senator McCain remarked "Human Cock Fighting". With few rules and a fair amount of perceived violence;

MMA was destined to stay an underground sport.

SEG, the Pay-Per-View provider, realized that if there was any potential for keeping the sport alive, they would have to get it sanctioned by the State Athletic Commissions. Over the following years SEG made move after move, from state to state, trying to gain compliance with Athletic Commissions. In 2001, facing Bankruptcy, SEG sold the rights to the sport to Station Casinos executives Frank and Lorenzo Fertitta, and aerobics instructor Dana White for 2 million dollars.

Over the next decade the Fertitta brothers and Dana White began to transform MMA into a mainstream sporting event. There were several key steps taken to get the company to that point, including great advertising, corporate sponsorship, increased cable pay-per view, and defined rules and regulations bringing the sport into compliance with sports commission standards nationwide.

Nevertheless, after several years the Fertitta brothers were millions of dollars in the red. The next move proved to be the pivotal moment for the UFC and MMA. The UFC introduced a reality series called "The Ultimate Fighter" (TUF). The sport high-lighted a group of fighters that trained and fought exhibition bouts in an elimination style event for the chance to compete for a six figure UFC contract. The final two finishers of TUF would fight in an official UFC bout. The reality series was an overnight success with thousands of followers.

During the following years, the UFC went from an underground sport to a main-stream sporting event that seems to have changed the world of sports as we know it. There are currently more bets placed on UFC fights than any of the boxing title matches in the last six years.

 UFC also seems to be garnering a higher class of followers than anyone would have expected. UFC events are sold out months in advance, and locations are actively sought by hotels and cities, as the amount of revenue generated by the fights is staggering. In Las Vegas the average individual will spend around $800 dollars during their trip, while UFC attendees spend nearly double that.

It is easy to look at the current success of the UFC and say that it appears to have been a stroke of luck. However, closer inspection shows that there are several Power Principles that were used to create this billion dollar giant. These principles are the same principles and techniques I have used again and again for business success.

POWER PRINCIPAL NUMBER 1:

The first answer is always NO! Many times I have seen people with a great idea or new concept and they are so excited to get the project moving that they will agree to anything to try and get/keep the company alive. Regardless of how tempting the first offer is, you need to make sure that you always say NO, or some variation thereof, to it.

In one meeting an associate shared with me the following story. He and his partner were faced with the possible collapse of a business venture they had spent hundreds of thousands to get 'off the ground'. However, after months and months of work, they needed a cash injection to keep the project moving. The first investor they meet with was very interested and agreed to inject the company with the needed funds. However, he wanted a 51% equity ownership in the company. My friends business partner prudently said "thank-you for your interest but I feel that we will be able to generate the funding without the loss of so much equity. We appreciate your time and interest, and we will keep you posted on our progress." The investor was visually taken back and quickly left the building, within 72 hours he had called them back and offered an increase in funding and only required 20% in equity.

Remember the first answer is always NO! Take time to evaluate all of your options and think over the best solution. <u>Do not allow yourself to be pressured into accepting an offer, business proposal, business system, or idea at the first presentation.</u> Take some time, think about the offer, and counter with the idea you feel gets you closest to your goal. Not only will this principle allow you the option to evaluate every alternative, but it keeps you in control.

In all negotiations, UFC president Dana White seems to have mastered this principle. He always expresses the way he wants things to work, and inevitably, people seem to come around to his idea or a variation thereof.

POWER PRINCIPAL NUMBER 2:

Expand your customer base as much as possible. This may seem to be an obvious part of any business plan, but it will surprise you how many people purposefully limit their product to certain groups or demographics. The UFC managed to penetrate every level of society, from utilizing trendy clothing worn by teens to groups of senior citizens flying to Vegas to attend live events.

Why limit your business to one type, age, or demographic? Think of the largest companies in the world, the majority of the time they try to open themselves up to as many clients as possible. It really is simple mathematics, the more people you have access to and who thus have access to your product, the more you will sell. As JC Penny once said: "People buy what they see where they walk" or, in modern terms, people will only buy what they are exposed to. The UFC managed to get their product in front of main-stream media, and although it literally took decades to get to that point, it was obviously a fight well worth it.

It's during tough economic times that major businesses really start to grow. You can capture more market share at a lower cost during an economic down turn than you can during a strong economy. As others are pulling back and going into survival mode, you need to be expanding your customer base as much as possible. General Electric, Hewlett Packard, IBM, and Microsoft were all companies that originated during a severe economic downturn. During challenging times we get caught up in… 'Let's just survive!" or "Let's just hunker down until this passes!" modes. When you go into survival mode you tend to stay in that mind set. <u>Don't just survive - *thrive!*</u> It takes just as much energy to worry about what is not going to happen as it does to focus on what will happen… *Psychologists have found that focusing on solutions, rather than our problems, increases our capacity to reach our goals.*

<u>POWER PRINCIPAL NUMBER 3:</u>

Hire your competition. One of the largest obstacles that the UFC faced was the sanctioning by the State Athletic Commissions, and although SEG had managed to get some states to sanction the sport, it was not until the Ferttita brothers and Dana White took over that the sport got universal sanctioning. In March 2006, the UFC announced that it had hired Marc Ratner, former Executive Director of the Nevada Athletic Commission, as Vice President of Regulatory Affairs. Ratner, once an ally of Senator McCain's campaign against *no holds barred* fighting, became a catalyst for the emergence of sanctioned Mixed Martial Arts in the United States. Ratner continues to educate numerous athletic commissions to help raise the UFC's media profile, in an attempt to legalize Mixed Martial Arts - in jurisdictions inside and outside the United States that have yet to sanction the sport.

The old Chinese proverb, 'Keep your friends close and your enemies closer' has never been more applicable. There is always some way to get your enemies on your side, and nothing gets people more motivated to help you than money. If someone can make money from your success, you can guarantee that the odds of success are in your favor. Remember when in doubt, *get your competition working for you rather than against you.*

POWER PRINCIPAL NUMBER 4:

People buy personality! We have been told again and again that people buy people, but we have been shown time and again that <u>what people really buy is personality</u>. People do not merely buy products; they buy the personality of the people selling the product.

The UFC was able to master this concept, creating amazing personalities. Fighters as a general rule are classic type "A" personalities and they all have egos bigger than the oversized trucks they drive; and the UFC feeds off those egos. The Ultimate Fighter allowed fighters to display their personalities and show interaction. In addition, anytime you lock that many fighters up inside a house, you can guarantee there is going to be conflict. It was the ultimate recipe for success: drama, intrigue and excitement all wrapped up in pounds of 'freakishly lean, testosterone filled, muscle bound' warriors.

With great marketing, the UFC created intriguing story lines that no one wanted to miss. This was prominently displayed by the simple fact that the bigger the grudge match they could create, the higher the number of attendees on each pay per view event. With names like "The Ice Man", "Razor", "Spider", "The California Kid", "GSP", and "The Ax Murderer", it was a masterpiece in selling personalities.

And, not only do the personalities draw-in spectators by the thousands, with ring side seats selling for thousands of dollars and venues packed to the limits, but the UFC has mastered the technique of selling personalities - and people are buying!

POWER PRINCIPLE NUMBER 5:

Never back down. Too many times people are confronted with obstacles and they give up on ideas or systems even though there is proven interest. The UFC faced enormous obstacles, disapproval by major political figures, lack of sports sanctioning, and millions in cash injections. Several people and businesses walked away from the idea over time, and yet it was the tenacity of the Fertitta brothers and Dana White that eventually created a billion dollar company.

Many times I have been faced with what appears to be insurmountable odds, but I have come to realize that the most important Power Principal is never to back down. There is always a solution no matter what the problem or obstacle. Sometimes the solution may not be immediately obvious, but if you take the time, consult with others, and devote some time to the situation, you will always come up with the best possible solution.

In addition, don't hesitate to get the perspective from somebody who may have a completely different viewpoint on the situation. Some of the greatest solutions we have found in our business often come from an employee, because they are looking at the problem from an entirely different angle.

In summary, these Power Principles can help you and your business get to the next level; whatever that next level happens to be for you. Understand that you are in the most competitive environment we have ever experienced, and you must stand out from the crowd to get noticed. With Facebook, Twitter, Linkedin, blog sites and all the other social media outlets, it is more important than ever to utilize these Power Principles and <u>set yourself apart as a Business Warrior</u>!

About Brad:

Brad Hess Co-Founder of My Mark, LLC

Business owner, entrepreneur, philanthropist, #1 best selling author, father and husband; Brad started his first company at the age of 21, which included designing a new product, acquiring investment capital necessary to finance the company's operations, contracting with the overseas manufactures, and heading up the US sales force. Shortly after this, he started his next company, which eventually created enough capital to get him into the real estate business. He spent the next few years working with investors from all over the country. These investors would come to small workshops where Brad and his Partners would teach specifics on how they were investing in real estate. Brad has always been interested in real estate and real estate financing. In 2005 he started his own commercial lending company, Hess Commercial Capital, Inc., which grew very quickly and was able to close over $10,000,000 in loans in its first year of operation.

After running several multi-million dollar real estate businesses and buying and selling over $200,000,000 worth of real estate, in 2009 Brad stepped down as CEO, and away from the day-to-day real estate activities; he still maintains his primary ownership position as well as a spot on the board of directors.

Brad is now involved with the development and growth of the exciting personal development and branding company, called My Mark, LLC. Reference: www.MyMark.com. Having created a considerable online brand and professional presence, Brad realized every individual needs their own Mark™. Brad understands the importance of creating, maintaining and defending your reputation, and is dedicated to helping every individual establish their own Mark™.

For more information on Brad Hess and My Mark, please visit www.MyMark.com

About Tyrell

Tyrell Gray Co-Founder of My Mark, LLC

Tyrell Gray graduated from Utah State University with a dual Bachelors Degrees in Economics and Business Finance. Once he graduated, he managed his first business, a flooring business that he and his partner took from a startup company to a thriving company bringing in over $550,000 in sales annually.

Tyrell then moved in to the financial arena, working for a branch of HSBC, the third largest bank in the world. As one of their account executives, he quickly rose through the ranks and recognized his aptitude for real estate finance. He was recruited from

HSBC to manage a local mortgage company closing over $3,000,000 dollars in real estate in their first year. Tyrell was again recruited to appear as a guest speaker and expert, explaining the intricacies of real estate and the mortgage industry.

Tyrell moved into the real estate arena full time in 2003 - building custom homes and developing properties in the real estate boom experienced across the United States. During that time Tyrell helped developed a business system where he and his business partner were able to purchase over $130 million dollars in REO properties in less than 11 months. They continue to use this business model to help investors and local residents stabilize the foreclosure market and provide solid returns for investors.

Tyrell has been recognized as one of the foremost leaders in the real estate industry. He has been a guest speaker on multiple radio stations, and featured on ABC, CBS, NBC, and Fox. He has also been published in USA Today, the Wall Street Journal and Newsweek. Tyrell was also one of the authors in the best selling Book "Shift Happens", that was published in the fall of 2009, helping business owners adjust to the major shifts to the economy.

For more information on Brad Hess and My E Mark, please visit www.MyMark.com

Power Principle #18

PREPARE FOR INSURANCE DISASTER

by James Murphy, Esq.

THE IMPORTANCE OF
UNINSURED MOTORIST COVERAGE

The importance of uninsured motorist coverage never really hit me until a few years ago when I got a call from my friend Brian's wife. She was in tears when she said, "Jim, Brian has been in a terrible car accident and the doctor's don't know if he is going to make it." I immediately stopped what I was doing and went directly to the emergency room to meet her. When I got there Brian was unconscious, and the police officer was just leaving after explaining to Michelle what had happened.

The officer explained that Brian was on a local highway when he got hit from behind, by a car that forced Brian's car out of control. The guy who hit him left the scene.

I tried to reassure Michelle that everything was going to be alright. After praying for my friend, my legal training forced me to think about the legal ramifications facing Brian and his family. I was thinking to myself that he had kids the same age as mine and they went to school together. I began to think about what my wife would do if that were me laying in the hospital bed.

Fortunately, after a few days Brian regained consciousness, and slowly began to recover. However, he was going to need extensive rehabilitation for serious injuries to his leg and arm. When the medical bills started to pour in, Michelle made an appointment to see me.

When she arrived at my office I tried to begin the conversation on a positive note, "Well Michelle I have some good news for you. The police found the driver that hit Brian." "Good" she said, "I am starting to get all these medical bills from the hospital. We need to sue this guy and make him pay." I responded, "Hold on a minute Michelle that is all going to take a while. Do you and Brian have health insurance?" "No," she said, "Brian just started a new job and we don't have health insurance right now. It does not kick in for six months. We can still sue the guy that hit Brian can't we?" My response was, "We can Michelle, but this guy who hit your husband only has the minimum liability coverage under Georgia law which is $25,000.00. You have uninsured motorist coverage don't you?" Michelle answered, "No I don't think so, we dropped our uninsured motorist coverage when Brian was out of work for several months and we tried to save money."

"I don't understand," Michelle stated, " why can't we go after this driver and make him pay for everything?" I explained by stating, "The guy who hit Brian is a young man with only $25,000.00 insurance coverage on his car and he is in jail now for driving under the influence at the time of the accident. Even if we sue him for a million dollars in court he can file bankruptcy and you won't ever receive anything more than $25,000.00." Michelle looked at me in disbelief asking, "How can I pay all these medical bills? The physical therapy facility will not provide rehabilitation without some type of health insurance or for me to pay them directly. We don't have the money for that." No one had ever explained to Brian and Michelle the importance of maintaining a high level of uninsured motorist coverage.

Over the years of representing people in serious automobile accidents, I have seen time and time again people not having enough uninsured motorist coverage to cover them in the event of injuries sustained in a serious car accident. From what I have seen most insurance companies do a terrible job of explaining what type of automobile insurance coverage you should have.

Here is what you should know. There are two major parts to your car insurance policy you need to understand:-

First, liability insurance protects you if you cause a car accident and someone else is hurt, and second, the liability coverage you have will protect you financially from the person you injured. The insurance company will defend you and hire an attorney for you, (if you are sued) and pay the injured person up to the limits of the liability coverage you purchased.

If you buy uninsured motorist insurance and a driver who injures you has no insurance, or not enough insurance, then your insurance company will pay you up to the limits of your uninsured motorist coverage. Since the other driver is underinsured or uninsured your company pays you. UM Coverage is also important in the event that you are struck by a hit-and-run driver and the other driver is never apprehended. In that event, your uninsured motorist coverage will protect you as well.

Finally, your uninsured motorist coverage will also protect you if the other party has less insurance than you. For instance, if you get hit by someone who purchased a relatively low amount of liability insurance (for instance $25,000.00), your own policy will protect you up to the amount that you purchased for yourself.

So for instance, if you were in a serious automobile accident like the husband that I described earlier, and the other driver only had $25,000.00 in liability coverage, but the husband had $1,000,000.00 (1 million) in damages from the accident, the other driver's insurance would pay the first $25,000.00, and the husband's UM coverage covering him for up to $1,000,000.00 for his losses.

It is also important to understand what the coverage limits mean in the event of an accident. What does it mean when your insurance policy says that you have $25,000.00/$50,000.000 liability coverage or $50,000.00/$100,000.00? Basically, what the policy is telling you is that the first number indicates what coverage is available per person in the event of an accident, and the second number is the total coverage available for one accident.

So, for instance, if there is $50,000.00/$100,000.00 in coverage, an injured person would be covered up to $50,000.00, but the total coverage available for the accident is only $100,000.00. If five people were hurt in the accident the most any one person could be paid is $50,000.00, but all five people together could not recover more than $100,000.00. In this situation, any one person's damages could not exceed $50,000.00 or the entire claim of all people in the accident could not exceed $100,000.00. You would be personally responsible for any amount above the policy limit if you caused the accident.

Just how much uninsured motorist coverage should you buy? To protect yourself in the event of a catastrophic accident as the one previously described, I recommend you buy as much coverage as you can afford.

How expensive is it? In most states your insurance company must offer UM coverage to you. However, they may not explain how important it is or the costs involved. There are some additional costs for higher UM coverage, but as we have previously explained it is very important to have this type of automobile insurance coverage. It's also not as expensive as you might think.

When I increased my UM coverage two years ago from $50,000.00 to $1,000,000.00 the additional coverage was only $300.00 per year. Is a few hundred dollars per year worth the piece of mind to know that if you or a family member is seriously injured in a wreck you are covered for up to a million dollars?

Why don't the insurance companies encourage you to have lots of uninsured motorist protection? **The reason insurance companies fail to advise you about UM coverage is because it is a good deal for you and a terrible deal for them.** As you can see from paying a nominal amount for an additional UM coverage you get a lot more protection.

I strongly recommend that you review your automobile insurance policy limits. If you have anything less than $1,000,000.00 in UM coverage I would strongly advise you to contact your insurance agent to find out what the costs would be to cover you for $1,000,000.00 in UM coverage. I don't think that I have to explain the danger out there on the roadways. You hear about terrible accidents everyday. With the increasing costs of medical expenses, hospital and doctor bills, doesn't it make sense to have as much coverage as you possibly can?

If you have any questions, please feel free to call us at (770) 577-3020.

If you found out about us through this book we will be glad to consult with you concerning your automobile insurance coverage through a free telephone conversation.

About James

James K. Murphy has practiced law for over 20 years. He is a Martindale Hubbell "BV" rated attorney who was admitted to the Georgia Bar in 1991, the U.S. District Court, North District of Georgia. He received his B.A. from the State University of New York at Geneseo. He received his J.D. from State University of New York at Buffalo. He was employed with the Georgia Legal Services Program for seven (7) years where he worked as a Supervising Attorney. He then entered private practice where he has focused on injury cases. He is a member of the Association of Trial Lawyers of America and Georgia Trial Lawyers. He has authored two reports on the insurance industry "How to Buy Car Insurance in Georgia" and "Mistakes to Avoid if You Want to Win Your Car Wreck Case", along with his latest publication "Counseling Loved Ones of Fatal Accidents."

POWER PRINCIPLE #19

"POWER A TAX-FREE FINANCIAL FUTURE"

by Chuck Oliver, President and CEO of The American Equity Advisory Group

"Anyone who chooses to be casual about their finances will become a financial casualty." ~ Anonymous

There is a dramatic change happening in America that you don't hear being talked about very much. It's one of the most colossal shifts in our history – but, between wars, natural disasters, politics, the recession, terrorist attacks, global warming, and all the other attention-grabbing topics, it tends to get little notice – if it gets any notice at all.

That dramatic change has to do with the "graying" of America. The huge baby boomer population is like an avalanche hurtling down a mountain, gathering speed and volume as it descends. Its sheer magnitude and intensity are tilting the economic scales, already currently strained, into an even more disastrous position. Think about this - every 8 seconds someone in the U.S. is turning 62 years of age, and that will hold true for *the next 19 years*. What do you think is the fastest bur-geoning population segment in America? Would you believe **centenar-ians**? Yes, people who are in their *100's*!

Most people have a vague realization that the majority of Americans are edging toward senior citizen status. But, the greatest faction of the popu-lation does not have the slightest idea of how that affects us *all* economi-cally – especially when it comes to financial planning for our retirement.

We've come to a point where conventional wisdom is not going to serve any of us well in terms of how we handle our money over the long haul. If we're going to power our financial futures, we will all have to employ methods that are both innovative and, at the same time, rock-solid - to ensure that we build the wealth we will need, in order to enjoy our retirement years to the fullest.

I've made it my company's priority to offer what we call The Personal Protected Pension Plan™ – legitimate low-risk, tax-free strategies to grow money that will sustain us for our new and longer lives. We can't do "business as usual" when it comes to planning for our futures – that's why our firm looks for innovative ways to create wealth without relying on traditionally risky markets and real estate bubbles that are bound to burst at some point.

We seek out these cutting-edge and reliable solutions to the big invest-ment challenges that lie in front of us all – because my Power Principle for a successful, prosperous and happy life is implementing the kind of foolproof retirement planning that minimizes your taxes, protects your principal and outmaneuvers inflation. It's what we teach other financial advisors and what we provide to our clients.

FROM CONSUMPTION TO CONSERVATION

First, however, let's talk about why the aging of America is a big deal to all of us – and why the economic volatility of recent years will continue for many years to come.

It's no secret that the baby boomer generation is beginning to move into the retirement phase of their lives. The oldest 'boomers' will turn 64 in 2010, and many younger 'boomers' have had an early retirement forced upon them by the tough job market.

As these roughly 80 million people move out of the active working phase of their lives, it will mean, counting those senior citizens who have already retired, that a full two-thirds (66%) of our population is moving into the "conservation mode" (retiring and holding on to their money as tightly as possible). This will leave only one-third (33%) in the "consumption mode" (working, making money and spending it).

That means that as the older population downsizes their real estate holdings – going from homes to apartments or condos or even into nursing homes or assisted care facilities – there won't be enough younger people to buy up those homes. The same is true with stocks and bonds. As the aging population sheds these riskier investments, there won't be enough younger investors to pick up the slack – not to mention the question of whether, in the Wall Street arena, they'll *want* to pick up the slack in the first place after the near-catastrophic crash in 2008.

This, of course, raises huge questions of where the stock market and the real estate market will be heading in the next few years. The scenario I just described will last, according to the demographics involved, until the next major consumption 'wave' in the year 2025. That means another *15 years* of economic volatility, where there just won't be enough younger consumers to compensate for the economic loss of our older retirees.

SOCIAL INSECURITY

Nothing reflects this coming mammoth age adjustment more than the Federal government's Social Security Program. When Franklin D. Roosevelt's administration created Social Security in the 1930's, times were different - the average man's life expectancy was *58*. Yes, that's right – 58 years old. And since benefits were scheduled to kick in when a person turned 65, you could argue it was a program that was created, in the majority of cases, to never have to pay a benefit.

Today, the typical male lives almost 30 years longer – life expectancy is now in the 80's. Not only that, but with a married couple, there is over a 50% chance that one of the spouses will live into their 90's. The growing pressure on the Social Security fund stems from two important factors: first, extreme economic conditions, as noted earlier, have forced more people into an early retirement, which means they will begin to draw their Social Security benefits earlier than expected, and second, there simply aren't as many young workers to fund the program properly.

In 2011, something unprecedented will happen, the harbinger of everything I've been talking about here. For the first time since the 1980's, Social Security will pay out more than it collects in contributions. This is not to say the government is going to let the program go broke, but it is an important signal that the two-thirds of the population that is in "conservation" mode is going to continue to be a big 'game-changer' in ways we're only beginning to see.

DISPELLING OLD FINANCIAL MYTHS

Please don't 'jump off the bridge' yet – I realize that what you've been reading so far seems to only forecast gloom and doom, but frankly, it's just more of a new reality – AND THE GOOD NEWS IS THAT THERE IS STILL AN INCREDIBLY EFFECTIVE AND VIABLE WAY TO BUILD AND PRESERVE YOUR WEALTH!

The question becomes, knowing all this, how do we work with this new paradigm to effectively protect and grow money over the long haul, as well as pass it on to generations to come? The first step to answering this question is to understand how our aging society will be developing over the next few years and react accordingly.

The second step is knowing what *not* to do; for example: if you're within ten years of retirement, then investing your money in stocks or mutual funds could be just as dangerous as playing *blackjack* in Vegas. Blackjack is a bet that usually doesn't pay off over the long run.

We'd rather you and your family **TRIUMPH**. So our philosophy is simply this: let's carve out what you're going to need to maintain your lifestyle and create income through The Personal Protected Pension Plan™ that's right for you and your loved ones - a pension that's safe from tax risk, inflation risk and market risk, and then put the remainder into more aggressive market products if you're inclined to take the gamble.

You could say I'm prejudiced. When I was considerably younger, I was worth a lot of money on paper. I could have even considered early retirement so I could enjoy the good life. Then, before I could turn around, the tech bubble popped in early 2000 and suddenly I was out several hundred thousand dollars. Gone. Disappeared into 'the ether'.

That's when I changed the mission of my business and the aim of my personal finances to adjust to the realization that to make money was ONLY HALF THE GOAL. The second half of the goal was that after making the money, to preserve it and protect it for one's future. That's now the approach I take in all my strategic planning with my personal money and that of my clients. That is why none of our clients are at risk of losing their money when following the plans we have laid out for them.

Of course, we all also know plenty of people who 'lost big' again in 2008. Thanks in part to those two big bubbles bursting, economists refer to the last ten years as "the lost decade" or "the big zero." Basically, there were no gains in the job market, no gains in real estate value, and most profoundly, exactly zero gains in the stock market - not exactly what was expected when the new millennium burst forth with such great promise.

The harsh truth is that no consumer has ever outperformed the market! Not even all-star mutual fund managers have ever outperformed the market long-term. If you've ever heard of a certain notorious "wealth management expert" named Bernie Madoff, you know what happens with people who tout stock market miracle pay-outs.

People would have made more money in treasury bonds than in the stock market during the last 40 years. The greatest 'bull run' in Wall Street history was from 1984 to 2003 – and, yes, the average overall return was 10%; but the average individual investor return was only 3.71% - because most people were buying at the peaks and selling in the valleys, rather than staying in it for the entire 20 year span.

Speaking for myself, I have a wonderful family which includes my wife who is a true life partner, and two great sons, whose financial futures I want to ensure, not put at risk. That's why our firm specializes in safe, secure and proven ways to build and preserve wealth. And, believe me, we've discovered them! I'll share some of our secrets a little later on in this chapter.

PENSION PANIC

The next step in looking at America's retirement situation is to understand how the pension structure has collapsed. The unraveling of the private pension is another huge aspect of our everyday lives that has gotten little coverage in the media.

The figures are pretty stark when viewed in black and white. From 1950 to 1979, the amount of American workers and salary-workers covered by pensions doubled. Since 1983, however, the trend has been completely downward – to the point where only 21 percent of Americans in the private sector have a defined-benefit pension plan funded by their employers.

And yet, to demonstrate how we can be a nation of dreamers, fully 61 percent of working Americans expect to somehow end up with that kind of benefit when they finally retire. As a researcher at the Employee Benefit Research Institute (a non-profit, non-partisan organization created in 1978 to study employee pensions) wryly put it, those benefits are "unlikely to materialize."

The failure to face retirement reality may just come from the fact that the current crop of workers are used to seeing their parents and grandparents retire with a pension that took care of them. Today's workers assume that pensions just happen somehow - kind of like the weather.

"The years 1965 to 1999 were the closest thing to economic golden years ever seen by this nation for those moving into retirement," says Employee Benefit Research Institute chief Dallas Salisbury, "and they will likely never be matched again for the bulk of the population unless savings behavior changes radically."

It's clear that, for most working Americans, creating a pension plan is their own personal responsibility. The earlier we all begin planning for our golden years, the better. The situation is unsettling, yes, but again, we've found great and revolutionary ways to use The Personal Protected Pension Plan™ to safeguard our clients' futures without any risk involved.

THE PERSONAL PROTECTED PENSION PLAN™ STRATEGIES

The main feature of The Personal Protected Pension Plan™ is that it secures the money you work all your life to save – and allows you to grow that money, withdraw that money and transfer that money to the next generation *tax-free*.

First and foremost, we help you to protect what you have and to build to what you'll need for your own retirement. Then, through The Family Legacy Life Plan™, we can also provide the same pension protection for you or your children and assure them a guaranteed secure financial future.

A hundred years ago, most American families lived on farms. The parents would pass on their farms to their children, who would will them to the next generation and so forth. There was a consistent transfer of family ownership over the years.

Today, we see real estate values in turmoil and we have little idea what inherited property might eventually be worth. We also can't be sure that 401k plans will actually end up growing money and how high taxes will be on them when we eventually draw funds from them. That triggers a real fear that the odds are stacked against all of our children's futures, including those of my own.

THE TRUTH IS, THERE'S NO NEED TO GAMBLE, ESPECIALLY WHEN A SURE BET IS AVAILABLE!

The only certainty is that we and our parents will eventually pass on. If one or both parents are able to qualify for The Family Legacy Life Plan™, it's a much better investment for those 25-35 years away from retirement to redirect their 401k contributions into The Family Legacy Life Plan™.

For example, say there are three children in their forties or fifties and that each of them puts about $6,000 into their 401k's annually. That's a total of $18,000 pre-tax or $14,000 after taxes if they put the money into their 401k's or other traditional market products.

If, instead, the kids put that money into a Family Legacy Life Plan™ policy on a parent and that policy has a million and a half dollar death benefit, the three children are guaranteed to make *$500,000 each,* free and clear, without having to worry about market risks or tax losses when that parent passes away. Keep in mind that the parents are likely to pass around the same time period when the children would be reaching retirement age.

In contrast, if they put that money into the stock market it would have to earn 8% or better every single year – without ever having a losing year – over those two or three decades to match that kind of pay-off.

These are, of course, approximate numbers, but they give you an idea of how you can do better. Not only would their stock market portfolio have to perform at a phenomenal level to achieve the same effect as the life insurance solution, but they are gambling that tax rates on that money won't have skyrocketed by the time they want to withdraw it, thus costing them a significant portion of their retirement fund.

THE 401K IS A BIG GAMBLE! THE LEGACY INSURANCE SOLUTION IS A TAX-FREE GUARANTEE!

With that million and a half dollar policy waiting to pay off with a tax-free transfer when the children approach their retirement age, everyone in the family can breathe easier and not sweat economic fluctuations. The money that will secure a prosperous future for themselves and future generations, in the midst of continuing economic uncertainty, is going to be there for them with a tax-free guarantee.

Obviously, when the time comes, you can then set up the same Family Legacy Life Plan™ for your children. They're still investing their money, not yours, for their future – you just happen to be the collateral.

By wisely redirecting resources and avoiding conventional financial choices that can easily end up backfiring, we don't have to worry about Wall Street bubbles blowing up. If someone has the funds to risk on a bull market, that's all well and good and we're certainly there to help. We do think, however, that protecting an essential portion of our clients' money to safeguard their future is crucial.

The Personal Protected Pension Plan™ also offers another strategy for a tax-free retirement if you own your own business. And, this is critically important, because, when it comes to retirement planning, entrepreneurs and business owners often put themselves in the worst position. They're so busy running their companies 24/7 and building up business value, they forget about their own personal financial position. Most of the time, they simply assume they can sell their business and take back out all the equity they put into it - so their retirement years will be covered.

There are more hard facts to deal with here. Over 1.2 million businesses go up for sale every year. Only *25%* will actually sell and most companies will end up going for a price that's below market value – or even below the value of the combined assets of the business, even if they're profitable and valuable on paper.

You may be one of the lucky ones who do 'score' with a business sale, but the odds are decidedly against you. You could easily end up with much less than you think and your golden years could end up being a big struggle when it comes to money.

By doing The Business Equity Retirement Solution™, you can begin putting your business equity to work for your retirement *right now* – so you don't have to worry about gambling everything on being able to complete a business sale down the line. You would be allowed tax-advantaged use of your business equity, and you would also receive tax-free growth on that money - which you can also withdraw tax-free when you retire.

And again, this isn't a new concept, nor is it akin to playing some kind of 'shell game' with the IRS. You're simply using your business equity for your retirement fund, instead of possibly losing that equity altogether if you have a problem selling your business.

These are just a few of the creative solutions we provide to our clients and develop in our work with our financial advisors. Yes, our country is changing. Most Americans no longer work at the same company for thirty to forty years and then retire comfortably on that company's pension program as they did in previous generations. Nor is the financial landscape as dependable as it once was - because of the shifting demographics and the aging of the baby boomers.

Yet, no matter where you are in life: retired, working for a company, or running your own business, the right wealth strategist can help you begin working today toward a prosperous and secure tomorrow. By the right wealth strategist, I mean one that is focused on the second half of your planning years. The first half was dedicated to the contribution and creation of wealth. The second half needs to be dedicated to withdrawing, distributing, and transferring that which you worked so hard to acquire in the first half. That is our objective, the mission of our company. Finding the right no-risk, tax-free solution is **not** as hard as you might think if you confide in and follow the appropriate wealth strategist, one that specializes and focuses on the second half of your financial game plan.

I strongly urge you to "Power Your Financial Future" with The Personal Protected Pension Plan™ so you can take care of yourself and your loved ones in the coming years. Visit us at: www.PersonalProtectedPensionPlan.com to begin securing your future and that of your loved ones.

About Chuck

Charles "Chuck" Oliver is an industry recognized wealth strategist who works with retirees and those who are about to be retired and their families who are uncertain about planning in and for retirement. Their concerns center around taxes, market risk, and the possibility of out living their income.

Mr. Oliver helps his clients gain clarity, balance, focus, and confidence about their wealth creation and preservation. Chuck refutes the wisdom of the importance of paying off mortgages and putting the money into IRA's, 403b's, and 401K's.

Chuck and his Team educate clients on how to increase their retirement income by 50% or more with little or no tax, with no market risk, and how to establish a tax free income for the rest of their lives, and one that will transfer tax free to future generations.

Accomplishments include:

- Founder and CEO of the American Equity Advisory Group, LLC and The Hidden Wealth System, the Chuck Oliver Team

- Fox TV News financial contributor

- Radio Show Host of Your Hidden Wealth on 540 WFLA

- Member of PREP the Partnership for Retirement Education and Planning

- Member NAIFA, National Association Insurance and Financial Advisors

- Member of the Winter Park Better Business Bureau

- Graduate of Capital University

- Working as a Wealth Strategist in the planning industry since 1992

- Member of NESA - Nationwide Elder Service Associates

- Named to America's PremierExperts® as a Wealth Strategist

- Faculty for The National Institute of Financial Education

- The Next Big Thing Radio, contributing provider

- Author, "Power Principles for Success," The Tax-Free Retirement

- Certified TEAM Member with Missed Fortune, Missed Fortune speaker, trainer and educator

- Founder of "The Money Sense Employer Program"

- MDRT Top of the Table-The Premier Association of Financial Professionals

- Co-author of Borrow Smart, Retire Rich with Todd Ballenger

Chuck is husband to Leanna and a father of two boys, Davis and Drake. He holds his family as one of his top priorities. Chuck is an avid golfer and runner. Chuck runs marathons to raise money for special causes.

Chuck's Unique Ability:

"Investing in the well-being of others through strategic planning and innovative solutions to help serve and transform financial and personal lives."

POWER PRINCIPLE #20

TAKE ACTION!

by Rutherford De Armas

"Obstacles don't have to stop you. If you run into a wall, don't turn around and give up. Figure out how to climb it, go through it, or work around it." ~ *Michael Jordan*

T he above quote from Michael Jordan is one of my favorites – and exemplifies the philosophy behind my Power Principle. If you want to achieve what you want in life, you should always focus on *how you can achieve it*, not on why you can't. Then follow through with consistent action to make your desired result a reality – take "Power Action" to get to where you want to go.

You may not get all the way there. Michael Jordan certainly didn't when he briefly swapped his Air Jordans for baseball cleats. But you will never know if you don't try.

Unfortunately, many people just lack the willpower to try. You can tell that by the non-stop barrage of television commercials that try to inspire viewers to make an effort – the late night infomercials that make it sound easy to lose weight, get in shape and make money, if you, of course, buy the products that are being advertised. The reason why there is such a big market for these products is the fact that the majority of times, the average person's reaction to taking on a big, hard challenge is, "I can't."

Motivational speaker Tom Krause says, "If you only do what you know you can do – you never do very much." I firmly believe that to be the case. The biggest battlefield is between our ears – which means every day we have to win the war against our own irrational fears and negative thoughts to fully realize our own potential.

NOT BECOMING A VICTIM

It's very tempting to surrender to those negative thoughts and take the path of least resistance. It's the easiest thing in the world. However, when we do that, we turn ourselves into victims because we haven't taken the necessary steps – the "Power Action" – that would have allowed us to take charge of our lives.

Here's an example of one special person who certainly could have chosen to live his life as a victim. He had an excellent excuse not to bother leading a useful and productive life – and it took an incredible effort, physically and mentally, to finally make it happen.

When Bill Porter was born in 1932, it was a difficult delivery and the doctor had to use forceps to complete the birth. There was some brain damage which led to the boy developing cerebral palsy. When Bill grew up, however, he wanted to work in a real job. No one would hire him, but he refused to accept disability payments and was intent on getting paid for real work.

He finally talked to a company in Portland, Oregon into hiring him as a door-to-door salesman. As he had incredible trouble merely getting dressed in the morning (it took him 3 to 4 hours just to get out the door), he had to stop by various places along the way - so friends could help him button his shirt, clip on his tie, tie his shoes and finish other tasks he physically couldn't handle.

In spite of all this, Bill went on to become *the top seller* for the company and received national recognition for his sales achievements. After his story was told in the local newspaper, Hollywood came calling and a TV movie, "Door to Door," starring award-winning actor William H. Macy as Bill, was aired on TNT to great acclaim.

In that day and age, society certainly did not encourage a boy with cerebral palsy to grow up and have such a successful, inspiring career.

Porter did it through sheer willpower by focusing on what he *could* do, not what he couldn't do. And he outshone thousands of other salesmen who didn't have that kind of disadvantage working against them.

MY OWN PERSONAL JOURNEY

I may come across so far in this chapter as a confident, self-motivating individual. But I also have had to fight my own wars in "the battlefield between my ears," just like everyone else.

My family moved to America from the Philippines when I was six years old. Because both of my parents worked hard to earn a living and take care of their family, they didn't have a lot of time to devote to my needs. In those days, parents such as mine were focused on work and not their children's emotional development. I certainly don't feel sorry for myself and there is no question I was loved – but, again, it was a different time and that was how parenting was approached.

My confidence suffered as a result. Even though I achieved a great deal playing tennis in high school – I was a varsity letterman for three years - I began to notice that, in very competitive matches, I began to look for a reason I *couldn't* win – rather than focus on what action I needed to take to enable me to come out on top.

Basically, it was giving myself an out – an excuse for losing. "The Ref made bad calls." "The sun was in my eyes." "I think I've got a flu bug." It was much easier to blame external factors than to actually examine what I personally could have done to win the match.

Finally, I saw, with a life-changing clarity, the mental mistake I was making. And I realized that working on justifications for failure would inevitably lead to failure – while taking the necessary Power Actions for success gave me the best chance at the outcome I desired.

TRUE WEALTH AND PROSPERITY

I want to take a little detour here and ask you, "What is real success?"

That's an important question to consider while mapping out what you want to do with your life – and figuring what Power Action to take in order to reach your goals. Because your actual goals may not be the ones you think they are.

When I titled this section "True Wealth and Prosperity," I wasn't just talking about what's in your bank account – but that's what many people think about when it comes to success. Yet, how many times do you read about celebrities and athletes worth millions and millions of dollars who are still miserable and unhappy – and behave like spoiled kids?

To me, life has to be about more than that. That's why, since I was 34, my most important clients have been my wife and kids. Prior to that, my adult life was devoted to the Fortune 500 corporation I worked for. I was working from 40 to 60 hours a week to advance myself and make as much money as possible. And, no question, I did very well at it.

But what was that success all about? Continuing to be promoted and working longer and harder? Or finding a way to properly balance my family and my work? My parents, unfortunately, were unable to achieve that balance, because they were new immigrants to America and had to work those kinds of hours. I was lucky enough to be in a different position.

That's why I made the decision to go out on my own and form a successful consulting company, Apogee Consulting Group™. That way I was in control of what hours I spent on business – and could work with my family's schedule, not against it. Before, my employer controlled what I did with my life – now, I can control it.

I really believe too many of us think we're helpless to shape our lives to what we want them to be. We think we have to work around the clock to achieve success – that we don't have a choice and we can't afford to give the time necessary to have complete relationships with family and friends. But, again, we're giving ourselves various excuses for failure – "The economy's bad", "This is what everybody has to do", or "I need as much money as possible."

All of those statements may be true to some extent – just as it may have been true that the Ref. did make a bad call during my tennis match – but it's not the *entire* situation. And, again, to focus on why you *can't* do something, rather than what you can do to make it happen, is to guarantee not to reach your goal.

I live a very comfortable life with great clients, great friends and a great family. I don't have all the money in the world, but I have more than enough. Because I believe I've achieved the kind of true prosperity I believe in – an overall happy balance of elements.

That's why I advise you to take Power Action to achieve the *life* you want to have – not just the career. <u>That brings true satisfaction</u>.

POWER ACTION IN BUSINESS

While I value my family time, I also obviously realize the importance of making a business work – and I'm very good at it, as my clients will tell you. The key to my effectiveness, I believe, is my philosophy on focusing on what you can do, rather than on what you can't do.

Many companies react to adversity the way I reacted in my difficult tennis matches – they focus on what could make them fail rather than what could make them succeed. If a business is losing marketing share or customers, they may react by simply trying to stop the bleeding and avoid failure, rather than reach for success.

Focusing on getting back the market share in a positive, pro-active way, forces innovation and new solutions. I work with a manufacturer that's been in business for over 100 years. Their revenue, however, was down by 40% - mostly because they hadn't tinkered with their outmoded distribution model, which entailed them selling though middlemen.

Those middlemen, who were also selling other products, had no obligation to market my client's line any more aggressively than anyone else's. They were 'getting lost in the shuffle'. And my client wasn't really dealing with how the world had changed – thanks to the internet, they could now communicate directly with consumers and develop processes to sell their products online. Blaming the situation on the middlemen was inviting failure. Creating new ways to directly sell and market their products to consumers was focusing on success.

Knee-jerk price cutting can also be another step on the road to sabotaging your own company. Some businesses I work with have seen their competition lower prices to a point that my clients just can't understand how they still turn a profit. And, yet, they immediately assume that the only answer for them is to lower their own prices to the danger point, even though it's going to kill their bottom line, or threaten quality to such an extent they could damage their brand and reputation.

Again, that's negative thinking – "I have to lower my prices, I don't have a choice." I tell my client companies to battle that kind of price point mindset. Instead, these companies should ask themselves, "What do I need to do to sell at the right price so I can provide outstanding value?" It's the kind of Power Action thought that forces a company to take a close look beyond the pricing issues to analyze overall what they're doing in comparison to everyone else in the marketplace.

The truth is that the consumer, even in these times, will pay a certain price if they're sure a certain threshold of value is met. One company I consult with works in the area of home improvement and was being underbid on many jobs. They were tempted to drop their rate, even though they really couldn't afford to.

My consulting firm always runs the SWOT process on every business we work with – we identify our clients' Strengths, their Weaknesses, their Opportunities and their Threats.

In this case, my client had their price point as a Weakness – and their outside Threat was the smaller fly-by-night contractors who could afford to charge less. Their Strength was their quality of work – they kept the same regular dependable workers on the payroll, paid worker's comp and insurance costs and made sure the jobs were done at a consistent level. The Opportunity was leveraging that Strength in a way that hit home for the consumer.

This company thought that all their potential customers cared about was price. Our research found out that they were wrong - quality is really what homeowners are after. The price, of course, still had to be reasonable - but nobody wants to have a remodeling job redone because it wasn't done right in the first place. Who wants their house torn up again?

In this case, we needed to educate the consumer on what to look for in a home improvement firm - that they needed to avoid firms that didn't carry the right insurance and simply subcontracted to 'day' workers who may not have the best qualifications. By subcontracting, these companies avoid responsibility for mistakes. And if, by chance, they don't pay the subcontractors, those subcontractors can have a general lien filed against the homeowner, even though the homeowner may have already paid the initial company that did the subcontracting!

By posting this kind of information on my client's website – and making available free downloadable PDFs with general facts about home improvement – we positioned them as a quality authoritative contracting business that consumers can rely on. My client needed to pursue these kinds of quality-driven potential customers, educate them and show them they were a reputable, reliable contractor they could trust. Yes, it took a little effort, but by doing that -- by focusing on what they could do to justify their prices rather than just cutting them -- they were able to continue their quality operation and expand their customer base, rather than watch it shrink.

Whatever any business is doing that's above common industry standards needs to be communicated to any potential customer, so they understand the extra value that's attached to the price tag. With the internet, it's so much easier to start a conversation with consumers – and that's an important evolution that many businesses need to begin taking more advantage of.

Finally, if there's a good thing about the kind of huge recession we've been experiencing, it's the fact that is helps get rid of wasted processes and outmoded ways of doing business that eat up time, manpower, and profits. When times are good, we're reluctant to challenge the way our businesses do things, even though they can usually be improved. When times are bad, however, we have no choice but to reevaluate – again, by looking at what a business *can* do to improve how it runs, rather than focusing on why it can't possibly succeed in a downturn. Retooling can be an incredibly positive and proactive move, depending on overall circumstances.

My business is to help other businesses take Power Action to turn things around, or improve on what's already good. What's the alternative? Why wouldn't you want your business to do as well as possible – and preserve its integrity and quality at the same time? There's no reason not to – unless the people running the company are too busy thinking up those negative reasons and excuses.

WINNING THE MIND GAME

I think we'd all be surprised at what we could accomplish if we didn't think it was impossible.

I can think of no better story to illustrate that than the one about how a graduate student at the University of California, Berkeley, arrived late one day to his statistics class. There were two problems already on the blackboard that he assumed were homework.

He copied the problems down in his notebook, took them back to his place, worked hard on them for a few days, solved them, and dropped the answers back on his professor's desk. Some time later, the stunned professor showed up at his room – and asked how the student had managed to solve the problems.

The shocking truth was the problems were actually examples of legendary math theorems that had never been solved – until the student unknowingly did what was thought impossible!

The student's name was George Dantzig and he became a legendary mathematician. Would Dantzig have ever taken on those problems if he had known no one else had solved them? Probably not. And he probably wouldn't have solved them as easily as he did if he had known that common wisdom was - they *couldn't* be solved.

Approach difficult problems as though there is a solution, both in your life and in your business. The path of least resistance usually just delays the inevitable – and by that time, the problem you've been avoiding has usually grown to monstrous proportions.

The ultimate resolution of the problem may be hard and painful – or it may be much simpler than you think. But taking Power Action brings about powerful results. Just ask Bill Porter – who, at the age of 77, is still online sales manager of that same company where he began as a door-to-door salesman.

About Rutherford

Rutherford De Armas has over 20 years of experience in sales and marketing, including sales management, sales training, and strategic planning. He has worked for large Fortune 500 companies and consulted with businesses of all sizes, handling various responsibilities in the areas of sales, sales management, marketing, and strategic business development.

He helps small and medium-sized businesses maximize their revenues and profitability by developing and implementing proven marketing, advertising, and sales strategies that get results.

He has played a key role in the expansion of businesses across several B2B and B2C industries including, but not limited to, Manufacturing, Professional, Retail, Wholesale, etc. with typical results of 4-8 times growth versus industry averages. Apogee Consulting Group™ shows its clients how to build a competitive advantage in their marketplace and then properly communicate those advantages to their prospects in the most efficient, effective, and profitable way.

For more information, go to www.RutherfordDeArmas.com or www.ApogeeConsultingGroup.com.

POWER PRINCIPLE #21

SET POWER GOALS

by Darrin T. Mish, Attorney

"Set your course by the stars, not by the lights of every passing ship." ~ *General Omar Bradley*

oals are funny things. They can be small - for example, it could be "I just want to get through today without a problem." Or they can be huge and overwhelming - such as, "I'm going to make a billion dollars by Tuesday." That's a pretty big range of objectives, I'm sure you'll agree.

And depending on who you are and what your circumstances might be, both goals can seem either completely intimidating and unachievable – or quite easy to accomplish. The first goal could be critical to an alcoholic trying to reform – the second goal might be 'easy as pie' for someone like Warren Buffet.

In short, goals are very personal things - they are essential to who you are, where you are and how you proceed with your life. They are meant to help you achieve more than you thought was ever possible with your life, but, strangely enough, they can end up causing you to *achieve less*.

For instance, if your goal in life is just to be able to own a comfortable house and a nice car, you're not going to think much beyond that. You're only going to advance yourself to a point where you can make enough money to attain that particular item. And that's fine, if that's all you really want.

I would imagine, however, and say that if you're reading this book, you want a lot more out of your career and your life. To me, that all starts with setting <u>bigger</u> goals – what I like to call *"Power Goals"* - than might be comfortable for you at the moment. They may, in fact, seem completely out of your reach – but that's the point of them. When you create *Power Goals*, you power up your life – because it affects how you approach every single aspect of your life, not just on a conscious, but also on an unconscious level.

MY POWER GOALS

About ten years ago, I took stock and wrote up my overall goals – and they were definitely big ones. I taped that piece of paper to my keyboard drawer of my computer desk and didn't really examine them that much. One of them - becoming one of the top earners in the country in my profession - I was very unsure of pulling off, and I hesitated before I committed to it. I finally decided not to let that uncertainty stop me – and, by having that goal always in the back of my mind, I made it happen. I also achieved all my other goals as a matter of fact, including owning a large new home and a brand new boat. To be completely honest, I was as surprised as anyone that I did it all – and much sooner than I ever thought possible.

Now, as I already mentioned, I didn't really look over those *"Power Goals"* very often. Nor did I lie in bed at night silently chanting them over and over, nor did I practice creative visualization or any other New Age techniques. What I did was make the choices, and do the work that was required - to make all my goals a reality.

Sounds too easy, right? Or maybe too hard, if you are heavily into "The Secret." But what I did – and what countless other entrepreneurs do – is certainly a real-world variation of that best-selling book.

Because I had such high goals set, I believe I approached my career at a higher level of determination. It may have been partly unconscious, but I wouldn't accept a career choice that would take me down a road that wouldn't get me to where I wanted to ultimately go. I wouldn't put myself in a position that didn't allow me to achieve what I wanted to achieve. In short, by having my *Power Goals* as a backstop, I was empowered to *not settle for less* – and to keep working towards making my dreams a reality.

HOW POWER GOALS GET SHORT-CIRCUITED

I just made myself sound pretty good so far, didn't I? Well, just to let you know that I am a real live human being and not some 'minor god'. I will admit that I wasn't always so wonderful at reaching my goals. As a matter of fact, there were several scary times in my life prior to that where I was in danger of not making it to the finish line at all. Those times taught me some valuable lessons, and I believe all of us have these kinds of "critical moments" in common.

One critical moment occurred when I was an undergraduate at college. My goal was to become a lawyer, like a lot of my classmates. Unfortunately, also like a lot of my classmates, studying wasn't my first priority. So when it came time to meet with my student counselor, he asked me what I wanted to do with my life. I told him. He looked down at my grade transcripts, looked back up at me and told me I didn't have 'a chance in hell' of becoming a lawyer. In other words, my *Power Goal* had gotten unplugged somewhere along the way.

That was my big wake-up call and it completely shook me to my core. I realized that wishing doesn't make it happen, and the Law of Attraction isn't real-life legislation. I buckled down and got straight A's the rest of my time as an undergrad, and ended up getting accepted into several law schools. So I was a little more prepared when I did start law school and got the standard John Houseman "Paper Chase" routine – when the professor tells you to look at the person to your left and look at the person to your right, because at the end of the semester one of those people won't be there.

That put the 'fire in my belly', so that I made sure I was there at the end of every semester of Law School – because I didn't take it for granted. Now, there were definitely some would-be lawyers that *did* take it for granted. In fact, some students who had gotten full scholarships ended up flunking out. Sometimes, when you get a free ride, you don't appreciate the value of it.

There was another time where my Power Goals were threatened – and this part is more than a little embarrassing, since I am now a tax lawyer. But, very early in my career, I had an IRS problem – not huge, there was a liability of about $10 thousand out there that, at the time, I could not pay. I was too anxious about it to deal with it, and it continually weighed on my mind. I really wanted it resolved – yet, I couldn't get myself to do what it took to resolve it.

Which brings me to another common threat to goals – *fear*. I was afraid to confront this ongoing debt and anxious about how to deal with the IRS. When I finally overcame this fear and sat down to negotiate, it did work out and it was a huge relief. But I could have had this relief months before, if I had gone ahead and taken the steps necessary to address the problem.

Facing difficult obstacles is, of course, a common factor when pursuing goals – especially *Power Goals*. And, to be fair, often it's not a matter of fear that stops you from dealing with many of those obstacles, it's a matter of practicality – you have to have the resources, knowledge and time to deal with certain ones. Losing fear, however, enables you to actually find out what it *does* take to overcome specific obstacles – and to plan accordingly.

WHEN REALISTIC ISN'T REALISTIC

When I created my own personal *Power Goals*, I really didn't know how many of them I could achieve. And some people might have said that they weren't "realistic." At the time, I might have agreed with those people. But what's the harm in setting goals that you think might be beyond your reach? Isn't that the whole point of goals? To push you past the furthest point that you feel you can go – so you can achieve even more with your life?

Obviously, putting down goals like, "I want to fly like Superman" or "I want to be the Queen of England" is completely unrealistic and silly. But for me to set becoming a top earner in my field was not – because it was something I might actually be able to do. If I had been "realistic," however, I might not have even seriously considered making that a goal. But I did, and I really believe it made a big difference to my career.

This goes back to one of my original points in this chapter – don't settle, especially, for what you can already do. What fun is that? <u>The</u>

<u>challenge in life is setting the bar higher and trying to keep jumping over it</u>. That's what inspires you, as well as the other people in your life, and keeps progress going. Otherwise, we'd all still be sitting in caves huddled around a fire. Even worse…we wouldn't have iPhones!

If you have the talent, and, just as importantly, the willpower, at some point you will be able to make things happen with the proper *Power Goals* in place – if you put in the necessary "sweat equity." Some people do get lucky and get it all without putting in the hours – but, I find, they have trouble holding on to it because they don't really know how they got it in the first place, so they don't understand how to hang on to it. It's kind of like those kids in my law school who didn't have to 'pay a dime' for their education – and couldn't make it.

Paying your dues is more than just a tiresome duty. It's what gives you the wisdom and the experience – not to mention the opportunity - to capitalize on your natural gifts in the most powerful way imaginable.

THE MYTH OF THE "OVERNIGHT SUCCESS"

I'm going to illustrate that last thought with what you might consider a weird example – the English singer Susan Boyle. She's what people call an "overnight success" – a term usually applied to celebrities or companies who seem to spring out of nowhere to become the center of massive attention, whether it's in the business or entertainment worlds.

For instance, Susan Boyle is someone whose music took the world by storm after appearing as a contestant on the "Britain's Got Talent" TV show. Suddenly she was a YouTube sensation and had incredible sales with her first album. For that to happen to someone like her, at her age, and with her complete lack of traditional "show business glamour," was seen as something of a miracle. To the international community, she was the ultimate "overnight success."

But "overnight success" implies that Susan Boyle just tried out for a TV show, happened to sing really well, and was recognized for it that one time. The truth of the matter is that this was a woman who *always* wanted to be a singer. As early as 14 years before, she was auditioning on a different British television show, and was ridiculed by the host at the time for her non-traditional looks and manner.

Being embarrassed on national television is the kind of thing that might make you never want to put yourself in that kind of situation ever again. And fear of that kind of ridicule could have easily stopped her right then and there. But she kept trying, kept singing in her church choir, and, in 2009, tried out for "Britain's Got Talent." That's when she became an "overnight sensation"…after 14 years of working at it, and putting herself out there under less-than-encouraging circumstances.

CHANGE YOUR LIFE – CHANGE YOUR GOALS

When I started out as a lawyer about 17 years ago, I had a small rented office, rented desk and as well as a rented phone and computer. My immediate goal was just to get my practice off the ground. When that stabilized, my next goal was to hire people to help me do a lot of the grunt work I didn't have the time or inclination to handle. I ended up with a reliable staff.

I also began my career as a criminal defense lawyer. I had to go to court first thing in the morning and first thing after lunch. It was hard work, grim, and sometimes I didn't even get paid. Out of that depressing experience came the goal 'to never have to set foot in a courtroom again' – unless I wanted to (you might call that an Anti-Goal – but sometimes they're just as effective!). Becoming a tax lawyer helped me achieve that goal – and learning how to *market* my tax practice into something bigger than my own personal practice finally vaulted me to my "top earner" Power Goal.

Throughout my professional life, when I've reached one goal, I've set a new one. I learned from each stage of my career how to reach the next one. And I don't want to stop – I want to continue to grow and achieve as I move forward. I strongly believe that, because your life is constantly changing, your goals should be changing right along with it. I advise you to make new goals and review previous ones every business quarter. If you don't measure progress, goals aren't goals – they're just wishes. Kind of like when I was wishing to be a lawyer as an undergrad, while not dealing with the fact that my grades weren't up to par.

Power Goals are incredibly important for entrepreneurs – without them, 'we could all end up adrift and chasing our own tails'. It's different when you work for a corporation - they'll set goals for you whether you like it or not, unless you're adept at hiding. But when you're out on your own, you have to be your own boss. And you have to be a *competent* boss – which means setting your own *Power Goals* that make sense for you and your business. If you can't figure out what those Power Goals should be, you may need to either change your business - or yourself.

I would also advise you to create not just professional *Power Goals*, but also family *Power Goals* and personal *Power Goals*. Your family *Power Goals*, for example, might be to make sure your kids are in good schools and your relationship with your spouse grows stronger and deeper. Your personal *Power Goals* could be anything from learning Sanskrit to improving your golf game. Having these in place in your head, again, changes your approach to your personal priorities – and makes you more proactive in terms of keeping your life a growing and dynamic venture.

The last thought I'd like to leave you with, when it comes to creating *Power Goals*, is don't do it when you're all-consumed with your day-to-day drudgery. Sometimes you need your own "time-out" to clear your head and find the right direction. I have a business friend who makes it a point to take a break every Friday afternoon. They cut themselves off from all calls and emails, then work, as they say, *on* their business and not *in* their business. This isn't to say inspiration can't strike when you are 'toiling away in the salt mines' – but, personally, I find time away from the office can really make a big difference.

Setting the proper *Power Goals* can spark you to new levels of personal and professional growth all throughout your life. Continuing to review your goals and evolve with them as your professional and personal life progresses is essential to making that growth happen. **Make sure your goals reflect who you are, what your abilities are and what you want out of your life - and you're sure to find success!**

About Darrin

Darrin Mish graduated from Golden Gate University, in San Francisco, California in 1993 with a Doctor of Jurisprudence. He was admitted to the Florida Bar in that same year and the Bar of the State of Colorado in 2002. He has earned an AV rating from Martindale-Hubbell, the country's most popular attorney rating service. An AV rating signifies an attorney that has "achieved the highest levels of professional skill and integrity." The AV rating is based upon peer reviews by other members of the Bar and the judiciary. Lawyers and judges in the larger community have been polled by Martindale-Hubbell and, based upon their submissions, the company has granted him the highest available rating for his legal skills, as well as for honesty and integrity. He has been honored to have his name placed in Martindale-Hubbell's Bar Register of Preeminent Lawyers as well.

This means that you, the client, receive aggressive representation from a young, energetic, honest, yet experienced attorney. Mr. Mish is permitted to practice before the United States Supreme Court; all courts of the State of Florida; the State of Colorado; the United States District Court, Middle District of Florida; United States Court of Appeals, 11th Circuit; United States Tax Court; United States Court of Federal Claims; the United States Court of Appeals, Federal Circuit; United States Court of Appeals, District of Columbia Circuit; and the United States District Court, Northern District of Florida. He has taken the extra steps to be admitted before all of these courts because he is committed to helping you with your IRS problems, including appeals.

In 2002, Mr. Mish was awarded "Practitioner of the Year" by the American Society of IRS Problem Solvers. He is a member of the Tax Freedom Institute, the American Bar Association, the National Association of Tax Professionals, the National Association of Criminal Defense Lawyers, the Florida Association of Criminal Defense Lawyers, and the Hillsborough County Bar Association. These memberships help him stay current with the law and enable him to protect your rights.

Power Principle #22

CONTENT IS STILL KING

by Lindsay Dicks

THE POWER OF YOUR CONTENT

Have you ever heard the saying, "Content is king on the Internet?" This statement is true, but it's missing a piece; marketing. Without the marketing aspect, it is like opening the doors to your business and doing no marketing whatsoever. The content is only as good as your marketing. The key behind getting good, qualified traffic is "Content Marketing," or to take it a step further, "personalized, targeted Content Marketing."

So what is **Content Marketing**? And better yet, what is **personalized, targeted Content Marketing**?

Content Marketing is simple but can be easily forgotten. It's based on two definitions, *content*, which is really just information about your particular niche, and *marketing,* which is the distribution and promotion of that information. In the business world, this means information created and targeted to your specific niche. The key to Content Marketing is that the content MUST be created specifically to either attract new customers or retain the ones you already have. If it doesn't do this, then it is simply a 'waster' of time, energy and money.

Today, the first thing anyone does when searching for more information about a person, company, product or service is to "Google" it. This concept is the reason why Content Marketing is so important; it's about getting your information out to the consumer whenever and wherever they look for it. In other words, be every place your consumer is, and today, most importantly, that's online.

TYPES OF CONTENT MARKETING

There are many types of Content Marketing, and while I sway toward online forms of Content Marketing, it is important to remember the offline types as well.

Examples of online Content Marketing:

- Downloadable White Papers

- Downloadable Special Reports

- Ebooks

- Videos

- Podcasts

- Ezines

- Blogs

- Articles

- Press Releases

Examples of offline Content Marketing:

- Books

- Magazines

- Newsletters

- Sales letters

- Post cards

- Other Direct Mail Pieces

One thing to keep in mind when developing Content Marketing for your industry is that some types of Content Marketing may work better than others for your niche. So, be sure to test each type, and if you are still unsure, ask your audience their preference. You don't necessarily need to implement all of these strategies if they do not fit your particular business, but if you are looking to gain more customers and are not utilizing one or more of these strategies, then it might be something to look at.

DISTRIBUTION OF CONTENT MARKETING

As I stated before, *content is king on the Internet*; however, it is only as good as your marketing. You must put your content into the hands of your prospects and be where they are… This, quite frankly, may not be on your website. It doesn't matter where they find your information, what matters is that they find it, and that it is valuable enough that they then visit your website or, better yet, contact you directly.

SEO (search engine optimization) and Content Marketing go hand-in-hand. SEO helps you improve your organic rankings in search engines. In other words, it is what allows you to come up in the search engine results when someone searches for keywords related to your product or service.

To properly promote your content and make sure it is in front of your searching prospects, you must understand (or hire someone who understands) SEO and the importance of seeding all content you produce with keywords – specifically, the correct keywords for your industry.

If you're unsure of your keywords, Google has an excellent keyword tool that helps you find out just what your prospects are searching for, visit: https://adwords.google.com/select/KeywordToolExternal.

Once you know your keywords, here are some ways to distribute your online Content Marketing pieces:

- **Social Media Sites-** The biggest ones out there right now that we are currently using are http://www.Twitter.com, http://www.Facebook.com and http://www.Linkedin.com

- **Social Bookmarking-** Social bookmarking allows you share your content online by publicly bookmarking your content. Think of it like bookmarking something in a magazine or book so it can easily be found later or shared with others. That's the idea behind social bookmarking, sharing useful content with others. The best tool we use is http://www.sociallist.net, which allows you to submit to approximately 50 bookmarking sites at one time including the biggest ones like http://www.digg.com, http://www.delicious.com, http://www.stumpleupon.com and http://www.reddit.com

- **Article Syndication**- One of the biggest article-syndication sites is http://www.ezinearticles.com. Another top article-syndication site we use is http://www.submityourarticle.com. It's a paid source, but with only a few clicks it allows you to submit your articles to 12-15 additional article-syndication sites. We also use http://knol.google.com/k, http://www.hubpages.com and http://www.squidoo.com to syndicate articles.

- **Video Syndication**- The biggest video syndications site is http://www.youtube.com. However, we also like http:///www.tubemogul.com, which not only allows you to submit videos to YouTube but also allows you to submit to about 15 other video sites at the same time. A complete time saver if you think about all of the uploads you would have to do (and it's FREE!).

- **Press Release Syndication**- Two of the biggest online press release syndication sources we use on a regular basis (and they are both free) are: http://www.prlog.org and http://www.pitch-engines.com.

- **Other Industry Related Blogs-** Find other blogs in your industry (or newspapers/magazines with columns in your industry) and offer to guest write a blog (or blog column) for them. You can develop a loyal following by providing great content to these additional blog sites. You can also comment on other blogs in your industry, and by commenting regularly and with good information you will see an increase in traffic to your site. Looking for a blog that you can guest blog on? Check out http://myblogguest.com.

MEASURING CONTENT MARKETING

Measuring Content Marketing can be a little tricky, as you are not always able to directly measure the value of someone "Googling" your name, company or keywords. What is the value of someone's confidence in you and your company by the information that they find? Not always easily measured, yet, VERY important. However, here are some things that you can track to determine the affect your Content Marketing is having on your business.

Think in terms of not direct profit numbers, but the effect that educating the consumer has on your website and your business.

- Repeat visitors

- Comments on your blog

- How long people stay on your website

- How many pages people view on your website

- Newsletter subscriptions

- Website downloads

- Referring sites (email, Social Bookmarking Sites, Social Media Sites)

- Gaining more "friends" on Twitter

- Gaining more "fans" or "friends" on Facebook

All of the above are signals that your Content Marketing strategies are working.

Although it can be tough to measure the power of someone "Googling" you and finding third-party verification of who you are and what you do, there are some ways that you can specifically measure your Content Marketing Strategies, here are a couple of examples:

- Separate 800 numbers (check out http://www.yourroiguy.com)

- Individual URLs for different projects

- Make sure every web page has a call to action that you track conversions on.

BENEFITS OF CONTENT MARKETING

The most important benefit about Content Marketing is that it allows you to compete with the "big dogs" in your industry. You may not be able to buy an ad for the Super Bowl, but with the Internet, distribution of content marketing has little or no cost. Here are some other benefits of Content Marketing:

- Generate more traffic to your website

- Build a loyal following

- Build a list from opt-ins on your website

- Increase brand awareness on the Internet

- Establish yourself (and your business) as the "go-to" expert in your niche

KEY THINGS TO HELP WITH CONTENT MARKETING:

- Content Marketing can seem a bit overwhelming, so make an action plan ahead of time - at least six months in advance, of what you are going to distribute to potential and current clients and also how you will distribute the information.

- Old rule of thumb, seven impressions to create awareness of an ad – so, in theory, this means that each piece of your Content Marketing should be created in a series. This means create a series of videos, a series of white papers, a series of blogs, etc.

- Content MUST be intrinsically important to your customer for it to play a vital role in your content marketing strategy. Don't just distribute content to distribute content, make sure it's valuable to your consumer or prospect.

- You MUST understand your customers and what is important to them - this includes any problems or frustrations they face. If you do not understand them, you cannot begin to deliver valuable relevant content.

- Content Marketing can be in conjunction with, or completely replace, traditional advertising.

- Great design adds value to Content Marketing by making it more appealing, accessible and easier to understand.

- Look both internally and externally for content - your employees may be your biggest asset when it comes to content marketing. What are they doing that you can repurpose into great content?

- Don't forget about direct mail as a part of content marketing, and the advantages that sending someone a magazine or post-card can have.

- Regardless of where your content ends up - the goal is to get your message out there. It ultimately doesn't matter if someone engages with your content on your website or someone else's, as long as it makes them take action.

- A good website with relevant and valuable content is the first step, but you MUST make it easy for them to buy and/or "raise their hand." Make sure your calls to action are on every page.

- Good cont*ent can trump big dollars*!

IN SUMMARY:

Remember, the entire principle of Content Marketing is that we have moved away from a sales position into an educational position. By sharing information vital to your niche, you become an authority and those in your target group will *want* to pursue a relationship with you. How do you do this? Educate the consumers by providing good, valuable and useful information, thus staying in the forefront of their minds and when they need your service…. ***THEY WILL THINK OF YOU!!!!***

About Lindsay

Lindsay Dicks helps her clients tell their stories in the online world. Being brought up around a family of marketers, but a product of Generation Y, Lindsay naturally gravitated to the new world of on-line marketing. Lindsay began freelance writing in 2000 and soon after launched her own PR firm that thrived by offering an in-your-face "Guaranteed PR" that was one of the first of its type in the nation.

Lindsay's new media career is centered on her philosophy that "people buy people." Her goal is to help her clients build a relationship with their prospects and customers. Once that relationship is built and they learn to trust them as the expert in their field then they will do business with them. Using Social Media and Search Engine Optimization, Lindsay takes that concept and builds upon it by working with her clients to create online "buzz" about them to convey their business and personal story. Lindsay's clientele span the entire business map and range from doctors and small business owners to Inc 500 CEOs.

Lindsay is a graduate of the University of Florida with a Bachelors Degree in Marketing. She is the CEO of CelebritySites™, an online marketing company specializing in social media and online personal branding. "The biggest mistake people make online is believing that their website is just an extension of their business cards and brochures. That approach is not only old fashion; today it's a waste of time and money. Your website has to be dynamic, grab attention, tell a compelling story and ultimately convert visitors into prospects and finally into customers. If not, that traffic that you've worked so hard to get to your website will move on within 10 seconds, never to be seen again. We help our clients avoid that pitfall to grow their business and their revenue streams."

Lindsay is co-author of the best-selling books, "Big Ideas for Your Business" and "Shift Happens." She was also selected as one of America's PremierExperts™ and has been quoted in Newsweek, the Wall Street Journal and USA Today, as well as featured on NBC, ABC, FOX and CBS television affiliates speaking on social media, search engine optimization and making more money online.

You can connect with Lindsay at:

Lindsay@CelebritySites.com

www.twitter.com/LindsayMDicks

www.facebook.com/LindsayDicks

Power Principle #23

DEVELOP FUNNEL VISION

by Scott Martineau

You probably already know that the Funnel is the metaphor we use to describe the system of capturing prospects and converting them into customers. Although many people think they have a "sales funnel" in place, the reality is that they really do not yet have "FUNNEL VISION".

In this section, we'll talk about how to get rid of "TUNNEL VISION" (a focus on today's sales) to true "FUNNEL VISION" (a proper focus on Filling, Converting, and Flipping your funnel).

TUNNEL VISION

(AKA "Straight For The Sale")

It's because of the fact that *not* everyone is ready to buy RIGHT NOW that the Funnel becomes so important. You see, most people think about "advertising." You place an ad somewhere. People see it. They know about your product, service or special offer.

And most people think about "sales." The sale is what you hope immediately follows advertising! People see the ad. They know about the product, service or special offer. Then they somehow contact the company—go to the website, visit the store, make a phone call—and then BUY SOMETHING!

And most people design their systems of selling using this "OLD way" (based on this concept that advertising leads straight to sales)

But the problem with this model is that you close the "Hot Prospects" (let's say that's a hefty 5%) and then everyone else (the other 95% of your traffic) just gets lost and goes to waste. This is the 'hunter' mentality—you eat what you can find today and kill… otherwise you starve.

But the truth is that people buy when they are ready to buy, not just when you are ready to sell! Most people think about doing the advertising and making the sale. But not enough people think about a systematic approach to generating and converting leads.

Did you know:

- …67% of the prospects that tell you "no" today will be ready to buy in the next year? —Gartner Research

- …80% of the leads you consider to be DEAD will buy within 2 years? —Sirius Decisions

You may have made the sale to your 5% of Hot Prospects…but where will YOU be when the OTHER 95% are ready to BUY????

TURNING "TUNNEL VISION" INTO "FUNNEL VISION"

Wow…63 of every 95 leads that don't buy immediately will buy within one year. So what are you going to do about all those leads? We've told you to "capture" them…but then what? Will you ignore them? Or can you expend the effort to keep in touch for 12 months (with automated follow up) until they decide to buy…from YOU? Because that's what the Funnel is all about…

…it's about being there when prospects ARE ready to buy.

This is the New Way of doing things. Because despite popular belief, **advertising is NOT marketing**. The Advertising & Sales model is not the best approach for a small business. Marketing is a long-term…and very profitable…harvest proposition. It's the Web 2.0 way of doing business.

You've supercharged your website, right? It's generating leads for you by offering a lead gen magnet and by capturing the contact information of all the people who download it. Obviously, if they don't opt in and download it…if they effectively say "no"…then nothing happens.

But if they opt in and say "yes," you present them with a sales offer. If they buy, you send them an email campaign and continue to follow up. If they don't buy, you still send them an email campaign—a different one, obviously—but you keep your name in front of all those leads until they are ready to buy.

If you don't have a system for harvesting and following up on the leads who aren't ready to buy now, you are delivering the sale to your competition. But the Funnel is designed to capture the leads who don't buy right away, and "funnel" them progressively toward greater and greater commitment to action through continuous, automated follow up campaigns.

Our goal is to redirect your advertising to Fill the Funnel, rather than just going for the sale.

It's kind of like getting married…no one says "Yes, I'll marry you!" the first time you meet them. Everybody knows that! (That's why no one's dumb enough to ask at that point in the game!) You've got to realize the same thing is true when it comes to making a sale.

Check out these statistics on how many "touches" it takes to close a sale:

- 2% close on the 1st call or touch

- 3% close on the 2nd call or touch

- 4% close on the 3rd call or touch (ironically, this is where most follow-up processes stop)

- 10% close on the 4th call

- 81% close ON OR AFTER the 5th call

So if you get a lead into your funnel but you fail to keep in "touch" beyond the third, fourth or fifth time, you stand to lose 81% of your potential sales. Wow! You're probably thinking people would be really motivated to follow up. Right? You might be surprised to see when most companies actually give up on their follow-up efforts:

- Nearly half quit after the first attempt

- 74% have given up after the 2nd call

- 86% are done after the 3rd call

- 90% have 'thrown in the towel' after the 4th call

- And only 10% attempt to call more than 5 times

This means that a majority of companies are creating a scenario to warm the lead and make them a prime target for the 2nd or 3rd company the prospect reaches out to. Now that's a real waste.

The goal of the Funnel is to allow you to nurture the relationship you have with your prospects and customers so you can maximize their life-time value.

Once you've filled the funnel with prospects, you want to use the Funnel to develop trust… to keep your name, services, products and expertise top of mind… to "convert" your prospects to customers through continuous positive and helpful contact with them. We call this Converting the Funnel. It happens because you have managed to "be there" when your prospects became ready to buy. You became the 'Master of the Moment'.

But after they make a purchase, you don't just throw a party and celebrate the end of the journey..…*You Flip Your Funnel*.

You start your new customer on the journey toward repeat purchases by keeping them in the database and targeting them with new email campaigns. Now we said earlier that the Funnel is the heart of your marketing strategy. It's what gives life to your business and keeps it alive.

In summary, the goal of Filling the Funnel is to:

- Keep in touch with your prospects until they are ready to buy (by capturing them in your funnel)

- Be there when they do buy (from you)

- Flip the Funnel by putting your new customer back into your funnel and converting them over and over again (repeat sales)

Because today's leads are tomorrow's…or next month's…or next year's customers…or repeat customers!

About Scott

Scott's dream is to revolutionize the way that small businesses grow. To him, this means that every person who has the entrepreneurial spark will have access to the tools they need to 'turn their spark into a raging fire of success'. He feels strongly that entrepreneurs need to stop looking around and just doing what everyone else is doing. Instead, he suggests that they should find their own mission in life, and then go build a great company around that dream.

Scott loves to watch and play basketball, play with his 6 children (throwing stuff, wrestling, dancing, computer games, reading stories, etc.), and go on dates with his beautiful wife.

...Oh yeah, and Scott wears jeans every day.

Power Principle #24

"THE POWER OF PARADOXICAL LIBERATION"

by Richard Seppala, "The ROI Guy"

"The tougher the job, the greater the reward."
~ George Allen

Since I brand myself as "The ROI Guy," I'm all about getting the best return on an investment. The first thing people think about, however, when they hear the word "investment" is money. And the mindset is, if I just put enough money into my marketing and my business, I should get a lot more money out.

Nothing to it, right?

Well, as you probably already guessed, it's nowhere close to being that simple. I've found that your investment in all aspects of your life has to be about a lot more than money. You have to invest time and effort – what's called "sweat equity" – and you have to apply focus and direction to that time and effort.

When I was growing up, my grandmother used to preach to me about "Paradoxical Liberation." Yeah, that's a mouthful – and when you're six or seven, as I was, it sounds like some weird cosmic thing Scotty

217

has to do to the engine room in a Star Trek episode to get the photon torpedoes back in action.

The complete phrase she used, *"Paradoxical Liberation Gained from the Discipline of the Order"*, explains it better: discipline, hard work and focus will enable you to reach your goals and free yourself from whatever was holding you back. Every time I felt like giving up on something, because I hadn't gotten what I wanted right away, I knew she would come at me with those words, especially the back half of the phrase.

And I've found time and time again that she was right – hard work does set you free. Bearing down and doing what you need to do in order to achieve the goals you're pursuing is what sees you through. Nobody hands you anything. And sometimes you just have to do things you don't want to do to get what you want.

In college, I heard a lot about 'Paradoxical Liberation' and discipline from my grandma – because I was more interested in partying all weekend instead of studying. Not that I was the only one who thought that way – otherwise, there wouldn't have been anyone to party with. Seriously, while I only thought about what I could get out of the day for myself, my grandmother was thinking about how what I did – or didn't do - that day could impact the rest of my life.

Taking on the concept of 'Paradoxical Liberation' may make you feel stressed and under the gun – and about as liberated as somebody locked up in Guantanamo. But if you don't give up and you follow through, you'll end up with the life you want – finally freed from your old, less-desirable circumstances.

My grandmother's idea of 'Paradoxical Liberation' affects what I do every day and every aspect of my business. But it wasn't always that way.

BECOMING THE ROI GUY

I never thought of going into business for myself after I graduated from college. It just didn't occur to me. Instead, I took the corporate route – and ended up being responsible for sales and marketing for some of the biggest 'senior' companies in America. Naturally, this resulted in an overwhelming amount of constant travel to the various senior communities across the country.

At the same time, I found myself in the position of single dad. With the mother out of the picture, I was responsible for my new son, Cole. And because I had to travel so extensively for my job, he developed separation anxiety – which became so severe he ended up being hospitalized because of it.

When that horrible event happened, there was no hesitation on my part – I knew I had to call up my boss and let him know I had to leave my position immediately. My son was obviously much more important than any job.

Quitting was the easy part – the big question now was what the heck was I going to do? I needed a job that suited my expertise but would enable me to stay local so I could take care of my son properly. I had also just met the love of my life, my current wife, Lisa, who was the most supportive person I had ever met – and I wanted be as close to her as well.

I finally realized that all I had learned about marketing and improving a company's ROI would probably be valuable to other businesses besides my former employer's. If I could sell those kinds of marketing solutions to other business owners, I would probably do pretty well.

But I forgot everything I had learned about 'Paradoxical Liberation Gained from the Discipline of the Order'.

I went to a lot of business seminars where successful people would talk about how the first year they launched a product, they made seven 'gazillion' dollars. That was the kind of speech that inspired me and I assumed that, hey, my first year in business, I should be able to make seven 'gazillion' dollars too. Yeah, *'I drank the Kool-Aid big time'*. And no, I didn't make even one 'gazillion' dollars that first year. Or second.

Because, the fact is that it really doesn't work that way – not for 99.9% of people starting their own business. Instant success is a rarity – and it takes hard work, discipline and focus when you're starting your own business. You're going to get knocked down a few times – and you don't get back up unless you have some great core values that give you the resiliency to go the distance.

I didn't know that at the time. For the first two years that I was in business for myself, I was convinced every product or service I launched was going to make me a millionaire. That didn't happen – and it was an eye-opener.

Grandma returned to my thoughts - and I finally embraced her idea of 'Paradoxical Liberation' for good (although I still can't say it fast three times). Once I began to bring more discipline and order to my work – and pushed myself to do all the little things I didn't want to do, but desperately needed to do - I turned my fortunes around and began to find the kind of success that had eluded me at the beginning. And it's really made me the ROI Guy I am today – along with the incredible support of my wife Lisa and my four amazing sons.

MORE PARADOXICAL THINKING

So how do you make 'Paradoxical Liberation Gained from the Discipline of the Order' a part of your life?

Well, you tackle yet another paradox – start with the finish. Where do you want to get to? What do you want to achieve with your business? How successful do you want to be and how hard are you willing to work to get that success?

Another paradox – these are simple questions that don't have very simple answers. Many people who start their own businesses initially think it's going to be 'a ton of fun' to be free of any employer demands and restrictions. In a sense, they're feeling too much liberation. There's a reason companies you work for have a lot of rules and restrictions – doing business at a high level requires a lot of discipline. The company enforces that discipline instead of trusting that you have it.

Which leads to one more paradox – the freedom that you go after by starting your own business can end up leaving you feeling more trapped than ever. Why? Because that very inflated sense of freedom you experience often gets in the way of setting clear goals. Business owners have almost too many possibilities when it comes to how they run their company – they have a multitude of options. Until they sort out those possibilities and find some clarity to their business "mission," they often end up 'spinning around in circles', lunging at some new venture whenever it presents itself without thinking it through first, like a kid distracted by a shiny new toy.

To be fair, it's complicated running a business – hey, I know that. For high achievers in some other fields, their goals are completely defined in advance for them. Take Olympic athletes, for example – they want to win the gold at the next Olympic games, that path is all laid out. It's a given. In business - just the opposite. There is no set goal, except to make money, of course. How much money you make and how you make that money is where it gets a little confusing.

Which is why clear goals are important. Otherwise, those of us who work for ourselves become the most infuriating bosses in the world - with no order to our madness, working incredibly hard, without ever paradoxically liberating ourselves. We, instead, get imprisoned by work that has no chance of paying off – which wouldn't make my grandma very happy.

The only chance to get the "liberation" part of the equation into play is to set those goals, make sure they're viable, and then work backwards (another paradox!) to plot out how you're going to achieve those objectives. It will take hard work, but it will be hard work with a purpose. And there's no paradox to that.

As I said at the beginning of this chapter, when it comes to the "Investment" part of ROI, I'm not just talking about investing money. It's also about investing thought, effort, and hard work. And you're not going to get a very good return on those investments unless you invest them wisely and make smart choices.

Employ the tools of 'Paradoxical Liberation Gained from the Discipline of the Order' in your own business and you can find success the way I did. You don't make millions listening to a guy at a seminar. You do it by putting in the work, day after day, building to your success. But, paradoxically, that man (or woman!) at that seminar just might give you some darn good ideas on how to do just that.

What am I personally building to? Well, my ambition is to put myself and my wife and kids on a big yacht and sail around the world.

That's the kind of extensive travel I can definitely deal with!

And here's one last paradox for you – ever see someone with Attention Deficit Disorder driving a Ford Focus???

About Richard

For over a decade, TCS President Richard Seppala has worked in the long term care arena as V.P. of sales and Marketing for top providers. During this time, he has developed unique and creative marketing programs consistently exceeding census goals and financial satisfaction.

As a result of his marketing and sales success, Richard has most recently formed Total Census Solutions -- a company helping others benefit from his innovative marketing techniques and the newest technologies that have just hit the long term care market.

Grounded by years of direct sales and marketing experience, Richard brings significant value to organizations - with creative insight, proven strategies and practical sales and marketing tools that generate results. These tools have generated thousands of inbound calls and qualified leads for multiple providers in multiple disciplines.

Richard has trained thousands of sales and marketing professionals from all over the country; to help them sell more effectively, generate more referrals and successfully convert callers to customers.

All this, combined with an appreciation for quality resident care, customer satisfaction and compassion, Richard Seppala 'sales and marketing innovations' are like no other.

Power Principle #25

'DARE TO BEGIN'

by Chuck Boyce

"All Glory Comes From Daring to Begin" ~ *Eugene F Ware*

At 12:01 am every day, we all get the same 1440 minutes for the next one. How you choose to use them, and what you choose to start right now, determines whether or not you will find success.

As a serial entrepreneur, I get approached with opportunities and ideas for joint ventures, partnerships and new businesses with some regularity. Many times the person that approaches has a reasonably good idea that they have been kicking around for some time, yet they've done nothing with it. They have made a choice to keep their idea locked up in a notebook or their head. They have never given it a chance by taking that first step and doing something with it.

I have three questions I ask of these individuals:-

1. How long have you had this idea?

2. What have you done with it so far?

3. What can be accomplished in the next two weeks?

The first question is usually answered pretty quickly. The answer is usually a very long time, months or years. I find that successful people don't generally sit around waiting to find someone else to help them get a project off the ground. They will start working on something immediately, and look for others that fill in critical gaps along the way. A commitment is made to move forward quickly, and they get started. *They dare to begin!*

The second and third questions are more often than not accompanied by blank stares. So as part of my personal weeding-out process, I ask them to get back to me within 3 days with those answers. Unfortunately, for many of these ideas or projects, this is the last time I will hear about it. It really is a shame, because I have heard some really good ideas over the years. On the rarest of occasions, they will get back to me, or they will find someone else that is willing to hold them by the hand, or do it for them.

This process also works in reverse. When I'm approaching someone else to do a deal, I have my answers to these three questions and I include the answer to "What's in it for them?"

Several years ago, I had the idea to open a computer based testing center as part of our executive business suite. One of my tenants was a small, regional IT staffing and consulting firm. I thought it would be a great fit in terms of our business needs. I laid a quick plan and wanted to open the doors within 3 weeks. My client agreed it was a good idea, and he could benefit by having a way to schedule his consultants in a priority queue and receive discounts for their certification exams. He indicated he'd get back to me shortly.

While he was performing his analysis, creating forecasts, working the calculations and looking at the project from every conceivable angle, I got to work. About 10 days later, he got back to me and indicated he still wasn't sure if it was a good idea for him, but he was willing to consider moving forward. In that same time he spent analyzing the project, I was done. The center was furnished, the equipment was in place, and we had qualified as an authorized testing center for the big three in computer based testing.

I shared with him that the center was done, and unfortunately he had missed out on the project. The testing center continues to generate a nice income stream as an add-on to that existing business. This project was a success, because while he was analyzing, I was doing. I had dared to begin.

Now just as this example was a success, there are many occasions where starting something that looks good at the outset turns out to be a mistake.

FAIL FORWARD FAST

"Fail faster. Succeed sooner." ~ *Tom Peters*

As I continue to meet other successful individuals, it becomes very apparent that they are very impatient bunch. They are constantly looking for ways to speed things up. They, like me, have decided that there is no benefit to SLOW. <u>There are no rewards for waiting.</u>

With the steady flow of starting new projects, and constant activity, it is important to know when to let go of a project or an idea. <u>There are times when it is just as important to call it quits.</u> The objective is to *Fail Forward FAST*.

When you are starting so many things, it is important to measure progress. If you are moving as quickly as possible, there will be times when a key market, partner or technology is just not ready, stable or receptive to your plans. There has to be a way for you to objectively decide to kill a project.

Recently, I decided to launch a two and a half day marketing seminar. This project moved very quickly, and within 3 weeks of the decision, hotel contracts were signed, a production company was on board to record the event, and several key presenters had been lined up. Over the following weeks, marketing was launched, budgets were established, and the remainder of the program was put to bed.

As the critical dates for our hotel contract drew near, it was clear that I was not going to make the numbers I needed to pull off the event. There were three critical measurements that I decided on at the beginning of the project, and if we didn't have a "go" indicator for at least two of the three criteria, I was going to pull the plug. As this was to be the first of what I hoped was going to be an annual event, it was crucial that the attendees at the first event were blown away by the content and the experience.

When decision day arrived, and I reviewed the three indicators, only one was in the "go" range I had set. At that point, I had to decide could we still pull off the event I had envisioned, what sacrifices would we need to make, and would the attendecs still have the experience we had promised. Unfortunately, the answer was a resounding NO.

So I pulled the plug, notified our registered attendees that we would push the event to the fall at the same location. Having established the success or Go/No Go criteria up front helped take some of the *angst* out of making a decision.

While this project was an initial failure for not making the grade in its current form, I learned a lot about our target market, and can make adjustments to the program and marketing materials to use what was learned.

Shortly, the process will start over again for the next iteration. My team will move forward FAST and I will have a set of criteria to make key decisions. If we Fail Forward Fast again, we will again use what we learned and reevaluate.

Keep in mind that this may not only be necessary at the start of a project, but should be considered in any project, product or service that may be getting a little 'long in the tooth'. If they aren't delivering to you the value you need to continue them, it is best to 'cut them loose'.

For many years I have represented a variety of products and services to a very tiny niche of about 2000 companies in North America. At the beginning, these products were new and very much in demand, so I had a very high return for the resources I committed to these products. As the market has aged and new competitors have sought to offer similar products to this micro-niche, the return on my resources dedicated to these products has diminished to a point where I will discontinue representing these products.

This was a tough, but necessary decision. Due to the extremely small size of the niche I have made many good friends and have become very well known to my customers. Again due to the size, and the many personal relationships, the business owners in the niche have come to expect that I will be personally handling the delivery of their products or service. Unfortunately, that is no longer the most beneficial way for me to spend my time.

So I must choose to get someone else on board, train them, and establish them as an upgraded substitute for me; or I must walk away. After a quick search, and discussions with key clients, I made the choice to leave this niche. Since I don't want to lose all of the goodwill and reputation that is built up in that niche, I must find new products and services to offer them that can serve their businesses and also have a broader appeal.

NO MORE WAITING!

One of my favorite quotes used by marketing gurus, consultants, coaches and 'arm chair philosophers' is "Insanity is doing the same thing over and over again and expecting different results." Having known my share of certified 'crazy folk', the idea is not really meant to be taken literally. It does point out that most people won't muster the energy required to change their habits and chart a new course. It takes hard work and perseverance to overcome the inertia created by doing the same old thing.

You however, can be different. You can choose right now to make the changes. Here are my recommendations to get you started:-

(…So now it is time to dust off that notebook, go to the whiteboard or jot down that idea you've been carrying around….)

- Write out the list of your three best ideas to bring yourself closer to personal success.

- Take a huge red pen, and cross out numbers two and three. Draw a huge circle, dollar signs, or a heart around number one.

- Put this list up in a prominent place so you see it at least several times per day.

- Take action on your Best Idea for Success right now.

- Make it a giant step and make a public commitment.

227

- Write down the ONE CRITERIA you will use to determine if this is a success, and the date you will evaluate the project. Chisel this date into a stone tablet, and be brutal when the day of reckoning arrives.

- Ask yourself constantly, "Is what I'm doing at this very moment moving me closer to achieving my goal of success?"

---- *Keep repeating this process until you've found success, by your definition!* ----

About Chuck

One of the top alternatives people are using to create wealth in this tough economy is through development of their own small businesses. Chuck Boyce and his organization are helping people do just that by providing online access to resources while assisting entrepreneurs fight some of the isolation associated with working from home.

"Our goal is to build a community of online resources, so if you find yourself, either by choice or necessity, starting a business out of your home, you won't have to figure out everything all by yourself. We have developed a place you can go to get access to the expert information you need. When you have a question you can ask people who have already faced the problems you're trying to overcome today."

Chuck says his site has attracted people from around the world who have found themselves working from home, either for a large company or in their own home-based business.

"The current unsteady economic situation is what initially inspired us to start this service because we've worked with independent professionals in the past and saw a growing need for this type of online community to be able to connect people with each other and critical resources. We continue to watch the unemployment rate moving higher, and people are finding themselves unemployed. Thousands of skilled laborers are out of work and many of these people just can't find jobs. Their alternative is to start their own businesses in order to secure their financial future."

Many times the first thing to be lost after losing a job is a person's self esteem and confidence. Chuck says they offer resources to help people develop the self-assurance they need to start moving forward again. "We try to show them that they are not alone by introducing them to others like themselves that have been in the same situation, have made clear decisions and moved forward and experienced success in a relatively short period of time."

Tip for Success

"I urge people to set their course and start something new if that is what the situation calls for. I started my own home-based business, a desktop publishing company, when I was 16 years old and have spent the majority of my career working for myself. This is the perfect time to start a small business; in fact many big companies today had their beginnings during the Great Depression of the 1930's. Small business is what drives our country and you could be a part of that legacy to help the nation return to prosperity. I know that if these potential entrepreneurs give themselves a chance and use our services and resources to build something new, they will also experience the freedom of working for themselves and the financial success we are all looking for today."

If you are interested in learning more about developing your own home-based business you can visit www.iahbb.org.

Power Principle #26

BE A JERK...WITH YOUR TIME

by Ben Glass, Esq.

As the father of nine who runs a busy personal injury law practice and two thriving information marketing businesses, the single most frequently asked question I get is: "How do you do it all?" People want to know how my wife, Sandi, and I, get the five elementary school aged children off to the bus stop each morning, attend virtually every high school sporting event and little league game, participate extensively in our church and charitable organizations that we are passionate about, and still manage to have dinner with the six children who are still at home virtually every night.

The challenges that I face each day in my businesses are no different than those faced by the hundreds of lawyers across the United States and Canada that I coach. I coach them on how to grow their practices effectively and ethically. They also do not vary greatly from those of the local small business owners and entrepreneurs with whom I meet monthly to share the best of "what's working in your business." Virtually every lawyer and small business owner I know point to "not enough quality time with family" as their chief angst in life.

How does your life look? If I followed you around for a couple days would I be impressed with how you use your time? Are you a hero to your family? Do your clients/customers get the fresh, creative, thoughtful you, or do they get the harried "always chasing the ball" you?

I know lots of entrepreneurs who are "maximizing life" and living without regret. They not only produce financial and emotional security for their families, but they continue to be the ones who are on the baseball and soccer fields, being leaders in their communities and heroes to their families.

Here's their secret: they are jerks—with their time. Like the little kid who battles ferociously in the sandbox to protect "what's his," they guard their time from those who think nothing of stealing it. Put more "delicately": effective control of your "time life" begins with how you think about time and how you think about your place in the world.

As an entrepreneur people are **depending** on you to be selfish with your time. I know that it does not seem that way as your clients, customers and staff vie for your attention by walking in your door, picking up the phone anytime they feel like it and expecting immediate responses to their email requests. Think about it – if not for you running a profitable, powerful, thriving business there would be no job for them to come to. There would be no reason to call you to ask for your product or service. Most importantly, there would be no financial security for your family. You are an economic engine in your community. You let EVERYONE down if you don't value your time appropriately.

JUST WHY DO YOU AND YOUR BUSINESS EXIST?

When you finish this book I would like you to go to your calendar and 'carve out' at least one day <u>for you</u>. I'm not talking about one day a month or one day a week or anything like that. I'm talking about getting started and carving out one day where you can go off – alone. Take nothing but a pad and paper and …think.

Ponder this: In order to know where to set your time priorities you need to be very sure about why you (first) and your business (second) exist in the world.

Need a cute question to 'jump start' your thinking?

If you knew you were going to die in exactly six months what would you do with the rest of your life?

You have to answer that question for yourself, but for me, I would want to secure the **emotional** and **financial** stability of my family. I would want them to remember, when I was gone, that the choices I made with my time were made with no regrets as to our relationship. There wasn't going to be any "Gee, I'm sorry I missed their teenage years" conversation running through my head or theirs. Second, I would want to know that through my efforts, the financial side of their lives was secure after I am gone.

Each and every day I recognize that these are my two highest priorities because ...guess what? I have no idea whether I have six hours or 60 years to live. I haven't been given the luxury of a "time frame."

YOU NEED TO TRULY VALUE YOUR TIME

OK, we *know* our time is important, but do we really know just how *valuable* our own time is? Can we put a price on it?

Dan Kennedy has a wonderful exercise at page 3 of his book, *No. B.S. Time Management for Entrepreneurs*. He challenges you to determine the value of your time by looking at your earnings goals and dividing it by the number of hours you work.

Simple.

Simple, except that as Dan points out, even though most of us "work" 40-60-80 hours a week, we are only really **productive** for only a couple of hours a day. Now, do the math to value your time by looking only at your *productive time.*

By they way, if you don't believe that your *productive time* is so small do this experiment: Call your best entrepreneurial buddy right now. For a week follow yourself around and write down what you're doing every 15 minutes. Keep a chart. At the end of a week send it to your buddy. Have him do the same for you. (The buddy system keeps you honest, because you wouldn't lie to your buddy.) Discuss which of those 15 minute increments was really geared towards creating the emotional and financial foundation for you, your family and your business. When productivity expert Lee Milteer (Milteer. com) taught this exercise to me and I did it, I was humbled by how much time I was wasting.

START BY SAYING "NO" TO EVERYTHING THAT IS NOT DIRECTLY RELATED TO YOUR GOALS

Why? Because those of us who are the most effective producers and doers in the community, are the ones that get asked to do and produce even more. We have a substantial challenge. Admit it. You accept more than you can handle because (1) your ego is stroked just because they asked you to serve on one more *important* committee, and (2) you feel guilty when you say *no*.

I'm telling you to get over your ego and I'm giving you permission to selfishly say "no."

Remember, your family is relying on you for that emotional and financial security, and your employees are relying on you to keep a thriving business going. Every time you get weak and give in to every business associate who wants to "pick your brain", and every community or professional group that thinks that "you would be the best to head our committee or come give a speech to our members", you first think "is this advancing the emotional and financial security of my family?" Unless the answer is clearly *yes,* you say *no*.

Feel bad about that? I did when I first started saying *no*. But then I got to thinking: these folks who are willing to help themselves to my time haven't said anything about being around when I am retired (or gone) to help with the emotional and financial security of my family. They aren't doing anything to keep paychecks flowing to my employees so that they can help support their families.

Okay, so how are we going to do this? Here's a list of the things that I do and don't do, in order to not let my time be wasted:

DON'T LET OTHERS DICTATE YOUR AGENDA

I have clear written goals that I have taken the time to write, review and revise. If I accept an additional obligational responsibility, it is because I have decided that it is good for me and my family …and not because it's something that I "ought" to do. The obligation is only accepted if it can be worked on my terms. This includes clients. This includes law clients. If your delay in making a decision to hire a lawyer has lead to a situation where you now not only need to hire a lawyer, but need him or her to do something immediately, then I'll give you a list of names to call …but I won't be that lawyer.

DO NOT ACCEPT OR MAKE UNPLANNED/ UNSCHEDULED PHONE CALLS

Many business professionals feel guilty when they are not seemingly available to their clients 24 hours a day, 7 days a week. They feel that they somehow need to obligate themselves to be constantly interrupted in order to maintain their position in the marketplace. Be courageous: never again accept an unplanned inbound phone call. Require everyone to make an appointment to speak to you. Your staff and friends will tell you that this is impossible. Its simply not true. In fact, it will elevate you status.

Here's our client communication policy:

Our promise to you is that while we are working on your case, we don't take inbound phone calls, faxcs or emails. Ben Glass takes no inbound unscheduled phone calls whatsoever. It makes him much more productive and helps get your case resolved faster. You can always call Ben's Assistant, Terry Patterson (703) 591-9829, and schedule an in-person or phone appointment, usually within 24-48 hours. This is a lot better than the endless game of "phone tag" played by most businesses today. Remember, too, that email is "quick," but is checked no more than twice a day. Replies are then scheduled into the calendar. So if it's really important, don't email – call Terry instead.

Here's what I learned when I implemented the policy: **Clients love it**. They become more respectful of your time and of the advice you give them when they do have that prescheduled telephone appointment with you. You are more productive because both you and they are prepared for the call.

DON'T WORK IN AN UNPRODUCTIVE ENVIRONMENT.

I have a cave. There are actually a couple of places that I go that are outside of my office and not in my home, where I can get away to work and to think. You might actually rent a small office somewhere between your house and your "real" office/place of business. Public and university libraries are also great places to "go and hide." Remember, you aren't going to be immediately accessible by email and telephone anyway. *Most of us can get six hours of productive time in 180 quality minutes of 'alone' time.*

LET GO AND DELEGATE

I know, I know. There are a lot of things in your life and in your business life which you feel could not be done by anyone but you. You are wrong. This is much more about discovering the process to find great reliable people than it is about your ego. In this "troubled economy", there are hundreds if not thousands of people in your community and around the world who would love to be able to do one small part of your business for you – and they will be really good at it. Teach the staff and employees who work for you in your physical office to think and act like entrepreneurs. Many of us won't do that because they fear that the employee will get so good at what their doing that they'll leave. If that happens, so be it. You want to teach the people around you not only how you want things done, but why. This allows them to be decision makers. There's actually probably very little in your business life that they could screw up so badly that it would be fatal to your economic existence. Trust them.

Also, remember that there are people around the world who will work for you. I have "virtual assistants" (contract workers who are great at everything from graphic design to writing to event planning) across the United States and around the world.

USE A CONVERSATION PLANNER

Carry a small notebook or a set of cards in which you make notes and begin to organize those communications with the primary contacts in your life. Know that you meet with your marketing staff three times a week? Every time you get an idea for them, rather than send off an email or run down the hall, just jot the note on a card. It will make your meetings run more efficiently.

TAME THE EMAIL

There are probably hundreds of books and white papers written on how to control email. The best I have ever read teaches you to teach your contacts how to handle email and how to communicate with you through email. It's <u>The Hamster Revolution</u>: How to Manage Your Email Before It Manages You. Like our firm communication policy, this is all about making a decision about how you are going to run your life, and then requiring everyone who works with you/associates with you/ buys from you, to play by your rules.

MAKE APPOINTMENTS WITH YOURSELF TO DO WORK AND INCLUDE THE ENDING TIME

As Dan Kennedy points out in his book, *No BS Time Management For The Entrepreneur*, people who set appointments to work for themselves, and make lists of things "to do", rarely put an end time on the appointment. They work until the "thing" is done. Far better to schedule the ending time and create pressure for yourself. I've even gone out and bought a $5.00 windup clock that ticks. Put that right in front of you while you work. Helps you concentrate.

Think this won't work? I once coached three youth soccer teams at once while in the startup phase of my solo law practice. I had to be out the door for practice at 4:30 p.m. Everything got done before 4:30. The only thing different between absolutely having to walk out the door to meet a bunch of teenage kids and setting an "end time" to the appointment you have made with yourself, is your own mindset.

CONCLUSION

Entrepreneurs are "doers." As such they get asked to do a lot of things. You must steadfastly reject taking on projects, clients, customers and any other obligation that is not steadfastly linked to your goals. Your community depends on you to value your time appropriately.

About Ben

Ben Glass is a practicing personal injury and medical malpractice attorney in Fairfax, Virginia. As the founder of Great Legal Marketing, Ben conducts sold-out seminars, and coached and mentored 326 attorneys across the U.S. and Canada. He has been written up and featured in *TRIAL* **magazine, Wall Street Journal Online** and the **Washington Post**, among others. Ben has also authored 7 books, including *The Truth About Lawyer Advertising* (available on Amazon).

He is the creator of "Militant Time Management for Lawyers" which is available at MilitantTimeManagement.com

To find out about Ben's Lawyer Marketing Company, visit www.GreatLegalMarketing.com. To visit Ben's law website, go to www.BenGlassLaw.com.

Power Principle #27

PRINCIPLES OF ENTREPRENEURIAL (SMALL BUSINESS) SUCCESS

by Kimberly Moore

As an entrepreneur, you can count yourself a significant part of the *economic* strength of America. According to the Small Business Administration, a small business is defined as having revenues under $5 million and fewer than 100 employees. Accordingly a report by the SBA's Office of Advocacy states that small business enterprises represented 50 percent of America's GDP from 1998 to 2007. Within this 'small business' definition is a sector of small business - for many of us, revenues are under $2M and we have less than 20 employees. We are home-based businesses or generally occupy less than 2,000 square feet of traditional office space, which is the focus of this article and my target audience.

Choosing to go into business for yourself can be immensely rewarding as well as challenging. I was fortunate enough to be nurtured in an entrepreneurial family of both white and blue-collar workers. Early on, I recognized the benefits as well as the difficulties in managing a small business. Family role models helped develop many of the skills I attribute to my success as well as my viewpoint in life from a business perspective. When I was 19, my grandfather gave me the opportunity to open, staff, and operate a 6,000 square foot convenience store with full-service deli and gas station under his tutelage. This was after more than 5 years of prior part-time cashier work in his automated carwashes - in addition to performing bookkeeping tasks in his general contracting business.

To supplement my practical experience, I acquired a computer science degree followed by a B.B.A. from Ohio University and an MBA from the University of Phoenix. Most recently I earned a professional designation as a Certified Mergers and Acquisitions Advisor.

When I moved to Colorado Springs in 1989, I quickly took a position as an administrative assistant for a property management firm. After only eight months, I convinced the asset manager of the property to allow me the opportunity to manage a struggling Business Center in the building. As a condition to the successful management of this Business Center, I negotiated a unique joint venture arrangement and after only a few months was able to turn a profit. After fifteen months, the joint venture expired and I began my debut as an independent business center owner with only 3,200 square feet and 11 office suites

This experience fueled my passion for business. It also drew me to the concept of providing shared professional space with flexible terms, services and amenities for entrepreneurial companies and professionals, as well as national and international companies seeking a local presence in the marketplace. With the global workplace emerging, the world was my market. The concept of sharing office space, infrastructure, talent and technology met my common sense entrepreneurial approach. This applied not only to myself but inspired me to offer the same service to other entrepreneurs and small business owners at various stages of their development – whether just beginning, expanding, relocating or operating an existing business. This model significantly minimizes capital expenditures, reduces risks and offers a competitive edge - while enabling an entrepreneurial professional to focus on their own unique skills, gifts and abilities which contributes specifically to the success of their own business.

During my early years as CEO of Executive Systems, I made an economic investment to bring to life my vision utilizing 'leading edge' communication technologies – this risky move definitely had its challenges as we deployed "bleeding-edge" technologies. However in the course of the last 15 years we have reaped the rewards and benefits of that decision and my clients have been given a competitive edge in their businesses.

Now, after nearly 20 years, we are in the process of re-branding our business to OfficeSuite360™. Our goal is to enable other small business owners the opportunity to take advantage of similar processes, systems and technologies to minimize operating and payroll costs, gain operational efficiencies, and increase revenue opportunities through our marketing strategies -- while converting more revenue to profit. Our platform gives a small business' entrepreneurial endeavors access to talent, technologies and infrastructure previously afforded only by large corporations. Small business can compete more efficiently and effectively, thereby gaining market share in their industry.

Through strategic acquisitions and sales, I expanded my available office space to over 36,000 square feet in four locations with over 120 office suites - including virtual office memberships both nationally and worldwide, and grew the company into a profitable business that produces over $1 million in annual revenues.

My knowledge and expertise expanded so that now I provide guidance to other small business owners. I evaluate business operations, systems and processes, then recommend re-alignments to improve efficiency and profit. I also provide valuations and intermediary services to match commercial buyers and sellers, to provide site location services as well as expansion, re-location, merger and acquisition opportunities. I offer 'turn-around' and business consulting services to prepare business owners for acquisition and/or to establish a more profitable position for continued ownership.

I have found eight principles that have guided my journey to success both personally and professionally. One thing I've learned - "life is short", even shorter as we get older (remember our parents saying this?) … arghh - so,

1. BE PASSIONATE about your profession. Hopefully your profession is what gets you up in the morning *(may often keep you awake at night)* and motivates you to re-invent yourself each day. In your working years, you will spend nearly a third of your life on the job, doing that thing you are passionate about – so, find your passion and make those hours more rewarding and fulfilling!

We've all read the benefits of goal setting so I must reiterate – set goals then do more. Draw them, color them, paste them on your mirror, really meditate on what it is you wish to accomplish in life. Start with the vision of the end game. What are you fabulous at doing? What is your unique gift? For my vocation, I chose business. I was good at it early on and I knew there was plenty of room at the top. I attribute my success primarily to a lot of common sense as well as a general understanding of the interrelatedness of all the various business disciplines.

For some of us, we're quite clever at a lot of "stuff", but in the end we are best at one or two things. Get to know yourself - identify your strengths, talents and unique contribution to your business, your industry, your team, your profession - as early in life as possible and stick with it. Remember, if you're good at something, don't do it for free. Search and be aware of opportunities to align your passion with profit. Keep in mind that passion without profit may make a better leisure pursuit than a vocation.

My first passion was actually an ambition to become an opera singer. Having been classically trained as a pianist, I had made quite a commitment to this endeavor starting at the very young age of 8. However, given my extremely competitive, over-achiever nature – I decided after only a couple years of college the probability of becoming the best opera singer - given the fierce competition - was a rather lackluster proposition for me. Given that I was unable to combine this passion for profit, I decided to enjoy a fabulous hobby in the privacy of my home.

2. BE PRAGMATIC in your endeavors. Is there a market for what you want to do? Is that market large enough for you to create the kind of success you envision for yourself? How will you measure that success? Profit may not be your motivator. Keep in mind your career choice should provide you with both the standard of living you desire and also the passion to commit and persevere in the face of adversity.

Assuming you have identified your passion, you need a strong dose of pragmatism. It's important to understand your strengths as well as your weaknesses. Surround yourself with competent professionals. Know when to hire a consultant or business coach to help you jump that hurdle that's keeping you from your success. If you can be so fortunate – find a mentor and emulate them. Begin building your little black book of contacts as early as possible; genuinely befriend these acquaintances, make a connection – this will serve you well in your career - whether you need a painter, a publisher or a new president for your organization …as you advance to CEO. Once you have identified the areas where you need outside assistance, build up your resources and align yourself with people who are experts in their field. It's not a numbers game. It is knowing a few qualified individuals who have a talent or skill that will complement you and enhance your success.

If you try one enterprise and it doesn't work out, pursue another passion. Most people have more than one. Opera singing didn't work out for me, but business has. Starting over is not a bad thing, however I would discourage switching careers too often, it may detract from your success.

3. BE RESOURCEFUL - Many small businesses have an expert entrepreneur at the helm. Again the challenge is they usually are an expert in a single discipline in their small business or segment of their industry. Identify, take note and evaluate your weaknesses. If your desk is piled with papers, maybe you need a professional organizer. If you are a scientist whose strength is not bookkeeping or selling, but you are a great inventor, seek out a salesperson and a bookkeeper - focus on your core strength. Smart companies concentrate on what they do best and outsource the rest.

Build Quickly – be aware of economic cycles, real estate cycles – any national or global implications on your business that may impact your short or long-term future business propositions and respond accordingly. Unpredictable markets, unforeseen trends, unexpected downturns can catch the entrepreneur by surprise. Gathering a mastermind group who can help guide the business is an invaluable resource for an aspiring entrepreneur to tap into.

4. PERSEVERENCE is more than not giving up at the first sign of resistance. Perseverance means researching solutions, knowing when to ask for help from your network or colleagues, possibly enlisting the assistance of professionals, coaches, consultants or mentors to gain the edge, the information you need to persevere through your business challenges. What is passion without persistence?

As you confront problems and find solutions, you will develop your analytical skills and internal resources and intuitions to 'block' and 'tackle' potential problems before they negatively affect you or your business - making each new challenge easier with a more successful outcome. Maintain a hopeful mindset, be positive and provide reassurance to staff and customers. They need to know you are going to stick with it. Once resolved, you will gain a personal sense of accomplishment and credibility.

Keeping up with the ever-changing workplace, technology, systems and processes, requires persistence and perseverance. Sometimes things don't turn out or work as you envision. Don't take the path of least resistance and fall back on what's worked in the past or old habits; push forward, learn, grow and persevere into the future.

5. PRODUCE RESULTS - whether you sell securities, manufacture widgets, or provide a service, the success of your business and America depends upon your ability to produce. America stands to lose much of its core business value if it quits producing a tangible product or valuable service. As entrepreneurs we can bring back production. For most businesses, nothing happens until a sale is made. To make a sale, create and communicate value to your intended customer by delivering the anticipated result.

I've always been a "systems" person. Even when I was young I found structure and process made it easy for me to find things, to be on time and even save me money. The structure process creates a set of habits. Find a system that works for you that produces results and enhances your performance -- then develop these habits to support your system. As a seasoned entrepreneur, I have found that systems produce enormous economies of scale, efficiencies, and consistency in your company and support a more productive and motivated team.

6. BE CREDIBLE - you gain credibility when you understand your product or service and how to communicate value to your potential client. Take steps to ensure your message is congruent with your result. If you say you have the largest selection of custom designed widgets, make it true. If you offer warranties, honor them. Do what you say you're going to do, follow-through and follow-up and then do it again!

It's also about your competencies; about knowing yourself, your limits and your capabilities. It's about knowing when to align yourself with additional talent. Dependability is important to your credibility. Stay the course, ensure your employees and clients know you will be there tomorrow. Expect more of yourself than anyone asks of you.

7. BE PROFESSIONAL - Professionalism differentiates you and your business to your customer and from your competition. Professional conduct shows in how you treat your customers, staff, colleagues and peers. It shows up in your appearance, how the phone is answered, your letters and emails, and in your speech and grammar. Observe other professionals in your industry. If you feel you have a weakness in any business or personal discipline, seek out assistance from an expert or emulate a colleague whom you respect.

Your business location also reflects a level of professionalism. So whether you are a small business start-up, a seasoned entrepreneur who needs a more professional service while working from home, or are at a point to relocate out of the home office, utilizing the space and service available to you in an Office Business Center makes an easy and economical segue to promote your success and professionalism. Make note, successful CEO's don't answer their own business calls – your image often defines your professionalism and credibility.

8. BE PRINCIPLED - You don't have to be perfect to be principled. I'm a bit of a perfectionist (working on recovery everyday). Be aware that perfection can be a distraction and even a deterrent to profit. Know when good enough is acceptable and be timely rather than underperform given a timeline while trying to obtain perfection. Determine your boundaries in how you conduct business. Are you a cut-throat competitor? Or more low key? Do you approach clients with the idea that you are doing them a favor? Or do you make them feel they are the most important part of your business? Again, do you honor your commitments to provide good service, warranties, and quality product?

Provide a clear value proposition to your clients. This affects your credibility, which reflects on your professionalism. Treat others the way you would want to be treated. Decisions should be objective, not subjective. It's easier to make decisions when you can obtain measurable results. Sometimes it is a gamble and you have to decide when to stick with it and follow through, and when to cut your losses. You can set the rules of conduct for yourself, but it will be the market that decides if those rules fit with whom they want to do business.

As you are faced with more difficult decisions, sometimes there are no clear right or wrong answers; I have found that rather than ascribing a right versus wrong value, I ask myself this "is this a wise versus a foolish decision?". Sometimes that small change in semantics pushes me to a better decision and on to a more suitable path.

A FINAL WORD

Believe in yourself. Give of yourself to others to whom you may be a mentor, friend, companion or encourager. Be curious – make it a point to read voraciously. Remember that no matter where you are in life, you are in the middle. There are always those with greater gifts, talents, accomplishments, money, etc., and there are always those with less.

Define your gift, find your niche, solidify your vision - pursue it with passion, perseverance and wild abandon! Good luck in your life!

K@Kmoore360.com
Twitter: KMoore360
303.719.8937

We enhance the professionalism and VIP status of small business, increase their speed to market, overcome capital intensive, expensive infrastructure and technology in a more cost effective manner, with less risk, whether your small business is home-based or located in traditional office space locally, nationally or internationally.

About Kim

Nurtured by an entrepreneurial family, Kimberly Moore gained business acumen early in life. A 6,000 square foot convenience store with full-service deli and gas station became her first enterprise. To add to this experience, she acquired a computer science degree followed by a Bachelor's degree from Ohio University and an MBA from the University of Phoenix. Most recently Kimberly earned a professional designation as a Certified Mergers and Acquisitions Advisor.

When Kimberly located to Colorado in 1989, she saw a need to provide small growing companies and entrepreneurs with space and back office support services in Class-A office buildings. She founded Executive Systems, a 5,500 square foot office business center. She also offered clients outsourced services such as financial and marketing strategies. During her years as CEO of Executive Systems, Kimberly proved to be an industry innovator through her use of unique telecom applications. She became an early adopter of communication technologies for the benefit of her clients, who found her solutions highly lucrative in payroll savings, operational efficiencies and increased revenue opportunities.

She expanded her available office space to 37,000 square feet in four locations and grew the company into a profitable business that produced over $1 million in annual revenues. In 2008, she sold that business, but returned in 2010, eager for the challenge to build it again.

Drawing on the skills she developed to successfully run an office business center, coupled with her education in telecom, technology and business management put her in a unique position to provide guidance to other small business owners. Her sharp mind gives her the ability to quickly evaluate business operations, systems and processes. She can then recommend re-alignments to create greater efficiencies and ultimately greater profits in many small to medium sized businesses. As an industry expert, she can provide valuations and intermediary services to match commercial buyers and sellers, to provide site location services as well as expansion and merger opportunities. Kimberly offers turn-around and consulting services to prepare business owners for acquisition and/or to establish a more profitable position for continued ownership.

Kimberly is a member and participates in many local and global industry organizations including Office Business Center Association International, Alliance Business Center Network, Global Office Network, Colorado Springs Executive Association, Peak Venture Group and Keep Colorado Springs Beautiful, a local "branch" of Keep America Beautiful.

Power Principle #28

MAXIMIZE THE DAY WITH PERSONAL MANAGEMENT SKILLS

by David A. Hoines, B.A., J.D., L.L.M.

A key to success in any career or business is efficient time utilization. If you work ten (10) hours per day, six (6) days per week, you have sixty (60) hours within which to accomplish the tasks necessary to be successful that week – or said another way, delivering the work to your customers and clients and reaping its rewards, which in the end, requires management skills.

Why do some persons seem to get more done than others? They have developed, organized, and acquired the techniques to be focused and prepared, and deliver the product or service as promised to the customer or client. On the other hand, we all have known persons who just can't get things done, or done in a timely manner – their performance always falls short, regardless of how smart they may be.

Success depends on the former – failure on the later. The skills therefore necessary for the successful person to develop include:

- Time Management
- Money Management

- Organization

- Marketing and Promotion

- Personnel or People Skills

- Communication Ability

- Goal Determination

<u>Time Management:</u> In essence, it is getting more out of the hours you work, NOT merely adding more hours at work, which means the making of <u>choices</u> concerning the best use of the hours spent at work, and choosing which tasks and decision-making are to be delegated.

<u>Money Management:</u> Involves budgets, accounting, billing, pricing and cost analysis. Certainly a basic understanding of accounting principles is fundamental – you have to be able to read and understand your business' profit and loss statement and balance sheet. In today's world, basic accounting programs (such as Quick Books) are affordable, easily utilized and not difficult to understand. If you can't keep track of the money, you surely won't have any.

<u>Organization:</u> Disorganization leads to chaos, increased stress, decreased productivity, and resulting failure. Organization leads to increasing productivity by proper structuring of work, putting tasks into sensible components, assigning work to those best suited to complete it, and declining work when not right for your organization or business. Getting and staying organized is a continuous undertaking that can only be mastered by constant awareness.

An easy and successful organizing tool is the creation and use of checklists. Even though everyone knows of checklists, they are often not utilized.

Dr. Atul Gawande, a professor of surgery at Harvard Medical School, relates the experience and success of checklist utilization at John Hopkins Hospital by physicians and nurses in his recent book, "The Checklist Manifesto: How to Get Things Right".

> "a five-point checklist implemented in 2001 virtually eradicated central line infections in the intensive care unit at Johns Hopkins Hospital, preventing an esti-

mated 43 infections and eight deaths over 27 months.

Dr. Gawande notes that when it was later tested in I.C.U.'s in Michigan, the checklist decreased infections by 66 percent within three months and probably saved more than 1,500 lives within a year and a half.

He further makes the case that checklists can help us manage the extreme complexity of the modern world. In medicine, he writes, the problem is "Making sure we apply the knowledge we have consistently and correctly". Failure, he argues, results not so much from ignorance (not knowing enough about what works) as from ineptitude (not properly applying what we know works).

If smart, educated and talented health care professionals can benefit from checklist implementation, so can we.

<u>Marketing and Promotion:</u> Marketing and promotion is much more than advertising. Indeed, it is often observed that the best marketing and promotion is a consequence of satisfied customers and clients. The keynote is a thorough understanding of WHO your prospective clients or customers are and WHY they are prospective customers. The goal is to develop a client base which refers you to other clients, enabling you to get and keep future business,

The fundamentals are:

1. Identify the clients or customers whom your services or products benefit

2. Communicate your value to these prospective clients or customers, and

3. Once a client or customer seeks your services or product, be certain to deliver the promised good or service in a timely and economical manner, thus closing the deal and securing repeat customers and referral business, which is by far the best source of future business.

The business owner is the primary ingredient for the success in numbers 1 and 2 above, but successful delivery of number 3 usually involves employees, which gives rise to a different set of skills – people management and motivation.

<u>Personnel and People Skills:</u> In the end, most everything is a people business in one way or another. The manager must understand that getting the most out of employees means involving employees: for example, giving feedback, seeking suggestions and demonstrating leadership are all powerful management tools. The one word that sums up people skills is RESPECT.

If you conduct yourself so that your management style is that of a "straw" boss who "barks" orders to employees, or otherwise conveys a condescending attitude toward employees, then you have the wrong persons in your employ.

Deborah Norville, anchor on the long-running syndicated TV newsmagazine, recently authored the book "The Power of Respect: Benefit for the Most Forgotten Element of Success". Therein she accurately observed that:

> When people feel respected, their sense of self-worth rises, a sensation so pleasant that they become predisposed to like and trust the respect giver. Often they will do everything in their power to aid whoever showed them respect in hopes that they will receive respect again.

> Showing respect can make family members feel closer to us…employees and colleagues work harder for us… and increase the odds that customer service reps, retail employees and waiters will treat us favorably.

> As a bonus, showing other people respect elevates our own outlook on life - it feels good to make others feel good. Improving our mood doesn't just brighten our day. It actually makes us smarter. Our brains release *dopamine* when we experience positive feelings. Dopamine receptors are located in the cerebral cortex, the part of the brain that handles strategic thinking and problem solving. When you "feel good", you have excited the decision-making part of your brain."

<u>Communication</u>: Effective communication, whether it be with customers and clients or subordinates, is not merely a matter of telling a person

what you want them to hear – you need to listen, to praise, to sympathize, to understand the other's point of view and needs. You must also be sensitive to the other person's time and time constraints – get to the point quickly. Also, be courteous – who listens to a 'yeller'?

<u>Goal Determination</u>: Knowing what you are good at is usually easy to identify and use to your advantage – equally important is understanding what you are NOT good at. Identifying these traits, which requires introspection and a careful analysis of yourself, is crucial to success. Some subjects you can avoid, others must be dealt with, and soliciting assistance when you need it is crucial in avoiding needless difficulty and maximizing success.

<u>Conclusion</u>: Personal management skills apply every day and must be continuously developed to experience success. Some believe that you either have these skills or you do not, which is wrong. The truth is that these skills can be learned and perfected over time. *What is required is a recognition of the importance of acquiring these skills followed by their implementation - every day, all the time.*

About David

The Law Offices of David A. Hoines has consistently delivered results in the areas of law in which he practices. David is respected by his clients and peers alike.

Most of us, at some point during our lives, need legal advice. Unfortunately, the legal system can be extremely difficult, intimidating, and frustrating, to many individuals; but it doesn't have to be that way. The right attorney is the best cure for these trying situations.

David Hoines has the education and the experience. He has been practicing law for decades and has handled all types of cases in many State and Federal courts and jurisdictions. It is his constant goal to bring a fair and equitable conclusion in all matters in which he is involved. In addition to a Bachelor of Arts degree and a Law degree (Juris Doctor), David also attained his Master of Law (L.L.M.).

David has been certified by the Florida Bar Association as a Specialist in Civil Litigation for each and every year since 1991. He is a member of the AARP (American Association of Retired Persons) Legal Services Network. He was recently nominated for and became a Fellow of the American Bar Association Foundation, joining a mere 1/3 of 1% of all lawyers in the U.S. In addition to membership in the Florida Bar, he is also a member in good standing of The California Bar and the State Bar of New York. He is also admitted to practice before the U.S. Supreme Court, U.S. Court of Claims, U.S. Tax Court, the U.S. Circuit Courts of Appeal for the 11th, 9th, 5th, 4th and Federal Circuits, and the U.S. District Court for the Northern and Central Districts of California, and the Southern and Middle Districts of Florida.

David will be happy to help you find the right solution for your situation or problem. And he promises that if for some reason he cannot be of assistance, he will point you in the direction of someone who might be able to help.

You can access his website, Hoineslaw.com, for more detailed information concerning his practice, background and experience.

Power Principle #29

THE POWER OF "THINKING FORWARD"

 Michael Biancone

Y ou are a superhero with invincible powers. Your ambitions are on a grand scale and no one can possibly defeat them. You have the power to dream and the power to eventually conquer the world with super human thoughts. No matter what step you take, you know it is always going to be the right one. The future holds limitless opportunities – and you are at the height of your tenacity, positive thinking and confidence.

You are six years old!

As I grew up from that invincible six year-old point, I faced the challenge of making my way through a society filled with rules and regulations, dealing with authorities whose own belief systems conflicted with my own. Of course, I wasn't alone in that journey – most of us are led down a path of irreversible negativity.

Unfortunately, most of us get worn down by the process. We believe it when we're told we *can't* accomplish our dreams. We take it onboard when we're told we're *not educated* enough to succeed. We let others create limitations for us and stop us from achieving all that we can do.

It's difficult to *not* give people that kind of power over you, especially when you're young. Everyone is older and more experienced – you assume they know what they're talking about and you give them power over you. It's the natural order of things.

Except it's really not. Much of it is just subjective and comes from people who have been beaten down themselves. They assume it's going to happen to you as well.

So, what happens when you get knocked down again and again? How can your own personal faith, beliefs and perseverance stand up to that kind of negativity and enable you to find success?

Let me share the secrets of how I overcame adversity. Let's talk about the Power of Thinking Forward.

THE MINDSET MAKES THE DIFFERENCE

Like any person with an imperfect education, I did not have a mountain of options. I applied for jobs, made a paycheck and worked to make a name for myself. It wasn't anything like when I was six years old; I did not have the same belief as a superhero anymore.

I persevered, because I did want more, and I wanted to succeed. To follow my thoughts, I answered a persuasive ad and began selling vacuum cleaners door-to-door – this was the beginning of my education in sales. I found success through belief, and continued to redevelop myself, and by not taking "no" for an answer.

Intelligence alone doesn't guarantee that you will find success - nor does talent. So many people with amazing amounts of both qualities never achieve their ultimate level of mental fulfillment.

For me, it's about the mental outlook. Your natural abilities will obviously help you get what you're after – but this is limited even if you do not have the attitude that allows you to overcome the various obstacles life throws your way. You need to have the Power of Thinking Forward - continuing to calculate what you need to advance yourself and acting on those thoughts, no matter how badly the deck is stacked against you, no matter how big the odds are against you. If you *Think* Forward, you will *Move* Forward.

To begin on a successful path, you should rid yourself of all the bad influences. When you are surrounded by good quality influences, you create premium surroundings. "You are the same person five years from now as you are today, except for the books you read and the people you meet". If you surround yourself with negative, disruptive, habitual or insolvent people, then you may or will become the same.

There are three guiding principles behind the Power of Thinking Forward that have enabled me to achieve:

1. TENACITY

Tenacity is all about having a "never give up" attitude. My tenacity has enabled me to travel down many productive, but difficult paths – enabling me to both learn valuable information and also to give me the experience and expertise to devise sales techniques that are literally changing people's lives.

If I did not have that tenacity, I might still be selling vacuum cleaners, or be stuck on somebody else's dream, never having accomplished the things I wanted to accomplish.

But how many people give up – as quickly as the first time they try?

When things get tough, many people fall short in learning what they need to overcome. We become afraid to try, we shy away from change, because we might fail in the effort – and that fear freezes us in our endeavors.

That fear also allows others to control our lives. Whether it's our boss, our government or even our next door neighbor, we too often give others the power and control - when people and institutions intimidate or halt us from moving forward.

Tenacity means you don't let anything stop you. Fight as hard as you can and never stop trying. If you use the Power of Thinking Forward and continue to generate the ideas and the self-discipline it takes to advance yourself, you will continue to get closer to your dreams and your goals.

Of course, it's not enough to Think Forward – you also have to complete the tasks that need to be done to Move Forward, no matter how difficult they may be and no matter how many times you have to try. Tenacity means you hang in there and keep at it until you complete the task. The important thing, when all is said and done, is that you can say, "I did my best." Anything short of this is an excuse.

With tenacity comes power. A fifteen round boxing match doesn't take less than fifteen rounds. When you're still standing at the end of the match, you feel complete. You went the distance; you accomplished what many others were unable to even start.

And if you happen not to finish a task, you still feel elated, and you look back on how you performed. This allows you to put in a superior effort and achieve more in subsequent challenges. Life should be looked at as a sporting event – be ready to execute a performance-based effort.

Zig Ziglar presented it this way: what if you were going on vacation and had one day to pack? You will do everything in your power to accomplish everything that's necessary, all day long, for as many hours as it takes. You will work beyond your capabilities to assure that you get everything done with your fullest effort. If this was the case - then why don't we treat *every* day like it's the day before vacation?

2. POSITIVE THOUGHT

This goes hand-in-hand with tenacity. Negative thinking is a big part of why people give up. They see all the things that can get in their way, all the things that can go wrong, and they stop before they start.

That's why positive thought is so critical to advancing yourself. It can't just be about you saying a Daily Affirmation in the morning and telling yourself that you can do it, whatever "it" is. No, it's living, breathing and feeling this positive energy.

We all want to get to the finish line as soon as possible. We all should know by now that life does not work that way. Still, we get discouraged and down about those bumps in the road and in our situations.

Today we possess a pessimistic trait allowing us to become discouraged, when it should be the reverse. For example, you manage to acquire a home by investing a down payment and making monthly payments for thirty years. But when it comes time to write the check every month, we grumble and complain. Why? Instead, each payment should be a joyful and positive moment – you are one step closer to your goal.

This is pleasurable by seeing your balance lower every 30 days. Every month should be a positive moment.

In our grandparent's days and during my childhood, I viewed an episode where families celebrated paying off their home by burning the mortgage note – this was a common practice long ago. What a momentous occasion for celebration. When's the last time you've heard of that happening? Today, everyone just wants to burn the house down – because our negative thinking doesn't see the value in working towards a goal. Instead, we're interested in instant gratification and short term profit. It should feel good to make that house payment – and build progress towards a joyful, powerful goal.

Positive thinking applies to the smallest of things in life, as well as the biggest. Be as happy about accomplishing little tasks as well as overcoming major challenges, and stop thinking your problems are worse than anyone else's.

Imagine that all the people of the world were each asked to put their problems in a paper bag, and then they were told to throw those bags out in the street. Then you were asked to go pick out any bag you want. I firmly believe you will make every attempt to find your own bag, because you don't want to have anyone else's problems. At that moment, you'll feel that your problems aren't so bad.

Positive thinking has a huge impact on anyone's life. My opinion is that 90% of people live as if trying will only lead to failure. Move on and be part of the ten percent that dares to make things happen.

3. CONFIDENCE

Confidence is the third piece to the Power of Thinking Forward. Have you ever noticed why are some people more successful than others? Confidence, together with tenacity and positive thinking, allows you to face a situation *without fear.*

Yes, you may have tenacity. Yes, you may be thinking positively. But if you don't have the confidence in yourself, you still won't be able to progress as far as you should – and you will end up second guessing yourself. Developing this takes hard work and conditioning.

The authority figures in our lives undercut our confidence. It is instilled in us, we somehow think we are less than they are. Which prevents us from moving toward a successful result?

Whoever you're talking to, whoever you're standing in front of, you should consider yourself on their level. Otherwise, you are putting yourself at an instant disadvantage in any negotiation – you are granting them power that you shouldn't.

I have been taught a great lesson from my mentors – "fake it 'till you make it – and if you don't know, pretend you do." I believe this will help you grow and become more than you are.

When you "fake it 'till you make it," it doesn't mean you do not have enough smarts. It means you have to push yourself to acquire the necessary knowledge or techniques for success. And pretending you know forces you to acquire the correct information. If you're nervous, pretend you're not. If you're sad, pretend you're happy.

Having confidence in yourself means you know that you can and will overcome these momentary weak moments. Having confidence gets you past the rough patches that make you doubt yourself – and takes you to the place where you know success is within reach. Having confidence allows you to think forward so you can move forward.

PUTTING IT ALL TOGETHER

I enjoy putting my Power of Thinking Forward to work with those that I teach – and seeing the awesome results it brings.

For instance, I helped one of my students who was in a scary situation – and who was unable to hold a conversation with anyone in authority. She was nervous about dealing with the rules that were to her own advantage. I told her to envision the best possible outcome. I wanted her to walk into the situation, exuding confidence, positive thinking and a belief that this is the way everything turns out. She was going to be "faking it until making it."

It worked. She ended up elated with her accomplishment. She overcame her fear, she overcame the obstacles and, in her mind, it seemed easy. The first person she approached, helped her - that's not always the case – if it wasn't with her, she simply needed to ask that person for someone else to talk to. And if that person didn't help her, she needed to ask for another person, until she found someone that would help her. That's the kind of tenacity that is needed in every situation. Remember to always ask – "If you cannot help me, please give me someone who can".

Practice my Power Principle and you may not win every task, but I promise you that you will win many. And you will also become a stronger individual who possesses a better outlook both about yourself and your life. It eventually makes everyday life effortless. You don't dwell on what's coming next and you don't admit defeat before the moment.

Implementing the Power of Thinking Forward has made me enjoy every moment of my life – and the day I put it into action was the day I became a winner. When a task was not completed - I didn't feel defeated – because I knew I had done my best, and that it was part of the learning process that eventually brings you success. It is better to try and fail then to never try at all.

The magical part? I accept that success is already at hand. I believe that I am one of *the* most positive individuals alive. After years of acquiring the wisdom and insight to reach this amazing place in my life, I feel privileged to be able to share these secrets and more with anyone in my "Free Advice Seminar." I enjoy delivering these powerful tools that have helped many break from the imaginary limits their own thoughts imposed on them with the smallest of efforts.

If you want to observe the *real* expert on the Power of Thinking Forward, watch a child. When children fall, they will get up and try again. They do not know the word "No" - it goes in one ear and out the other; they are relentless and fearless because they haven't yet "learned" to be afraid and to question themselves.

Let's teach ourselves to be more like that six year-old. Let's not give up until we get what we want.

Be a superhero. Conquer the world.

About Michael

In 1978, Michael Biancone sold vacuums door to door. It was a moving and rewarding experience. Since then, he has been able to cultivate different successful sales opportunities throughout the next few years.

In 1983, he joined Ahnert Enterprises, involved with land, timeshare and campground sales. He was accelerated and promoted in seven months to Sales Director - holding achievements that cannot be duplicated today. He held numerous positions in management and achieved the highest honors by receiving every possible award and recognition offered. He was given the opportunity to be educated by Marketing Experts.

In 1989, The Rank Organization, a multi-billion dollar company from Europe, purchased Ahnert Enterprises. He quickly moved into their land division for the next three years. He successfully achieved the highest honors by exceeding their lofty goals and desires.

In 1993, he was hired by The Flagship Resort of Atlantic City to work in their Internal Sales Department. His accomplishment and talents had placed him directly in front of the President of the organization to be offered a position as Vice President. He respectfully refused.

In 1995, he accepted a position with Fairfield Communities in Myrtle Beach, SC. Having eminently acclaimed training and education in Management Sales, he disagreed with tactics used and moved to a more adapting company. He was hired by Plantation Resort of Myrtle Beach, SC where he accepted a position as Director of Sales. In June of 1996, Spinnaker Resort of Hilton Head was contracted as the Sales and Marketing Company. Within five years, he managed to excel in positions from Sales Manager to Project Director - achieving feats that were not obtained by any other major company in Myrtle Beach (i.e. Fairfield Communities, Bluegreen Corporation, Vistana Resort of Florida, and Marriott). They achieved over $48 million in gross revenue with over 6600 sales in a non-ocean front property. His most heartfelt achievement was giving his personnel the attention and opportunity to be successful. He had the desire to help more men and women become successful sales people and managers than any person or company in his field.

During his tenure with Spinnaker Resorts, he had spearheaded developments in various locations as a consultant, advisor and trainer to place these Developments on a healing and successful track in a short period of time. With experience and proven track record, he traveled to Charleston, SC and Hilton Head, SC for the next few years, bringing designated resorts up to par and beyond.

In 2004, with his talents and achievements, he was united with a Land Sales Development Company. They wasted no time successfully generating over 70 million dollars in sales the first year. From there, he helped manage various projects with unprecedented successful results. Projects involved were Charleston Landing, Myrtle Beach; South Island Plantation, Georgetown; Crystal Blue Resort, Myrtle Beach; La Capilla and Rancho Buena Vista, Los Barriles, Mexico; Arrowhead Grand, Myrtle Beach; and Villas Garden, Myrtle Beach. As a Special Projects Director, he sought out valuable projects and properties through acquisitions, both domestically and internationally, along with producing and creating new and current marketing, as well as using innovative selling methods.

His continuing achievement accredited to his work is being a successful investor and helping others invest successfully since 1985. He has been a consultant to many individuals and companies for more than 20 years, an inventor for the Auto Industry and medical field, and a father to a wonderful little girl named Taylor. He is in the midst of writing a book on sales and negotiating techniques that he devised over the years. He plans to continue his road to success and his passion of helping others.

"I HAVE BEEN TAUGHT BY THE BEST TO DELIVER THE BEST!"

- Michael R. Biancone

Power Principle #30

UNLOCK YOUR EARNING POTENTIAL ... JOIN THE VIRTUAL REVOLUTION!

by Kimberly VA

"The task ahead of us is never as great as the power behind us." ~ *Author Unknown*

HAS THE WHOLE WORLD GONE VIRTUAL?

From the small business owner who is staring out of a home office to the multi-million dollar companies, everyone is discovering the VALUE OF VIRTUAL ASSISTANTS! So what do they know that you don't? They have discovered how to maximize their profits and minimize their expenses by utilizing the myriad of skills that Virtual Assistants have to offer.

WHAT IS A VA?

By definition, a Virtual Assistant, aka VA, is a home-based entrepreneur who generalizes or specializes in a variety of business support duties and services that can benefit both small and large businesses. In general, VAs are professionals who bring with them not only the business skills and expertise that you are looking for, but also bring the knowledge that they have gained from working with other business professionals. They are someone you can call on to do the tasks that you do not have time to do, or simply do not know how.

YOU CANNOT BUY MORE TIME, BUT YOU CAN CREATE MORE TIME BY HIRING A VIRTUAL ASSISTANT ... THE NEXT BEST THING!

It does not take long for an entrepreneur to realize the need to delegate. We've all been there - late nights, long hours, and an overwhelming feeling that you will never be able to get it all done. You find yourself in the midst of a never-ending cycle of busyness, becoming so preoccupied with the time-consuming tasks required to keep your business alive that you begin to neglect the things of greater importance. Frustrated, you try learning this and organizing that, but there is just not enough time to do everything; and, the more successful you become, the worse it gets! Suddenly it becomes clear that you are fighting a losing battle and you are faced with the decision to begin using your time wisely to grow your business or get caught up in the busywork that inevitably keeps it from growing.

WHAT IS YOUR TIME WORTH?

Successful professionals know that you should only be doing what only you can do! You spent a lot of time and training to becoming a professional in your field and as such, your time is quite valuable. That's why it is just not lucrative for you to continue doing things that someone else can do in their area of expertise for much, much less than what your time is worth.

ATTEMPTING TO DO THE OFFICE DUTIES IN ADDITION TO YOUR REGULAR DUTIES DISCREDITS YOUR PROFESSIONALISM AND IS NOT A PRODUCTIVE USE OF YOUR TIME.

Your reputation as a trained professional is also quite valuable, so why compromise it by doing tasks that discredit everything that you have worked for? With a Virtual Assistant you can delegate those projects that are "beneath" you and preserve the level of professionalism that you have strived so hard to achieve. Really, how many professionals do you know who are answering their own phones, running their own marketing campaigns, building their own website, designing their own newsletter/ezine, managing their own books, and still finding time to productively engage clients? That is simply not a business model for success!

Once you come to realize your own value, you will be much better prepared to set forth with the delegation. To decide what needs to be delegated, you will want to start by dividing your workplace tasks into two categories: intellectual tasks and menial tasks. The intellectual tasks are the tasks in your business that only you can do. They encompass the duties that you use to generate revenue and utilize the skills that you paid thousands upon thousands of dollars and numerous years acquiring.

IT'S TIME TO CEASE ALL THE TASKS THAT ARE KEEPING YOU FROM YOUR EARNING POTENTIAL AND RELINQUISH THEM TO A CAPABLE AND EXPERIENCED VIRTUAL ASSISTANT.

As for the menial tasks, well, the term itself is a bit of a misnomer, as these tasks are not menial at all as it pertains to your business —provided you are not the one attempting to implement them. These are the job duties that are currently diverting your attention, stealing your time, and keeping you from succeeding. They include the tasks that you are capable of doing, and those that you are attempting to learn for the sake of your business, but are outside of your valuable intellectual skills. For example, an attorney would not be using his time wisely if he chose to handle his own bookkeeping needs including: payables, receivables, collections, bank reconciliations, and the like. Nor would it benefit him to undertake all the workings of his marketing campaign such as: designing the ad/flyer, securing the distribution list/sites, creating the corresponding webpage and message line, answering and returning related calls, etc.

Are you visualizing similar scenarios in your business practices and realizing your own folly? Then it is time to create a more efficient business. Grab your menial tasks list and begin putting delegation into action!

Delegating the projects on your menial task list will work best if you determine, in advance, how many hours you want to assign to each project and identify the expertise and experience required to do those tasks. You will want to jot down clear steps to achieving your objectives. These will be important when you choose your VA and assign your project(s).

PREPARING TO DELEGATE WILL REQUIRE SOME ORGANIZING.

Before you even begin searching for your VA, make sure that you are well organized and ready to undertake the evaluation process that will ensue. Delegating is not necessarily handing off a project to someone; rather, you will want to have clearly defined instructions as well as expectations if you wish to obtain your desired results.

The more you put into preparing to delegate, the more you will get out of it. Therefore, it is wise to draw up a detailed set of procedures for each menial task that you intend to allocate, along with specific instructions of how to accomplish the project(s). Much like a job description, this is where you will list out each aspect of the assignment: duties, responsibilities, qualifications, expected results, compensation types (hourly or by project), time projections and limitations, and other pertinent information. This list can also be referred to when evaluating prospective VAs or you may choose to formulate a list of "interview" questions from it.

IT'S TIME TO FIND YOUR VA!

Nowadays, finding a Virtual Assistant is relatively simple. Most professionals have used VAs or know someone who has, so asking your colleagues, your business networking group, or friends in your social circles is really where you want to begin your quest to find your VA. If you strike out with the word-of-mouth referrals, you can find hundreds, even thousands of VAs through an internet search. This may make the screening process a bit more arduous, but by no means complex. Begin by searching for those who have the skill set required for the project at hand and the level of expertise to boot. Your overall goal is to find a VA who can integrate her skills and your tasks to work cohesively with you to produce positive results on you project.

Select someone whom you can relate to and communicate with well. Like any other workplace relationship, you will want to establish good working relations with your Virtual Assistant. This is especially important since you may never actually meet in person. Pay particular attention to personality and working style. It is imperative that each meet your expectations from the very beginning, so as to avoid any difficulties later on, say in the midst of an important project.

Most Virtual Assistants have a niche of duties in which they prefer to work and really enjoy. Focus your search on a VA who has a passion for the type of work you are offering; and, if possible, the experience of working with others in your field of business. Keep in mind that the VA you choose will be directly involved with your business. If she cannot grasp the value of what you do, her lack of passion will come through in her work and hinder your success.

SCHEDULING A CONSULTATION WILL GIVE YOU THE OPPORTUNITY TO EVALUATE YOUR VA CANDIDATES, WHILE ALLOWING THEM TO DEMONSTRATE THEIR QUALIFICATIONS.

A Virtual Assistant will be more than happy to provide you with a free phone consultation to determine if your needs and her skills are a good match. Use this time wisely to evaluate your VA candidate. This is your opportunity to gauge the interaction as you discuss your project and the significance it has on your business. Clearly explain the duties that are required and the expectations that are sought. Clarify the specifics of what you are looking for in an assistant and what skills and experience you require. Expound upon how you envision the role of the VA on the project and in your business. Then, allow her to share her experience and qualifications.

A professional Virtual Assistant understands that this is her chance to demonstrate her abilities, her personality, and her related experience. The conversation should take a natural progression of give-and-take as she inquires to learn more about you, your business, and the project. You should be able to hear professionalism in her voice from the onset - along with an enthusiasm and a genuine interest to help you succeed - as she discusses the skills and qualifications that she will bring to the job. Ideally, she will offer her experience with similar projects as she takes the lead to determine a proposed approach to accomplish your task. Listen for cues that indicate her capability and her compatibility, as these are both important.

Expect the consultation to bring about a natural brainstorming session that will draw on both of your experiences and guide you into making an educated assessment the VA. Seek to identify competency and aptitude as they are key indicators of what it will be like to work to-gether. If you find that you are guiding the VA along with no real input or value being offered by her, it's time to move on to the next candidate. It is important to eliminate those who do not meet your expectations or possess adequate qualifications. You want to only consider those quali-fied candidates who show a genuine interest in the project(s) at hand, have similar work experience, and express the know-how and the char-acter to get the job done right. And, trust your instincts. If you have an uneasy feeling or you do not have chemistry, don't waste your time or hers muddling through the interview, move on!

YOU'LL HAVE LESS THAN AN HOUR TO ASSESS YOUR VA CANDIDATE … STAY FOCUSED!

A typical consultation will run about 30 to 60 minutes, so you need to stay on target as you evaluate your candidate. Be sure to inquire about all aspects of her business: the manner in which she attends to her clients and projects, her background, references, workload, and rates. Ask about her years in business as a VA, any former work experience that she draws upon, her field and level of education, and any certifi-cations or specialized trainings that she has earned. Note, it is always best to evaluate overall experience and education along with earned certificates, as some certifications can be a bit generalized and may not always carry the merit of a more specialized certificate.

Get all of your questions answered while you have her on the line, including time constraints, project deadlines, price, payment arrange-ments, and terms. Identify whether this is her sole business or some-thing that she is doing on the side. Ask about her workload and her capacity to accept new clients. Clarify the maximum number of hours per week/month that you are allotting the project(s) and make sure it fits within her availability. Find out how she prioritizes her clients and where you fit in the order of things. Discuss her rates and whether she charges by the hour or by the project. You will want to know if she requires an upfront retainer fee or if payment is due once services are rendered. Also, check if she offers any discounts for membership or for buying a block of time in advance.

It's important that your Virtual Assistant be responsive and easy to reach when working together on a project. Although she may not be at your beck-and-call from 8-5 like an employee, she will, in all probability, check her emails and voicemails day and night and be available to respond even when she is not on the clock for your project. Check with her about her anticipated response time and her preferred means of communication: phone, email, or IM. Consider time zone differences for both personal contact and as it pertains to the project. Discuss also the manner in which she intends to keep you updated on the progress of the project (e.g.: a regular basis, a periodic basis, or as necessary).

Most of all, make sure that you have clearly communicated the entirety of the project and that the VA knows what is expected. Have her restate her understanding so that you know there are no miscommunications. A lot of time, energy, and money can be wasted on misunderstandings. It may be also a good idea to ask if you can email her with further questions that may arise, thus opening the lines of communication. This will give you another opportunity to evaluate her on response time and writing style should you have more questions when narrowing down your VA choices. Ultimately, your goal is to choose a VA with whom you can foresee yourself having a good and productive working relationship and walk away feeling secure in your decision.

LETTING GO…

"The best executive is the one who has sense enough to pick good men to do what he wants done, and self-restraint enough to keep from meddling with them while they do it." ~ Theodore Roosevelt

As a business owner/manager, you'll be tempted to want to run all facets of your business, especially in the beginning. That's only natural. But, as a professional, you know that you clearly cannot afford to. Letting go is one of the hardest things to do and requires a level of trust that often is beyond your comfort zone. Your innate inclination will be to worry. …worry if you selected the right VA …worry if your VA understood the project in the way that you had envisioned it …worry about the results. The truth is, the only way to know is to give it a try.

You have spent time to evaluate VA candidates and have chosen to hire the Virtual Assistant with whom you have made a connection and felt best demonstrated her abilities. She has won your approval and qualified herself as an expert in her field. She comes to you skill-ready and has agreed to undertake the menial tasks that have been weighing you down in your business. Her help will allow you to focus on your field of expertise, thus increasing your profitability and growing your business. It's time for you to ease up and let go.

YOUR VA'S SUCCESS IS CONTINGENT UPON YOUR SUCCESS.

Rest assured, your Virtual Assistant is a highly trained entrepreneur with the experience and expertise to carry out the duties that she accepts. She will have her own systems in place and be ready to get started right away. Although there may be a slight learning curve in the beginning, with the detailed instructions that you have provided her, she can tap into her strengths and focus on the work that she loves doing and only come to you for clarification as needed.

To make you feel more at ease when working with your new VA, you may choose to set up routine communication in which to discuss project progression and results. Schedule a time each week to chat about the project and review its progress or have her submit a schedule of duties performed and progress made. This will keep you up-to-date on the project details and costs and will provide an overall sense of accountability. These updates will take a natural progression as you become more comfortable with your VA's quality of work and consistently productive results.

It's important to note that as a business owner herself, this is not just a job to her; it's her business, her reputation, and her livelihood that she is working to protect and preserve. She genuinely wants to make sure that you succeed, as your success keeps her in business. And, by gaining your trust and respect, she may also gain more of your projects or even new clients from your word-of-mouth referrals.

THE SWITCH TO VIRTUAL COMES WITH OTHER HIDDEN VALUES.

As a profession, Virtual Assistants encompass a very diverse field to include marketing, customer and public relations, client services, personal contact calling, email screening, online research, event planning, graphic design, writing/editing, website design, bookkeeping, and the list goes on. But do not expect that one VA will be able to do it all. Depending on your project list and your in-house staff, you may only need to hire one VA or you may be better suited with a team of VAs. But there is no need to worry, Virtual Assistants make it easy for you to stick to your budget. You are in complete control of the cost. Whether you require 1 hour only or 60 hours weekly, you can hire a VA to do as much or as little as you need and only when you need it.

Virtual Assistants afford you the use of highly trained professionals for less than you would typically spend on an employee or a 'temp' with presumably less experience. VAs are the obvious solution when faced with a workload that is not quite big enough to justify the hiring of in-house help and is just big enough that it's 'stealing' more time than you are willing to lose. This is particularly valuable when you find yourself faced with a specialized project that no one in the office has the skills or training to accomplish.

At first, the thought of hiring a Virtual Assistant seems expensive. A qualified VA will run you in the range of $30/hr and up, which may sound exorbitant and counterproductive as it pertains to cost control; however, the hidden value is in what you are not paying for: training, supervision, down time, taxes, benefits, office space, furniture, equipment, overhead, and more.

When you hire a Virtual Assistant, you are not hiring an employee; rather, you are engaging a professional. Unlike traditional employees, Virtual Assistants bill you only for the time that they spend working on your project(s). Whether you secure your VA by the project or by the hour, you will never be billed for breaks, workplace distractions, water-cooler time, personal calls, sick pay, vacation days, or down time. And, because they are virtual, VAs require no office space, no desk, no computer, no phone, no supplies, and no additional overhead.

Virtual Assistants are self-employed entrepreneurs who operate as independent contractors. As such, there will be no expenditures for personnel staff to provide them with orientation, new hire paperwork, or training. There will be no cost or administration for health insurance, retirement plans, disability insurance, or other benefits. You will be free from employer taxes, workers compensation insurance, OSHA compliance, Federal Fair Labor Standards, and the like.

Moreover, there is no need to spend time and money to advertise for help, review resumes, schedule and conduct rounds of interviews in hopes of getting through the probationary period with a good employee so you won't have to begin the process all over again. You can simply avoid the time, cost, and frustration that accompany hiring, training, and supervising a new employee when you hire a Virtual Assistant.

With a VA, you choose the one(s) who have the skill set for your project(s), discuss the aspects of the job with them, and let them do what they do best ... soon you will find yourself wondering how you ever got along without your VA!

Now you are now ready to join the VIRTUAL REVOLUTION!!!

About Kimberly

Kimberly VA's thriving Virtual Office provides a variety of business support duties and services to dozens of professionals around the United States. She takes pride in helping new and established professionals let go of the busyness that is holding them back from their earning potential.

With nearly 30 years of business and professional experience to draw upon, Kimberly has developed a knack for tailoring each assignment to successfully meet the needs and budget of her clients. The passion that she has for her work comes through in everything that she does. Notably, she was dubbed "Kimberly VA" by an attorney collaborative she works with –an honorary title that is becoming widely acclaimed.

Kimberly holds an AA Degree in Business Administration and a BA in Psychology. Coupled, they provide her a well rounded education with the know-how to tackle projects professionally and the people skills to relate well on a personal level while doing so. Her dedication to hard work shines in her college achievements—having reached Summa Cum Laude status with her 4.0 GPA, while taking up to 30 units per semester.

She brings this same dedication to every project that she accepts. Kimberly has found her niche is focusing on the personal relationship building aspects of business –promoting professionals in their community, setting up speaking engagements, turning prospects into clients, and so forth. And, as an added service to her clients, she collaborates with VAs in varying fields to offer an overall support team.

Kimberly's most recent VA work has been with service professionals – Estate Planning, Business, Divorce, & Other Law Practices, Wellness Professionals, and Non-Profits serving senior & teen populations. Her professional experience also includes the following industries: International Real Estate & Relocation Services, Commercial Interior Design Services, Retail, Construction, Surgical Supply, Community College, the District Attorney's Office, an Auto Dealership, a Manufacturing Plant, and a Foundry.

To learn more about Kimberly VA and to receive a free Checklist to use when evaluating your VA candidates visit www.KimberlyVA.com. Mention Power Principles to receive discounts and special offers.

POWER PRINCIPLE #31

"FLIP IT LIKE A PANCAKE!"

by William D. Umansky, Attorney

"If you don't like something change it; if you can't change it, change the way you think about it." ~ *Mary Engelbreit*

'm not your average attorney. As a matter of fact, I'm not your average guy.

Would the average guy dress up like the Pope to try and get thrown out of a Jewish high school? Don't think so, dude. But I did. And when that didn't work, I dressed up like another famous person – scratch that, I should say, *infamous* person - who I knew would *really* not go over well. You may have seen him in Quentin Tarentino's last movie, "Inglourious Basterds" – he had a dopey little moustache and people kept shouting "Heil" whenever he came into a room.

Not the most *tasteful* thing to do, I'll admit, but it did the trick.

I'll get back to why I pulled that crazy stunt in a moment. First, I want to talk about my particular Power Principle – which, despite the title of the chapter, doesn't have anything to do with breakfast food. When I say, "Flip it like a pancake," I mean that, when you find yourself in an incredibly negative situation, you sometimes need to turn it on its head – at least in *your* head.

277

Because you usually can't change what's going on around you – but you can change how you deal with it. That's been my 'm.o.' for a long time – and it's worked for me. It's not about positive thinking – it's about positive *action* and making a situation work for you, rather than letting a situation work you! It's how we learn, grow, adapt and *survive*. Actually, scratch "survive." It's how we *succeed* - personally, I'm not satisfied with just survival. Otherwise, I might as well just be a bug on a rock somewhere.

Look, let's be honest – life never goes completely right. Not for *me*, anyway; send me a postcard if nothing's wrong on your end. Because of all the 'crap' that gets thrown at us all on a daily basis, it's easy to see yourself as a victim - to crawl up in a little ball, wish it would all go away, and wait for somebody to take care of you. *Ultimately, though, that keeps you in a powerless position. That's not where you want to be.*

Especially if you're reading a book about Power Principles, right?

Now, let me discuss in more detail just how 'nuts' I really am.

I REVERSE REVERSE DISCRIMINATION

When I was a kid growing up in a New York neighborhood, I wasn't in what you'd call a very healthy part of town – at least not for a skinny, white, Jewish boy like me. I ended up in a high school where most of the students were African American, many of whom were pissed off at the way they were treated by society. That left me to assume the position of Target of the Day – every day. For that first week, I was beaten up, slammed into lockers and, if I wasn't exactly left for dead, it certainly wouldn't have disrupted the school day much if I had attained that condition. Well, maybe someone would have eventually asked, "Whatever happened to that Jewboy?"

This was not an enjoyable situation - understatment. But, rather than go for "Most Likely to Have Permanent Head Damage" in the yearbook, I decided to try and make it work. My first method was not the best. I tried to fight back. So I jumped a bully from behind and tried to knock him down with a chair, just like in the movies. Literally I hit the kid with a solid chair and he should have gone down. Problem was, unlike the movies, I had that chair turned right back against me and suddenly I had the biggest bloody nose of my life.

I began taking on the teachers in classes – razzing them in front of the other students. There was one teacher that was even more unpopular than me – so I put a dead rat in his desk. I hid tape players around the classroom that would just start yelling curses or inane comments, like "Look at that idiot at the teacher's desk!" By fighting the power, I put the kids on my side, no matter what race or religion they were. By becoming the class clown, everybody thought I was gutsy and hilarious – and I earned their respect. I'm not so sure about the teachers, but, hey, they weren't the ones beating me up.

Outcome? I didn't want to leave that school ever. I suddenly had too many great buds that I loved hanging out with. Began to love hip hop and east coast rap (still do!). As a matter of fact, I *was* actually voted "Most Funny" and "2nd Most Popular" – a pretty big achievement for a skinny Jewish kid in a school where gangs were cool and sports were for geeks.

Which was, of course, when my mother decided I needed to be in a better school – that Jewish high school I mentioned at the beginning of the chapter. Well, nothing against that school – but it wasn't *my* school. It was too buttoned down and not nearly as wild and fun as my previous educational Mecca. No, I wasn't getting beaten up – but, instead, it felt like I was getting beaten down, by learning how to be a victim and accepting the notion that the rest of the world was out to get us. Every day Rabbis warned us "Never to forget." Forget what? That we were slaughtered by millions of Nazi's! Who could forget that. I asked my mom numerous times to get me out – she said, "No way!" To her, I was finally in the right kind of school at last.

Once again, I felt like I had to make a radical move – which is why I came into school dressed like Uncle Adolph. It's the kind of thing you do when you're too young to know better. But, hey, it worked.

I GET FLIPPED LIKE A PANCAKE

When the bad times hit a couple of years ago, I'll admit I felt like the scared kid in that school who kept getting 'dumped on', and didn't know how to stop the punches from raining down on my head.

Before that, I was a fanatical person in terms of pursuing excellence and success; completely driven. I was diagnosed with eight herniated discs about five years ago, so I wake up with pain every morning – which didn't stop me from doing my workout every day. As a matter of fact, the pain, weirdly enough, turned me into more of an optimist (I told you I was crazy). I don't believe in whining or complaining and I see myself as taking charge of my own destiny. I dealt with the pain, I faced up to my professional challenges, I built up a successful practice and I worked on making it better every day.

Then the bad times hit - what's now being called "The Great Recession," the worst economic landmine since "The Great Depression." I'm still not so sure why the word "Great" is used as the adjective for all these horrible downturns, since they're anything *but* that in most people's book. But, anyway, the banks imploded, credit crashed and money was (and still is) 'tighter than Lady Gaga's pants'.

That hit all businesses big time, including my own. Suddenly, everyone in my profession (criminal defense lawyers) was slashing their prices to make up for lost revenues. My fees, which I hadn't raised once during my entire 17 year career, were being undercut left and right by the competition. My profits were going down, my percentages were declining and suddenly I had the same kind of fear and anxiety as many of my clients.

Not only that, but the rise of "lawyer marketing," where millions of dollars were spent by firms on relentless advertising designed to convince everyone who had bruised themselves in a fall that they deserved six or seven figure payouts meant that (a) these mega-firms that worked off volume were taking away more of my business and (b) the quality of the cases were going down. Whiners and complainers were beginning to show up in my office that may have suffered minor personal injuries, but didn't take any responsibility for their own health or well-being. And of course, there were the ones who were trying to commit fraud and weren't hurt at all. They just wanted people to pay all their bills and buy the new Escalade without question.

And that started me questioning *everything*. How could I compete with these marketing behemoths? How could I deal with clients I didn't *like*? How could I make the money I should be making after all these years in the business? I started hating those lawyers, I started hating those clients and I started hating people who couldn't afford to pay my fees. Yeah, even though I no longer dressed up like Hitler, I was becoming as much of a hater as him. And that tends to affect how you relate to people, right?

Totally right.

You can't go on like that. At least I couldn't. I knew it was time once again to flip it like a pancake. And, once again, do the craziest thing I could think of.

I DO THE STUPIDEST (SMARTEST) THING POSSIBLE

As you can tell, my initial instinct is to usually go against the grain and do what everyone else is *not* doing.

So, in the midst of the worst economic times in over 70 years, I raised my fees and spent all my money on a giant new office building. Oh, and by the way, I also put in a working courtroom in that office building. Gotta have your own courtroom, right? Did I mention I also hired more lawyers and staff and about doubled the people working in my practice?

So why the hell would I do all that when business was mind-numbingly *horrible*?

I did it because I was tired of my negative thinking that the recession had brought on. I was tired of the low rent clients I was getting and tired of competing with the discount law firms that were going to out-market me no matter what I did. Trying to take on all that would have been like trying to take on those high school kids who were beating me for being white and Jewish. Don't fight the fight on everyone else's terms. Fight it on your own terms.

The point is that I once again flipped it like a pancake. I took the situation and turned it around to one that played to my advantages. I went into 'hock' and leveraged everything I had to buy that office building (which I got for an amazing price under market. Have to thank the Great Recession for some things…). I raised my fees significantly. And I changed how I sold my services to prospective clients.

Let's first talk about my new and improved fees. Yeah, I raised them up! Really for the first time in 10 years. But I didn't just raise my fees to make more money or rip people off. I did it because the Great Recession and the low-fee marketing-maniac lawyers gave me the opportunity to reposition myself. By pushing up my firm's quality quotient, my clients could benefit from all the extra services we had to offer, as well as my proven talents, expertise and extensive experience. Expanding our practice distinguished us from the competition – allowed us to charge people based on our abilities, not on our fear of the economy.

And yeah, there were people that couldn't afford the new prices. But I remained flexible – when I had to cut a deal, I did so. But you know what? Even when I lowered my new fee, *I was still making more than my old fee*. Not only that, but I got good will out of it from the clients I cut my fees for - even though I was still charging more than I had before. The best of all possible worlds.

I also began to change my approach to clients. I began to stop patronizing and sympathizing with everything they said – instead, I started to be straight with them about what they needed to do to change their lives, not just win their cases. Again, I was tired of hearing endless complaining about their myriad problems – when it seemed like obvious solutions were available. For instance, someone came in and complained their surgery was going to cost more because they were overweight, so they needed more money. I told them they should try to lose weight.

Again, this isn't the usual way to make friends and influence people – often the quickest way to ruin a relationship is to tell the truth. So I lost some clients – but I gained others and I also gained their respect. And I realized this was the niche I should be pursuing – not just working on winning personal injury cases, but also working on giving my clients new and productive lives. I didn't want them to let an accident ruin the rest of their lives – instead, I wanted to help them find a whole new start. A second chance. Help *them* <u>flip it like a pancake</u>. I was an expert on it, right?

So I hired a new marketing director to help me do some grassroots marketing. I began speaking at charity and community events – not about slip-and-fall or car crash injury cases, but about how you don't have to live like a victim, and how an accident can be an opportunity, if you visualize a better future for yourself. How compensation through legal action can change your temporary circumstances, but only a change of attitude can ensure a positive, productive life. It was a risky approach. I don't know of any other lawyers doing it. But it works for me.

I've redone my practice with a small niche of quality clients who have been hurt by the negligence of others. I have no trouble going after compensation for their injuries – and for compensation that will help reestablish them in a new career. We want to give people a second chance if they're hurt and help transform how they look at their futures. We don't just deal with their legal issues – we deal with their life issues.

I like my new practice – because it comes directly out of my personal passion to take negative situations and make them work for someone. I think it's the ultimate Power Principle. Let's face it, when things are going good, who the hell needs a Power Principle? When you've got the brains and guts to handle things when everything goes south, however, you can face your life every day with the confidence you're going to deal with whatever challenge comes your way.

Look, I'm not Superman. As I admit several times here, I faced some pretty good jolts in my life that threw me off-course momentarily. But those moments are what it takes to absorb the bad things that happen and to figure out what to do about them.

My main thing is that you can't take on a new situation the same old way. You either change up your approach or you get lost in the shuffle. You flip it like a pancake.

You know what happens when you don't flip a pancake, right? It gets *really, really* burnt!

About William

William D. Umansky has over a decade of experience to offer any client, especially in the area of criminal defense and personal injury. He has an insight into the workings of the prosecution because his career includes experience as both a former Assistant State Attorney in Florida and The City Prosecutor for the City of Orlando. As a former prosecutor, Mr. Umansky was in charge of the Domestic Violence Misdemeanor Division. He has also been a Police Academy Instructor, an Adjunct Professor at Florida Metropolitan University, and a Legislative Assistant to a United States Senator. Mr. Umansky's entire career has centered on the legal process, both as a prosecutor and now a defender of those accused of illegal behavior.

During his career, Mr. Umansky has remained involved in his community and is an active part of Florida's legal system. He belongs to the Orange Bar Association, acting as Co-Chair of the Orange County Bar Criminal Law Committee for several years. He is a member of the Academy of Florida Trial Lawyers, Florida Association of Criminal Defense Lawyers and the Central Florida Criminal Defense Attorneys Association.

Mr. Umansky graduated cum laude from the University of South Florida with a bachelor's degree in Psychology and obtained his law degree from the University of Florida College of Law. During law school, Mr. Umansky was a member of the University of Florida Trial Team and received a Certificate of Recognition for Outstanding Contribution to the University of Florida Law School. He also earned an award for achieving the top grade for his work in Negotiations and Dispute Settlement. Mr. Umansky also attended the Tulane Institute of European Legal Studies.

Mr. Umansky is admitted to practice in the Florida State Courts and the U.S. District Court Middle District of Florida.